WITHDRAWN

HARVARD LIBRARY

WITHDRAWN

Reading Moby-Dick and Other Essays

American University Studies

Series IV
English Language and Literature
Vol. 69

PETER LANG
New York • Bern • Frankfurt am Main • Paris

William Hamilton

Reading Moby-Dick and Other Essays

PETER LANG
New York • Bern • Frankfurt am Main • Paris

Library of Congress Cataloging-in-Publication Data

Hamilton, William
    Reading Moby-Dick and other essays / William Hamilton.
        p. cm. — (American university studies. Series IV, English language and literature ; vol. 69)
        Bibliography: p.
        1. Death of God theology. 2. Melville, Herman, 1819-1891. Moby Dick. 3. Christianity and the arts. 4. Theology. I. Title. II. Series: American university studies. Series IV. English language and literature : v. 69.
BT83.5.H32   1989   231–dc19   88-12122
ISBN 0-8204-0613-9   CIP
ISSN 0741-0700

CIP-Titelaufnahme der Deutschen Bibliothek

Hamilton, William:
Reading Moby-Dick and other essays / William Hamilton. — New York; Bern; Frankfurt am Main; Paris: Lang, 1988.
    (American University Studies: Ser. 4, English Language and Literature; Vol. 69)
    ISBN 0-8204-0613-9

NE: American University Studies / 04

© Peter Lang Publishing, Inc., New York 1989

All rights reserved.
Reprint or reproduction, even partially, in all forms such as microfilm, xerography, microfiche, microcard, offset strictly prohibited.

Printed by Weihert-Druck GmbH, Darmstadt, West Germany

Contents

Preface ix
   I. Reading *Moby-Dick* 1
  II. The Conversions of Michelangelo 79
 III. Shakespearean Death 127
 IV. The Inquisitor's Argument 151
  V. God as Monica's Breast? 167
 VI. To Cast Fire Upon The Earth: a baccalaureate sermon 171
VII. The Second Coming of the Death of God 177
VIII. Consenting to Die: A Meditation on Mortality 181
Notes 245

Illustrations

Figure 1. Michelangelo, The Separation of Light from Darkness, Sistine Chapel ceiling, fresco, Vatican.

Figure 2. Michelangelo, Madonna, Medici Chapel, marble, Florence, San Lorenzo.

Figure 3. Michelangelo, The Temptation and Expulsion from Paradise (detail), Sistine Chapel ceiling, fresco, Vatican.

Figure 4. Michelangelo, Last Judgment (detail), Sistine Chapel, fresco, Vatican.

Figure 5. Michelangelo, Rondanini Pietà, marble, Castello Sforzesco, Milan.

All photographs and permissions to use them are from Alinari/Art Resource, New York.

Preface

The larger part of this collection consists of essays in the area of religion and the arts; the rest are more generally theological and cultural. The first four essays record one theologian's engagement with a series of texts, or what David Tracy calls classics. The reader will observe that the author has been unable to succumb to the latest (or next-to-the-latest?) piece of literary-critical relevance—the Paris-New Haven connection. The reason for this inability is not moral: it is not that I am too humble to claim that my critical speech is as interesting and playful as the speech of the novelists and poets. The reason is simply autobiographical. My first severe training in the reading of texts was training in the reading of the Bible. In that training one sat— in fear and trembling, as we said then—before an objective Word, alien in both time and meaning; enemy, obstacle, other, never to be mastered or confused with our own inept words about it. That training apparently cannot be washed off, and I still find it in operation when I turn to texts in literature and art.

This collection does, I think, have a connecting theme. Of course, all authors say that about their collections, and sometimes they can be believed. Each of these pieces, in one way or another, directly or indirectly, tries to attend to the cultural implications of the experience of the death of God, an experience which I hold to be a decisive twentieth-century religious event.

This can be seen especially in the title essay, the long piece on Melville's *Moby-Dick*. The death of God, in a complex way, is at the center of my understanding of this novel. The title essay is in the form of a reader's or study guide, which means it can be read before, during, and after (but never instead of) the reading of the novel itself. The content of each chapter is briefly indicated, then follows anything from a brief comment to an extended essay suggested by the chapter. Some of the themes and images playing through the novel are discussed at the point of their initial appearance.

Two pieces of Melville material, contemporary with *Moby-Dick*, are virtually essential for a full reading of the book: the review essay, "Hawthorne and His Mosses," and the 1851 letters to Hawthorne; I have drawn on this material when appropriate. I cannot avoid expressing my deep indebtedness to the work of Dr. Henry A. Murray, whose essays on Melville surely belong on everyone's short list of the finest literary criticism of our century.

I probably would not have dared to venture into the forbidden territory of Michelangelo were it not for the work and example of Professor Leo Steinberg. If this distinguished art historian can manage such convincing raids into my field without getting into trouble, perhaps the reverse movement is also possible. In any case, I am deeply in his debt. My own particular interest is in Michelangelo's poetry, which I believe has been too heavily neo-platonized in recent interpretion, and when my Italian and courage improve, I intend to continue my explorations.

The Shakespeare essay, and the long concluding essay on mortality, give form to an interest in the subject of death itself that has been with me for many years. The Shakespeare piece puts me alongside those critics suspicious of theological interpretations which find radiant redemption in every death and Jesus in every heroine. *King Lear* has become for me over the years an indispensable instrument by which I try to make sense of myself and my time.

Dostoevsky's "The Grand Inquisitor" has suffered grievous over-interpretation in our century (some of it my own), and my reading of it here attempts to counter that tradition.

The essay on Augustine is my one attempt to invent a new genre in theological–critical writing. The genre is called "serious spoof," and it is either to be taken seriously or not.

Preface

"To Cast Fire Upon the Earth" is a baccalaureate sermon delivered on May 25, 1986, at Northland College in Ashland, Wisconsin, on the occasion of the award of an honorary Doctor of Divinity by the college. I wish to express my gratitude to the trustees of the college, to the former president Malcolm McLean, and to Professor Lloyd Steffen for their kindness and hospitality during the visit to their campus.

I wish to thank the following authors and publishers for permission to quote from their copyrighted work:

New Directions Publishing Corporation, for a passage from Dylan Thomas: *Poems of Dylan Thomas*, Copyright 1952 by Dylan Thomas.

Random House, Inc., for a passage from "For The Time Being, A Christmas Oratorio," from W. H. Auden, *Collected Poems by W. H. Auden*, ed. by Edward Mendelson, copyrighted 1944 and renewed 1972 by W. H. Auden.

Scholars Press, for several pages from my monograph *Melville and the Gods*.

Harcourt Brace Jovanovich, Inc., for a passage from Mary McCarthy, *The Stones of Florence*.

The College Art Association and Professor Leo Steinberg, for permission to use a passage from his article, "Michelangelo's Florentine Pietà," in *Art Bulletin* (December, 1968).

Holt, Rinehart and Winston, for a passage from Theodore Reik, *Thirty Years With Freud*.

Harry N. Abrams, for a passage from Frederick Hartt, *Michelangelo's Drawings*.

The New Yorker, for a passage from the issue of April 22, 1972.

John Wiley and Sons, for a passage from Loren Baritz, *City on a Hill*.

Yale University Press, for several passages from Robert S. Liebert, *Michelangelo*.

Princeton University Press, for a passage from Richard F. Gustafson, *Leo Tolstoy, Resident and Stranger*; for several passages from Volumes II and V of Charles de Tolnay, *Michelangelo*.

Oxford University Press, and Professor Leo Steinberg, for permission to use a passage from his *Michelangelo's Last Paintings*.

Creighton Gilbert, for permission to quote from his translations of Michelangelo's poetry in *The Complete Poems and Selected Letters of Michaelangelo*, edited by Robert N. Linscott.

I am fortunate to have two good friends who have weathered the journey from "former student" to colleague and friend with understanding and grace. Over the years I have come to owe a very great deal indeed to Dr. John A. Phillips of Amherst, Massachusetts, and Dr. Ronald Carson of Galveston, Texas.

My indebtedness to Mary Jean is, as ever, beyond calculation. She has always been there, during the good times and the bad, with exactly the right mixture of understanding and skepticism. Without her. . . .

I want to dedicate my first post-retirement book to our children: Ross, Donald, Catherine, Patrick, and Jean, who, like Caliban's isle, are "full of noises; Sounds and sweet airs that give delight and hurt not."

"I, for one, don't see how Herman Melville relates to our life style."

• •

I
Reading *Moby-Dick*

Moby-Dick is not a difficult book and does not really need a guide. But what is not necessary can be enjoyable (as owners of red Porsches can attest), and so this dispensable essay may claim a modest reason for being. But once it gets readers into *Moby-Dick* itself, it ought to be forgotten, for they are then ready to re-read without a guide or with one of their own.

There are (at least) three ways to read *Moby-Dick*: the poetic, the political, and the theological. Since my reading is probably closest to the third, a word about the other quite appropriate approaches is in order.

The *poetic* reading takes the novel as a language system. It may do its work by looking at fundamental images: shoving off from land to sea, or circles (coils, whirlpools, vortexes, sharks or nursing whales swimming in circles), or something of the sort. It may more generally see the novel as a book about language, about the names we give to natural objects; indeed, as a book about the nature of nature itself. What, this reading sometimes asks, is an object in the natural order? Is it simply a value-free fact, there to be measured or mastered, as scientists like to do? Or is it a sign of something deeper or higher? It has been observed that the real teaching of *Moby-Dick* is

> that a man invites destruction if he accepts the transcendental theory of knowledge which makes physical objects emblematic of some spiritual reality. Yet it does not follow that this teaching represents Melville's own firm belief.... It was the author's emotional sympathy for a character of whom he intellectually disapproved [i.e. Ahab] which gave *Moby-Dick* much of its ambiguity and dramatic intensity.[1]

What is a whale; what is *the* whale for Ahab, Ishmael, Starbuck, Melville?

The *political* reading defines the *Pequod*'s search as a search for a visible America: Ahab may be read as a corrupt entrepreneur, the "mariners, renegades, castaways" as oppressed labor. One of the most eloquent passages ever written about Melville articulates this secular-political reading.

> Melville understood the idea of the new; he understood that the discovery of the final New World ended, rather than began, man's eternal dream of a happy land where sorrow and pain would be no more. He knew that the New World, because it was the last, would necessarily be the place where men would have to face themselves without the comfort of that ancient faith that elsewhere life could be better. America meant that there was no place left to go, no more escapes, no more freedom growing in virgin lands. The gift of new space was finished, and henceforth men would have to make instead of receive their felicity. Melville knew that they would fail. American comfort had been genuine so long as Americans received it, so long as the land had been fertile and unoccupied. With the end of land came the beginning of true civilization, came men's need to fashion ways to live together. Melville's own life overlapped the lives of both John Adams and Franklin Roosevelt. He had witnessed the growth of America from a primitive to an industrial order. He had seen the passing of the land and the development of civilization. With civilization in America came the ultimate tragedy: the eternal passing of the Typee valley from mankind's sober hope. America now took her place among the nations as a land like any other. Americans now were merely men. The land had come of age, and age was time and tragedy and the end.[2]

The *theological* reading asks yet another set of questions. What are the various faiths of Ishmael? What religious styles does he adopt and set aside? What is the relation of Ahab to God and the gods? What god is he fighting, what kind of god does he become in his seeking and destroying? What sort of god, if any, is the white whale himself, and are there any other divinities lurking in the novel besides Ahab and the whale?

There is evidence—within *Moby-Dick* and elsewhere—that Melville was gripped by a deep exhaustion and despair as he worked on the book. In the important June 1(?), 1851, letter to

Hawthorne, he writes: "I feel I am now come to the inmost leaf of the bulb, and that shortly the flower must fall to the ground." An almost suicidal note for a young man not yet thirty-two. Later in the same letter he writes that if an author were really to tell the truth, his fate would be poverty. And then, most poignantly:

> Dollars damn me; and the malicious Devil is forever grinning in upon me, holding the door ajar. My dear Sir, a presentiment is on me,—I shall at last be worn out and perish, like an old nutmeg-grater, grated to pieces by the constant attrition of the wood, that is, the nutmeg. What I feel most moved to write, that is banned,—it will not pay. Yet, altogether, write the *other* way I cannot. So the product is a final hash, and all my books are botches. . . . Though I wrote the Gospels in this century, I should die in the gutter.

Beyond this classic statement of the author's dilemma, Melville appears haunted by the spectacle of nature, history and self all threatened by disorder and meaninglessness. Men may be sustained, but they are also destroyed, by nature. The historical optimism of his fellow countrymen is a lie. Neither the inherited Calvinism (for all his asides that he found much there quite useful) nor the newer romantic optimism of transcendentalism that found intimations of the divine all through nature, history, and self, could fully illumine his dark view of life in nineteenth-century America. So when old myths die, you make new ones. Life is a voyage, ending in catastrophe; sea is both destruction and life; land is both safety and peril; fire is to be defied and adored; wind is benign and malignant. And at the center of this new myth is the white whale itself, whatever that may be.

1

> Ishmael introduces himself and tells us why he goes to sea, of his restlessness, and of "the overwhelming idea of the great whale himself." Moby-Dick himself is hinted at in the last sentence of what has been called the finest first chapter in English. Incidentally, Melville began his second sea voyage, his first on a whaler, in January 1841, out of New Bedford. It is both necessary and perilous to identify the author and narrator.

"Call me Ishmael." We might ask: Why didn't Melville begin simply with "My name is Ishmael"? Is there a hint that Ishmael may not be the narrator's real name? In any case, the effect of this opening command is to drag us at once into the story.

Ishmael takes to the sea, he tells us—perhaps seriously—to escape from suicidal depression. The sea becomes at once something like healing or salvation, so we will not be surprised if the gods come to play an important part in this tale. Here the sea is freedom, "the image of the ungraspable phantom of life"; the city, New York City in this case, is the evil from which man needs redemption. A bit later, Ishmael will re-affirm his contempt for the "turnpike earth."

Isn't this "everlasting itch for things remote" that sent Ishmael to sea a universal one, or at least a very American one? We are tempted to solve our problems in history by flights to nature (i.e., boats, streams, mountains), to heal by vacations the damage done by work, to dissolve the self's bondage to time by movement in space. If the gods cannot save us, perhaps a trip can.

The nearest Melville seems to come to revealing *his* interpretation of *Moby-Dick* is in the elusive, and inaccurate, reference to Narcissus. Narcissus is "the key to it all," he says—a myth about destructive pride and about water that kills. But in most versions of the story, Narcissus does not drown, he pines away because he cannot embrace the alluring image in the water. Perhaps myths are there for us to productively misuse.

2

Ishmael goes from Manhattan to New Bedford. Arriving on Saturday, he finds he has to wait until Monday for the Nantucket boat. After wandering into a church where the black preacher is discoursing symbolically on the blackness of darkness, he finally finds a suitable inn.

Ishmael's accidental visit to the black church marks the first instance of a theme that dominates *Moby-Dick*: the idea of "black," the idea of "white," and the relation between the two. In Melville's review-essay, "Hawthorne and His Mosses," he warmly approves of Hawthorne's affinity for blackness. This is a passage important for an understanding of the metaphorical climate of *Moby-Dick*.

> For spite of all the Indian-summer sunlight on the hither side of Hawthorne's soul, the other side—like the dark half of the physical sphere—is shrouded in a blackness, ten times black. But this darkness but gives more effect to the everlasting dawn that forever advances through it, and circumnavigates his world. Whether Hawthorne has simply availed himself of this mystical blackness as a means to the wondrous effects he makes it to produce in his lights and shades; or whether there really lurks in him, perhaps unknown to himself, a touch of Puritanic gloom,—this I cannot altogether tell. Certain it is, however, that this great power of blackness in him derives its force from its appeals to that Calvinistic sense of Innate Depravity and Original Sin, from whose visitations, in some shape or other, no deeply thinking mind is always and wholly free. . . . Now it is that blackness in Hawthorne, of which I have spoken, that so fixes and fascinates me.

This early reference to "the blackness of darkness" in *Moby-Dick* prepares the way for the later meditation on the even greater terror of the color white. Both before and after *Moby-Dick*, Melville was fascinated by the black–white relationship. With but two exceptions, the black man was strong, trustworthy, profound, while the white was inmature, weak, injured, or mad.

This theme first comes up in Melville's first novel, *Typee*, where Tommo, suffering from a mysterious, perhaps psychosomatic, leg injury, is carried around the valley on the shoulders of his friend Kory-Kory. *Moby-Dick* has its own set of black man–white man images. We will shortly see a kind of marriage between the white Ishmael and the native Queequeg. We will find them yoked together in the monkey-rope device (chapter 72), and on the final page of the novel Ishmael is saved from the destructive vortex by holding on to the coffin of Ishmael which has been transformed into a life-buoy. Black and white together even at the end.

Flask perches on black Daggoo's shoulders at the first lowering (chapter 48), while the mad white (and Christian) Ahab has two black alter egos: mad Pip, who touches some decent center in Ahab and whom Ahab rejects as something "too curing to my malady"; and the Zoroastrian (i.e., light is good and black is evil!) Fedallah who achieves final spiritual domination over his captain.

In "Benito Cereno," shortly after *Moby-Dick*, Melville returns to the black–white theme in his portrait of the weak, white, demoralized Don Benito receiving constant attention and physical support from Babo, the violent leader of the slave rebellion. After the other innocent white captain, Delano, finally sees the reality that has been played out before his eyes, he captures Babo and frees Cereno from his unwilling captivity to the slaves. Delano cannot understand why Cereno is not delighted by his freedom. "What has cast such a shadow upon you"? asks the good-natured American who cannot believe in sin. "The Negro," Cereno mysteriously replies, referring no doubt to the actual Negro Babo, to the idea of slavery that has deeply corrupted both owner and owned, and to "blackness" itself—that tragic sense of things that Delano lacked, that Cereno learned, and that Melville so deeply admired.

It is characteristic that Melville was not content with a simply moralistic translation of black and white. Never was black evil and white good, and not always was the reverse the case. One recalls that Melville was later to become uneasy with the views of the abolitionists because he felt they subtly demeaned the black race by denying to them the possibility of sin, and thus the possibility of full humanity.

3
Ishmael describes the inn, and particularly a painting in the lobby of a whale and a storm-wrecked ship. Other sailors come into the inn, and we have a brief look at Bulkington, who will become Ishmael's shipmate. He gets a room for the night, one he shares with his future shipmate, Queequeg.

Here is our introduction to the central human relationship in *Moby-Dick*, that between Ishmael and Queequeg, white and black. Dr. Henry A. Murray, our greatest contemporary Melvillean, has called attention to Melville's life-long "craving for the responsive, undivided utter love of somebody whom he loves with his whole heart."[3] Melville lost his father at the age of twelve, who had suffered both bankruptcy and madness before his death. Small wonder that so many observers have detected in Melville's work an incessant search of son for father, of something to fill the void left by the father's death. Melville's household, both before and after his marriage, was dominated by women, particularly by a powerful mother who lived with him for some time after his marriage. When he was an old man, he said of his mother,"she hated me." As we will see, throughout *Moby-Dick* Queequeg will turn out to be a more effective redeemer of Ishmael than the sea ever was.

4

Ishmael wakes up the next morning and describes a strange childhood dream.

This chapter describes the beginning of a friendship, even a kind of love, between Queequeg and Ishmael. Notice the description of Queequeg's hand in his as something "supernatural." Queequeg, meeting Ishmael's landlocked depression, serves as both spouse and god.

Ishmael's recollection of falling into "a troubled nightmare of a doze" that so terrified him as a child brings us to the first of several important "dreams" in *Moby-Dick*. After this first one of Ishmael, the next is that of Jonah the prophet in Father Mapple's celebrated sermon. Here is the preacher's portrait of the guilt-ridden dream of the reluctant prophet.

> Like one who after a night of drunken revelry hies to his bed, still reeling, but with conscience yet pricking him, as the plungings of the Roman race-horse but so much the more strike his steel tags into him; as one who in that miserable plight still turns and turns in giddy anguish, praying God for annihilation until the fit be passed; and at last amid the whirl of woe he feels, a deep stupor steals over him, as over the man who bleeds to death, for conscience is the wound, and there's naught to staunch it; so, after sore wrestlings in his berth, Jonah's prodigy of ponderous misery drags him drowning down to sleep (chapter 9).

There is no dream, and no guilt, in the biblical Jonah; Mapple's invented dream of Jonah is tormented, anxiety-ridden, restless. So are most of the other *Moby-Dick* dreams. Ahab has slept restlessly from the beginning of the voyage, and Stubb speaks of the captain's sleeping habits in chapter 29.

> Didn't that Dough-Boy, the steward, tell me that of a morning he always finds the old man's hammock clothes all rumpled and tumbled, and the sheets down at the foot, and the coverlid almost tied into knots, and the pillow a sort of frightful hot, as though a baked brick had been on it? A hot old man! I guess he's got what some folks ashore call a conscience; it's a kind of Tic-Dolly-row they say—worse nor a toothache.

Later (chapter 31), Stubb has a dream of his own in which he is kicked by Captain Ahab. Stubb is not inclined to propose any deep interpretations of his dream.

Dreams, guilt, and conscience seem all yoked together in this book. In chapter 44 a terrifying and revelatory dream of Ahab, sleeping with clenched fists and bloody palms, is recorded.

> Often, when forced from his hammock by exhausting and intolerably vivid dreams of the night, which, resuming his own intense thoughts through the day, carried them on amid a clashing of phrensies, and whirled them round and round in his blazing brain, till the very throbbing of his life-spot became insufferable anguish; and when, as was sometimes the case, these spiritual throes in him heaved his being up from its base, and a chasm seemed opening in him, from which forked flames and lightnings shot up, and accursed fiends beckoned him to leap down among them; when this hell in himself yawned beneath him, a wild cry would be heard through the ship; and with glaring eyes Ahab would burst from his state room, as though escaping from a bed that was on fire. Yet these, perhaps, instead of being the unsuppressable symptoms of some latent weakness, or fright at his own resolve, were but the plainest tokens of its intensity. For, at such times, crazy Ahab, the scheming, unappeasedly steadfast hunter of the white whale; this Ahab that had gone to his hammock, was not the agent that so caused him to burst from it in horror again. The latter was the eternal, living principle or soul in him; and in sleep, being for the time dissociated from the characterizing mind, which at other times employed it for its outer vehicle or agent, it spontaneously sought escape from the scorching contiguity of the frantic thing, of which, for the time, it was no longer an integral. But as the mind does not exist unless leagued with the soul, therefore it must have been

that, in Ahab's case, yielding up all his thoughts and fancies to his one supreme purpose; that purpose, by its own sheer inveteracy of will, forced itself against gods and devils into a kind of self-assumed, independent being of its own. Nay, could grimly live and burn, while the common vitality to which it was conjoined, fled horror-stricken from the unbidden and unfathered birth. Therefore, the tormented spirit that glared out of bodily eyes, when what seemed Ahab rushed from his room, was for the time but a vacated thing, a formless somnambulistic being, a ray of living light, to be sure, but without an object to color, and therefore a blankness in itself. God help thee, old man, thy thoughts have created a creature in thee; and he whose intense thinking thus makes him a Prometheus; a vulture feeds upon that heart for ever; that vulture the very creature he creates.

This is not an easy knot to untie. There is a dualistic psychology at work here. Ahab has both an eternal living principle or soul (which functions like the modern unconscious in this passage) *plus* a mind, characterizing, frantic, and mad (ego?). Awake, the mad mind dominated the sane soul—thus the voyage of the *Pequod*. But asleep (guiltily, like Jonah?) the sane but normally dominated soul briefly escapes from the mad mind's tyranny. But there is a striking overlap between sleeping and waking. Just after awakening from his exhausting dream-torment, Ahab is in fact a soulless monster—vacated, formless, until the mad mind reasserts its mastery over the soul or self. Thus sleep, however tormented, gives to Ahab the only intimations of sanity he is to know. (It is striking to see, in chapter 51, that the "sea" sleeps with the same tormented movements as does Ahab—and Jonah.)

One is tempted to guess that Melville was sleeping very badly during the work on *Moby-Dick*. Sleep here is always dream-laden, and the dreams are connected to both torment and conscience.

5–6
Ishmael takes his Sunday breakfast and goes for a walk in New Bedford (where there is now a Herman Melville shopping plaza, by the way).

There is an interesting and slightly odd remark on humor at the beginning of chapter 5.

> So if any one man, in his own proper person, afford stuff for a good joke to anybody, let him not be backward, but let him cheerfully allow himself to spend and be spent in that way. And the man that has anything bountifully laughable about him, be sure there is more in that man than you perhaps think for.

This is not the conventional wisdom that one ought to cultivate a sense of humor or "be a clown." It recommends being a victim of someone else's joke. There is a touching note of both compassion and admiration for anyone willing to become such a victim.

Later (chapter 49), after spending all night in a water-logged whale-boat, Ishmael expands this early analysis of humor into a desperate philosophy of life. Ishmael may mean this, or he may just be trying it on to see if it fits. Real or feigned, it doesn't last long.

> There are certain queer times and occasions in this strange mixed affair we call life when a man takes this whole universe for a vast practical joke, though the wit thereof he but dimly discerns, and more than suspects that the joke is at nobody's expense but his own. However, nothing dispirits, and nothing seems worth while disputing. . . . And as for small difficulties and worryings, prospects of sudden disaster, peril of life and limb; all these, and death itself, seem to him only sly, good-natured hits, and jolly punches in the side bestowed by the unseen and unaccountable old joker.

Ishmael's words on humor seem at once bitter, sad, and angry.

7
Ishmael decides to go to church and offers a description of the interior of the Whaleman's Chapel.

Ishmael's piety will prove to have many forms and this chapter begins to explore them. Sitting in the chapel he reflects on death at sea. How fortunate, he thinks, is the survivor who can say—"just here lies my beloved." Those "who have placelessly perished without a grave" distress their survivors beyond normal grief, he thinks. The continuing emotional intensity surrounding our own missing-in-action soldiers in Southeast

Asia underscores Ishmael's insight that there is a kind of comfort in knowing just where the dead one lies.

This leads Ishmael to remark that a belief in immortality rarely seems to comfort the grieving one. Then, in an aside of striking bitterness:

> But Faith, like a jackal, feeds among the tombs, and even from these dead doubts, she gathers her most vital hope.

What is he saying? Partly this is a conventional comment that reflection on death can often be the beginning of religion. But to call faith a scavenger of animal and human corpses is hardly to praise it. A piece of conventional anthropology seems to explode into hatred of such a scavenging kind of religion.

This mood abruptly shifts at the close of the chapter when a (now) conventionally religious Ishmael decides, with a suspicious touch of bravado, that he is not afraid of death since his soul is immortal. We know a good deal about Melville's own religious inheritance. It was curiously mixed. From his father came a bland liberal Unitarianism, though most of his childhood church experiences were of his mother's Dutch Reformed Calvinism. This inherited Protestant mixture was slipping away at the time of the writing of *Moby-Dick* (1850–1851), but Melville was never to escape the questions that Calvinism posed, even when he could not accept the answers. A few years after *Moby-Dick*, Hawthorne noted in his journal that Melville "had pretty much made up his mind to be annihilated"; that is, he had given up his belief in personal immortality. It may be that Melville was slightly more deconverted than Ishmael at this time.

8
Father Mapple, and the chapel's pulpit, are described.

Meeting Queequeg has made Ishmael reflective. Father Mapple, preaching from his elevated pulpit, must—he muses—"symbolize something unseen." This is the first appearance in the novel of the idea of a symbolic nature; nature's meaning lies not in what it is, but what it signifies. This pervasive idea can be found in Plato, and in another form in Calvin's theology of the sacraments. In Melville's day this idea of nature is associated with transcendentalism which can be traced back through German romanticism to seventeenth-century Puritan preaching. Ishmael admits here that he is drawn to this view of nature, and later, standing watch at the mast-head, this view will tempt him again. Transcendentalism dominates Ahab's thinking about the white whale, and we might observe that Ishmael survives the catastrophe brought about by Ahab's transcendentalist madness because he is finally able to overcome the view of nature that he first toys with in this chapter. Later, Ishmael will have a closer look at Ahab's idea of nature as a series of masks concealing a deeper truth behind them. He will be both attracted and finally repelled by this view. Melville himself seems both fascinated and repelled by Ahab, and this partly explains why it is possible to read the captain as both devil and hero.

At the close of the chapter Ishmael describes a painting decorating the back of Mapple's pulpit in which an angel casts a spot of light on a floundering ship. (A second use of the device of a painting to set the atmosphere.)

> "Ah, noble ship," the angel seemed to say, "beat on, thou noble ship, and bear a hardy helm; for lo! the sun is breaking through; the clouds are rolling off—serenest azure is at hand."

Here is the first appearance in *Moby-Dick* of an important image in Melville's imagination: that of a ship or seaman or both, pressing bravely, often vainly, forward through the water. We first saw this in Melville's first book *Typee* where it is the dominant image of the book. There the narrator tells us of his frequent visits to a statue at a mausoleum of a dead native warrior. He is in his canoe, looking intently ahead, with a skull mounted on the prow facing him. Tommo cries out to this effigy:

> Aye, paddle away, brave chieftain, to the land of spirits! To the material eye thou makest but little progress; but with the eye of faith, I see thy canoe cleaving the bright waves, which die away on those dimly looming shores of Paradise.

The chieftain's journey is through death and beyond, ironically blessed by the grinning skull facing him. At the end of *Mardi*, Melville's third novel, the narrator Taji, rejecting the security of the land that beguiled his friend Babbalanja, is alone in his boat at sea, looking just like the Marquesan chieftain, plunging forward to freedom and to death.

In *Moby-Dick* this image is picked up in the apostrophe to Bulkington and landlessness (see note to chapter 23, below). Bulkington's courage is defined as his resistance to the temptations of "the treacherous, slavish shore" and his drive to push forward, against the wind which would force him to land, to the sea and (as it happens) to death.

When Ishmael first catches sight of Captain Ahab he is positioned just like the effigy of the chieftain. Erect at the prow, looking out over the water with "a determinate, unsurrendering willfulness, in the fixed and fearless, forward dedication of that glance" (chapter 28).

This image is a deeply sad one, for the pictured journey seems always to be a doomed one. At the end of chapter 52, Ishmael reflects on the idea of going around the world:

> But in pursuit of those far mysteries we dream of, or in tormented chase of that demon phantom that, some time or other, swims before all human hearts; while chasing such over this round globe, they [i.e. those far mysteries we dream of, our goals or ideals] either lead us on in barren mazes or midway leave us whelmed.

Of course one must undertake journeys, mythic and real, and they are all doomed to fail. The boat in the painting in Mapple's pulpit is but a part of this nearly compulsive, and certainly fascinating, image in Melville's work.

9
Mapple's sermon. A lyrical, free-wheeling, not particularly biblical meditation on the book of Jonah.

What we have in this sermon is an accurate picture of a central theme in Calvinist theology: the transcendence of God and the need of man to abase himself utterly before that God. It is not a picture of the author's faith, but it may well be a picture of what he was fleeing from. Mapple's magnificent sovereign God will ultimately be perceived by Ishmael as dangerous, even evil, and Ahab's white whale is another form of that dangerous and evil God. Perhaps we cannot evaluate Melville's real attitude to Mapple's God until we take account of two later moments in the novel: there is a second sermon in *Moby-Dick* (chapter 64) when the black cook, Fleece, preaches a sermon to the sharks. This seems to suggest that all sermons are as useless as words directed to sharks to stop eating. And second, we probably ought to observe both that "delight" is the key word in this sermon's final peroration, and that *Delight* is also the name of the most forlorn and tragic ship the Pequod will meet at sea.

As a one-time maker and consumer of sermons, I am tempted to add a note on Father Mapple as homiletician. This is really a very peculiar sermon: in theology, impeccably Puritan–Calvinist; in exegesis, incurably liberal, modernist, as relevance-mongering and unbiblical as any contemporary Protestant hymn to positive thinking.

The book of Jonah is an odd little book, better seen as a fiction or a parable than as narrative history. Mapple gives a credible, if elaborated, approximation of what goes on in the first two chapters. Jonah is called by God to preach inevitable judgment to the foreign (i.e. Assyrian) city of Nineveh, and he flees from this call. He arrives in Joppa, a coastal town south of Mount Carmel, and boards a ship for Spain. A storm comes up, and the sailors suspect that Jonah's sin is the storm's cause. He admits it and courageously offers himself as a sacrifice. He is thrown overboard and swallowed by a divinely appointed fish from whose belly he utters a devout hymn of praise with absolutely no note or repentance in it. God liked the prayer and instructed the fish to find some land to vomit Jonah upon.

This is the part of the story that Mapple treats in his splendidly careless way. He brings in an array of embellishments to the spare biblical narrative to underline Jonah's guilty flight from God. He invents that magnificent guilt-ridden nap for Jonah that the Bible knows nothing of. The function of these embellishments, apparently, is to set Jonah before his congregation as a model for repentance. The biblical text, on the other hand, makes not the slightest mention of repentance.

Mapple's first point: Jonah is a model of repentance for us all. Answer: no, in the book of Jonah he is nothing of the sort. Point two of the preacher: by his failure to do so, Jonah reminds me of my function to preach Truth to the face of falsehood. Answer: this is profoundly true, though Mapple found it in the book of Jonah by noting what the prophet Jonah did not do.

In dealing so elegantly and imperfectly with chapters one and two, Mapple manages to ignore the real problem in the book of Jonah. Other Hebrew prophets, Amos for one, preached judgment to other nations, but the most radical judgment went to Israel. Jonah is asked to preach only to a foreign city; his message is to be judgment, not redemption through repentence. When Nineveh finally does repent (in Jonah 4) in response to Jonah's word of judgment, the prophet is furious with God's softheadedness. Foreigners should not be permitted to repent and be saved; this should be a privilege reserved for Israel alone. The book of Jonah must be seen as a post-exilic study in narrow nationalistic pride and deep hostility to all nations outside of Israel's borders. Jonah is a perfect exemplar of that narrow chauvinism.

Jonah as chauvinist becomes, in the parable of the book of Jonah, Israel itself—stupid in its provincial rejection of God's sovereignty over all the nations. Jonah's chastisement of God for accepting the repentance of Nineveh is even more stupid than his initial flight from God's call in chapter 1. Jonah's (i.e. Israel's) hatred of the Assyrians is so profound that he would rather die than face the fact that their repentance is a response to his own effective preaching!

So Mapple manages to miss most of what is going on in this strange little Old Testament book. He is wrong about Jonah as a model for repentance, but he is right that real prophets (like Mapple) should do what Jonah was initially afraid of doing. Mapple, in his superb peroration, assumes that speaking truth to falsehood will always fail in worldly terms.[4] It may be, though

Mapple might have noted how successful his beloved Jonah was, and how ungraciously he handled his success.

There is an alluring whiff of heresy at the close of the sermon's peroration.

> Woe to him whom this world charms from Gospel duty! Woe to him who seeks to pour oil upon the waters when God has brewed them into a gale! Woe to him who seeks to please rather than to appal! Woe to him whose good name is more to him than goodness! Woe to him who, in this world, courts not dishonor! Woe to him who would not be true, even though to be false were salvation! Yea, woe to him who, as the great Pilot Paul has it, while preaching to others is himself a castaway!"
>
> He dropped and fell away from himself for a moment; then lifting his face to them again, showed a deep joy in his eyes, as he cried out with a heavenly enthusiasm,—"But oh! shipmates! on the starboard hand of every woe, there is a sure delight; and higher the top of that delight, than the bottom of the woe is deep. Is not the main-truck higher than the kelson is low? Delight is to him—a far, far upward, and inward delight—who against the proud gods and commodores of this earth, ever stands forth his own inexorable self. Delight is to him whose strong arms yet support him, when the ship of this base treacherous world has gone down beneath him. Delight is to him, who gives no quarter in the truth, and kills, burns, and destroys all sin though he pluck it out from under the robes of Senators and Judges. Delight,—top-gallant delight is to him, who acknowledges no law or lord, but the Lord his God, and is only a patriot to heaven. Delight is to him, whom all the waves of the billows of the seas of the boisterous mob can never shake from this sure Keel of the Ages. And eternal delight and deliciousness will be his, who coming to lay him down, can say with his final breath—O Father!—chiefly known to me by Thy rod—mortal or immortal, here I die. I have striven to be Thine, more than to be this world's, or mine own. Yet this is nothing; I leave eternity to Thee; for what is man that he should live out the lifetime of his God?"

Just after Ishmael has dusted off his half-hearted belief in the soul's immortality to help him deal with his fear of death, Mapple closes his sermon—often called "orthodox" by untheological critics—by denying that very immortality. "Mortal or immortal, here I die," he cries. And then: "I leave eternity to Thee; for what is man that he should live out the lifetime of his God?" Man is not, and should not claim to be, immortal. A fascinating heresy, or unbelief, at the heart of Mapple's belief. Eloquent preacher; as exegete, not so hot.

10-11
After church, Ishmael returns to the inn. His admiration for Queequeg deepens.

When Ishmael remarks that "Queequeg was George Washington cannibalistically developed," we are reminded of a line in the June 1(?), 1851, letter to Hawthorne: "It is but nature to be shy of a mortal who boldly declares that a thief in jail is as honorable a personage as Gen. George Washington."

Mapple's sermon does not seem to have deepened Ishmael's Christian faith. He turns to Queequeg, not God. "I'll try a pagan friend," he remarks bitterly, "since Christian kindness has proved but hollow courtesy." Melville clearly enjoys describing Ishmael's decision to share Queequeg's worship. Doesn't the golden rule state that we should do to others what we wish others to do to us? Well, I wish Queequeg would join me in my worship, so I should join him in his. Christians can justify anything, Melville suggests, and he will make this charge again.

Queequeg further emerges here as Ishmael's true redeemer, more effective than the "sea" to which he initially fled. They have smoked together, they were "married" and became "a cosy, loving pair."

> I felt a melting in me [Ishmael confesses]. No more my splintered heart and maddened hand were turned against the wolfish world. This soothing savage had redeemed it.

12
In a brief biographical chapter on Queequeg, Melville is unable to withhold his opinion, also held in *Typee*, that pagans are generally to be preferred to Christians.

13
On the packet-ship from New Bedford to Nantucket, Ishmael reflects again on his restlessness on land, and on "the magnanimity of the sea."

On this trip, Queequeg's natural superiority to Christians is again illustrated. A man on the ship insults him, is accidentally thrown overboard, and Queequeg saves the man's life, loving his enemies. "We cannibals must help these Christians," says Queequeg, and at the novel's close Queequeg, in the form of his floating coffin, does indeed help Ishmael.

14–15

Some historical remarks on Nantucket. Ishmael and Queequeg look for a place to stay, and chowder is discussed.

16

Ishmael seeks out a whaler for himself and Queequeg. He meets Captain Peleg and Bildad, the Quaker-owners of the *Pequod*, and reflects on the significance of the sea-going Quaker character-type who learns from the sea "a bold and nervous lofty language." (An apposite description of Melville's own language in *Moby-Dick*.) Captain Ahab is described, and Ishmael signs up.

In his aside on the special kind of character produced by Nantucket, the Quaker tradition, and the sea, Ishmael reflects on power and ambition, the first of a series of interesting and subversive reflections on power in the novel. "Be sure of this," he declares, "O young ambition, all mortal greatness is but disease." This may not become entirely clear until we set it alongside this remark on Ahab and power in chapter 33:

> That certain sultanism of his brain, which had otherwise in a good degree remained unmanifested; through those forms that same sultanism became incarnate in an irresistible dictatorship. For be a man's intellectual superiority what it will, it can never assume the practical, available supremacy over other men, without the aide of some sort of external arts and entrenchments, always, in themselves, more or less paltry and base. This it is, that for ever keeps God's true princes of the Empire from the world's hustings; and leaves the highest honors that this air can give, to those men who become famous more through their infinite inferiority to the choice hidden handful of the Divine Inert, than through their undoubted superiority over the dead level of the mass.

This means, I take it, that however intellectually impressive Ahab may have been, there is a moral inferiority, a mediocrity, in anyone like him who deliberately seeks power or mastery over others. This is a fascinating, and very Protestant indictment of the world of secular politics.

This moralistic rejection of power is also found in one of Melville's reflections on the power of the sperm whale. Take that whale's skull, he suggests in chapter 80, and set it alongside a human skull (which it greatly resembles) and a sound phrenological analysis would oblige you to say of the former owner of that whale skull: "This man had no self-esteem, and no veneration." Thus, he obscurely concludes, "you can best form to yourself the truest, though not the most exhilarating conception of what the most exalted potency is." True power is therefore immoral, sought for only by the insecure and self-hating.

Yet Melville was not consistent in his repudiation of power. In the meditation (chapter 86) on the sperm whale's tail, he speaks of its "Titanism of power" and then he adds: "Real strength never impairs beauty or harmony, but it often bestows it. . . ." And when that supreme embodiment of power, *Moby-Dick*, finally appears, there is no suggestion of evil at all. He is all power, joy, mildness, beauty. "A gentle joyousness—a mighty mildness of repose in swiftness, invested the gliding whale" (chapter 133).

One is tempted to conclude that for Melville power is properly invested only in whales; when mere men like Ahab seek it, they prove themselves morally crippled.

The comic and unflattering portraits of Peleg and Bildad (the biblical Bildad was one of Job's pious comforters) underline Melville's attitude to organized religion. Note Bildad's impeccable American piety: "a man's religion is one thing, and this practical world quite another. This world pays dividends."

At the close of the chapter, Captain Peleg calls Ahab "ungodly, God-like," anticipating an Ahab we will shortly see for ourselves—the claimant to and destroyer of divinity. "Ungodly, God-like" suggests Hawthorne's description of Melville himself as both religious and irreligious, comfortable neither in belief nor unbelief.

Peleg has a comment in this chapter that prepares us for the strange criticism of Starbuck shortly to appear: "Pious harpooners never make good voyagers—it takes the shark out of 'em. . . ." Christian piety fits one badly for the real world: a theme wandering through all of Melville's writing, from his attacks on missionaries in *Typee* to the flawed innocence of Billy Budd. This is not simply an attack on Christianity. It is as much an attack on the wolfish world for its inability to receive such sublime irrelevance.

17
Ishmael observes Queequeg's fasting and discusses again the differences between Christianity and paganism.

18
Queequeg signs on as a harpooner with the *Pequod*.

19
A mad stranger named Elijah accosts Ishmael as he is leaving the *Pequod* with Queequeg. Elijah warns about Ahab.

We should recall two things from the Old Testament at this point. In 1 Kings 17–21, the prophet Elijah's criticism of the wicked king Ahab is described. Further, the Old Testament asserted that before the Messiah comes, Elijah must return and prepare the way. Here is Elijah's return, and the *Pequod* sets sail on Christmas day.

20
In an innocuous chapter about the *Pequod*'s final preparations for sea, Melville throws off a sentence that may remind modern readers of one of the strategies of what we call repression.

> But when a man suspects any wrong, it sometimes happens that if he be already involved in the matter, he insensibly strives to cover up his suspicions even from himself.

It is early Christmas morning, and the ship's company begins to come aboard.

21
The mystery of the elusive sailors at the opening of this chapter is cleared up at the close of chapter 47.

22
Peleg and Bildad finally leave the ship as it sets sail, and Ishmael expresses his delight in leaving the land for the open sea.

23
Bulkington is at the wheel, and this chapter is a memorial to him. The reader will feel, perhaps for the first time, the sense of doom that hovers over the *Pequod*.

Here is another form of the land–sea relationship that Ishmael expressed at the beginning of the novel. Bulkington may or may not have been a character Melville intended to develop, but in any case he disappears after this chapter. Here again land is all oppressive conformism; sea absolute freedom. In a little while, Ishmael will become uneasy with this simple dualism. Sea will become for him as much death as freedom; land will be a longed-for domesticity. The emotional intensity of the language here suggests that there was a good deal of Bulkington in Melville.

> Know ye, now, Bulkington? Glimpses do ye seem to see of that mortally intolerable truth; that all deep, earnest thinking is but the intrepid effort of the soul to keep the open independence of her sea; while the wildest winds of heaven and earth conspire to cast her on the treacherous, slavish shore?
>
> But as in landlessness alone resides the highest truth, shoreless, indefinite as God—so, better is it to perish in the howling infinite, than be ingloriously dashed upon the lee, even if that were safety!

The divinity of the sea is being prepared. This chapter marks the end of what can be called the Ishmael section. The narrator voice of Ishmael recedes after this, becoming more objective and detached.

24
Whaling as a profession is defended.

Here is a new kind of material, and we will find more like it as we move on. It comes more from books than from experience, and it may be that this chapter and the other factual compilations like it were inserted late in the composition of the book. The reader may be tempted to skip over this factual material, but the temptation should be resisted. To the most detailed discussions of whales and whaling Melville can attach his most symbolic flights. While at work on *Moby-Dick*, Melville wrote about this symbol-making process to Richard H. Dana, Jr. (in a letter dated May 1, 1850):

> It will be a strange sort of book, tho', I fear; blubber is blubber you know; tho' you may get oil out of it, the poetry runs as hard as sap from a frozen maple tree;—& to cook the thing up, one must needs throw in a little fancy, which from the nature of the thing, must be ungainly as the gambols of the whales themselves. Yet I mean to give the truth of the thing, spite of this.

In this chapter Melville makes use of an argument he has used before. Are whalemen butchers, he asks? Yes, of course, but the great military commanders are even greater butchers.

Later (in chapter 87) the argument is expanded: "there is no folly of the beasts of the earth which is not infinitely outdone by the madness of men." In *Typee*, Melville had justified the cannibalism of his native friends on the grounds that modern civilized soldiers are more bloodthirsty. Some years ago, Father Daniel Berrigan used this argument in defending his destruction of draft board records: I am burning paper, not children. The argument is more rhetorical than moral, but Melville always found it hard to resist attacks on militarism, particularly when defended by piety.

This chapter contains the first reference to the great Leviathan—symbol of God's power—in chapter 41 of the Book of Job. It is the union of power and divinity in the Christian God that apparently most offended Melville.

25
Furthermore, whale oil is probably used at coronations.

26–27
The mates and the harpooners are introduced.

Something symbolic is going on. The three mates are white, one from each of the great New England whaling centers—Nantucket, Cape Cod, Martha's Vineyard. The harpooners are non-white, and representative: Queequeg a Pacific islander, Tashtego an American Indian, Daggoo an African. The *Pequod*'s journey is political as well as theological. The mates are the American managerial class, the harpooners and crew are the ordinary workers.

Melville's sketch of Starbuck is worth close attention. He is an attractive man; a Quaker, competent and courageous. But there is a hint in him of something fatally, even tragically, weak.

> And brave as he might be, it was that sort of bravery, chiefly visible in some intrepid men, which, while generally abiding firm in the conflict with seas, or winds, or whales, or any of the ordinary irrational horrors of the world, yet cannot withstand those more terrific, because more spiritual terrors, which sometimes menace you from the concentrating brow of an enraged and mighty man.
>
> But were the coming narrative to reveal, in any instance, the complete abasement of poor Starbuck's fortitude, scarce might I have the heart to write it; for it is a thing most sorrowful, nay shocking, to expose the fall of valor in the soul.

A hard indictment of the chief mate, and the author never really lives up to his promise to describe this tragic fall of valor. We are thus uncertain about what this weakness of Starbuck is supposed to be. He does not take any steps to prevent Ahab's final destructive act; that is true. He admits (in chapter 38) that he is quite overpowered by his captain; that his office is simply "to obey, rebelling." And in chapter 123 he resists the temptation to capture or to kill his feared commanding officer. Is this his weakness? Is this the "fall" that Melville refers to in this chapter?

We do know that Starbuck is a Christian. Is it this the author wishes us to identify as Starbuck's fatal weakness: that as a Christian he is incapable of murder? (It would be uncharacteristic of Melville to think this, for while he may have felt deeply alienated from Christianity in mid- and late life, he always admired its pacifist principles.) Indeed, Starbuck's Christianity is at least an analytical advantage; he rightly discerns Ahab as blasphemer, that his purpose is "heaven-insulting."

Melville's final word on Starbuck's piety is to criticize it as bland and reactionary orthodoxy. Looking out at the enchanting ocean surface (chapter 114), Starbuck meekily declares: "Let faith oust fact; let fancy oust memory; I look deep down and do believe." This is not a confession of faith with which Melville would have had much sympathy. It may be that Melville is arguing that Starbuck is morally flawed *because* he is a Christian. We do know that Melville consistently wanted his Christian characters to be weak, almost feminine in their passivity, not wholly in order to patronize them, but in part to admire their impotent and unworldly folly.

One reason this moral indictment bewilders the reader is that there is a part of Starbuck that is worthy of admiration, that cannot be construed as ruined or tragically weak. He stands up to Ahab, and finally gets his own way, on the (admittedly trivial) matter of the oil leak (chapter 109), and, at the very end of the novel, just before the sighting of Moby-Dick, Ahab treats his chief mate as the one solid note of sanity in an otherwise mad world. "Let me look into a human eye," Ahab asks (chapter 132). Starbuck, touched by this show of affection, tries for one last time to turn Ahab away from his mad search. He fails, but not surely because of some special weakness. He fails because rational suasion can never deflect determined madness from its goal. The problem of Starbuck's weakness, introduced here, is indeed an elusive one.

At the close of chapter 26 we find an example, as fine as you'll find anywhere in Melville's work, of his command of rhetorical speech. Someone has said that if Melville's poetry aspires to the condition of prose, his prose—as here—aspires to the condition of poetry.

> Men may seem detestable as joint stock-companies and nations; knaves, fools, and murderers there may be; men may have mean and meagre faces; but man, in the ideal, is so noble and so sparkling, such a grand and glowing creature, that over any ignominious blemish in him all his fellows should run to throw their costliest robes. That immaculate

manliness we feel within ourselves, so far within us, that it remains intact though all the outer character seem gone; bleeds with keenest anguish at the undraped spectacle of a valor-ruined man. Nor can piety itself, at such a shameful sight, completely stifle her upbraidings against the permitting stars. But this august dignity I treat of, is not the dignity of kings and robes, but that abounding dignity which has no robed investiture. Thou shalt see it shining in the arm that wields a pick or drives a spike; that democratic dignity which, on all hands, radiates without end from God; Himself! The great God absolute! The centre and circumference of all democracy! His omnipresence, our divine equality!

If, then, to meanest mariners, and renegades and castaways, I shall hereafter ascribe high qualities, though dark; weave round them tragic graces; if even the most mournful, perchance the most abased, among them all, shall at times lift himself to the exalted mounts; if I shall touch that workman's arm with some ethereal light; if I shall spread a rainbow over his disastrous set of sun; then against all mortal critics bear me out in it, thou just Spirit of Equality, which hast spread one royal mantle of humanity over all my kind! Bear me out in it, thou great democratic God! who didst not refuse to the swart convict, Bunyan, the pale, poetic pearl; Thou who didst clothe with doubly hammered leaves of finest gold, the stumped and paupered arm of old Cervantes; Thou who didst pick up Andrew Jackson from the pebbles; who didst hurl him upon a war-horse; who didst thunder him higher than a throne! Thou who, in all Thy mighty, earthly marchings, ever cullest Thy selectest champions from the kingly commons; bear me out in it, O God!

This meditation on God and democracy is part of the story of Ishmael's piety. It is neither particularly Christian nor particularly transcendentalist. It is a radical religious–political vision, or eschatology, based on the ordinary American.[5] In this vision the transcendent Puritan God of mother and Mapple has incarnated himself, not in the life of a single Jew, but in the lives of ordinary seamen. The Captain may turn out to be, like the old God, omnipotent and mad; the mates may be trivial or debilitated by their Christianity; but apparently in the harpooners and crew, black and white, American and non-American, the true god has come to rest. This new god is defined as "thou just Spirit of Equality," but Melville is unusual in that he bases his idea of equality in Jacksonian America on human sin, not on the fashionable moral optimism of the time. Connections between this religious–political vision and those of such contemporaries

as Whitman and Marx would not be difficult to draw. In such a vision, America can still be loved, for all its present vulgarity, largely because of its promise. This barely lovable America is the nation to which Melville, still hopeful, returned after his stay in the terrifying Eden of the Typee valley. America will not always elicit such love from Herman Melville.

He concludes chapter 27 by remarking that most whalemen are islanders, Isolatoes. "I call them this," Ishmael says, "because they do not acknowledge the common continent of men, but each Isolato [is] living on a separate continent of his own." Ishmael himself is such an Isolato; so, acutely, was Melville himself, until his death. It was a fate he never acquiesced in.

How strange to find in the same chapter a powerful vision of human community and an equally powerful rejection of it.

28

Ahab finally makes his appearance on the quarter-deck. Melville writes: "He looked like a man cut away from the stake, when the fire has overunningly wasted all the limbs without consuming them. . . ."

We first see Ahab associated with fire, and he stays with fire throughout the novel. Even his white scar will prove (chapter 119) to have been caused by a sacramental burn of some kind. One is almost tempted to suggest that Melville designed the imaginative structure of his book around the four elements:

earth:	land—first depressing, then longed-for; Ishmael
air:	gentle winds, birds, sky, always feminine, always beneficent
fire:	Ahab, his scar and his prayer; the try-works
water:	the hoped-for redeemer and the ultimate killer; Bulkington

In "The Try-Works" (chapter 96), the glowing fire of the try-pots transforms the *Pequod* into a floating hell. Ishmael, at the helm, is overcome with drowsiness after looking too intently at the fire and he nearly loses control of the ship. Ahab as fire equals the ship as fire; both resemble the fire of hell and stand for both death and judgment. At the close of chapter 96 is a powerful meditation on the nature of fire—and therefore on Ahab.

> Look not too long in the face of the fire, O man! Never dream with thy hand on the helm! Turn not thy back to the compass; accept the first hint of the hitching tiller; believe not the artificial fire, when its redness makes all things look ghastly. To-morrow, in the natural sun, the skies will be bright; those who glared like devils in the forking flames, the morn will show in far other, at least gentler, relief; the glorious, glad sun, the only true lamp—all others but liars!
>
> Nevertheless the sun hides not Virginia's Dismal Swamp, nor Rome's accursed Campagna, nor wide Sahara, nor all the millions of miles of deserts and of griefs beneath the moon. The sun hides not the ocean, which is the dark side of this earth, and which is two thirds of this earth. So, therefore, that mortal man who hath more of joy than sorrow in him, that mortal man cannot be true—not true, or undeveloped. With books the same. The truest of all men was the Man of Sorrows, and the truest of all books is Solomon's, and Ecclesiastes is the fine hammered steel of woe. "All is vanity." ALL. This wilful world hath not got hold of unchristian Solomon's wisdom yet. But he who dodges hospitals and jails, and walks fast crossing grave-yards, and would rather talk of operas than hell; calls Cowper, Young, Pascal, Rousseau, poor devils all of sick men; and throughout a care-free lifetime swears by Rabelais as passing wise, and therefore jolly;—not that man is fitted to sit down on tomb-stones, and break the green damp mould with unfathomably wondrous Solomon.
>
> But even Solomon, he says, "the man that wandereth out of the way of understanding shall remain" (*i. e.* even while living) "in the congregation of the dead." Give not thyself up, then, to fire, lest it invert thee, deaden thee; as for the time it did me. There is a wisdom that is woe; but there is a woe that is madness. And there is a Catskill eagle in some souls that can alike dive down into the blackest gorges, and soar out of them again and become invisible in the sunny spaces. And even if he for ever flies within the gorge, that gorge is in the mountains; so that even in his lowest swoop the mountain eagle is still higher than other birds upon the plain, even though they soar.

Fire is the tragic side of life, the first paragraph implies, but it also suggests that tragedy is not the last word and that a hopeful morning shall come.

The second paragraph seems to take back the lesson of the first. Here joy is demeaned, sorrow is praised, the radical pessimism of the book of Ecclesiastes is *the* truth, and even madness is preferred to naive jollity.

In the final paragraph, fire is warned against, and apparently woe, sorrow, and Ecclesiastes are not unambiguous truth, after all. There is a good woe, a good pessimism that is wise; and there is a dangerous pessimism that is madness and that must be transcended. The author's shifting attitude to fire and all it stands for reflects his shifting attitude to the character so supremely identified with fire.

A final word on fire. In chapter 116, the dying whale turns toward the sun, and shortly after (chapter 118), Ahab destroys his quadrant. The quadrant had pointed to the fiery sun above Ahab, and Ahab cannot acknowledge the right of anything to be above him. In Ahab's great fire-sermon, or better, fire-prayer, the transformation of Ahab into fire is completed. The typhoon has blown up, the corpusants appear at the ends of the yard-arms, the actual sun is denied, and the only light or fire or sun remaining is Ahab. In this apostrophe all the fiery themes are tied together; Ahab's scar, Ishmael's fearful experience at the wheel of fire as hell, and the identification of fire and evil in the Zoroastrian faith of Fedallah, Ahab's harpooner and soul.

> Oh! thou clear spirit of clear fire, whom on these seas I as Persian once did worship, till in the sacramental act so burned by thee, that to this hour I bear the scar; I now know thee, thou clear spirit, and I now know that thy right worship is defiance. To neither love nor reverence wilt thou be kind; and e'en for hate thou canst but kill; and all are killed. No fearless fool now fronts thee. I own thy speechless, placeless power; but to the last gasp of my earthquake life will dispute its unconditional, unintegral mastery in me. In the midst of the personified impersonal, a personality stands here. Though but a point at best; whencesoe'er I came; wheresoe'er I go; yet while I earthly live, the queenly personality lives in me, and feels her royal rights. But war is pain, and hate is woe. Come in thy lowest form of love, and I will kneel and kiss thee; but at thy highest, come as mere supernal power; and though thou launchest navies of full-freighted worlds, there's that in here that still remains indifferent. Oh, thou clear spirit, of thy fire thou madest me, and like a true child of fire, I breathe it back to thee.

To worship fire is to worship what destroys, and that worship Ahab defines as defiance. Not defiance of the fire-god, not defiance of evil—this would be orthodoxy. But defiance of all humanity, all ethics, all decency that weakly protests against the evil journey. Fire can come as love, but this is not the form of divinity Ahab is addressing. His god is infinitely destructive power—"and all are killed." That is the divinity Ahab here assumes. "I own thy speechless, placeless power": I am one with you, god, and I will dispute forever any claims for mastery over me. Ahab confesses that he is in fact made of fire, and at the close of this striking prayer Ahab returns his fire, his self, to the fire-god that made him. Is even that fire-god to be destroyed by Ahab's fire?

This prayer marks Ahab's final preparation for the dread encounter he is expecting. Fire is his god, and it permits but one form of faith, defiance. Fire is his god, standing not for love but for uncontrollable power. Fire is his god, his father, for Ahab knows no mother, no mother's graces. Fire is his god, purifying and destroying him, as fire will do. At last Ahab is truly redeemed, fire is his "clear spirit"; he is one with himself and with fire, ready to destroy. "I came to cast fire upon the earth; and would that it were already kindled!" (Luke 12:49).

The "girlish air" at the close of chapter 28 is re-affirmed at the beginning of chapter 132 in an unforgettable image. The sea is, as always, masculine, robust, heaving. "The pensive air was transparently pure and soft, with a woman's look." And then, in a striking union of these two images:

> Aloft, like a royal czar and king, the sun seemed giving this gentle air to this bold and rolling sea; even as bride to groom. And at the girdling line of the horizon, a soft and tremulous motion—[orgasm?] most seen here at the equator—denoted the fond, throbbing trust, the loving alarms, with which the poor bride gave her bosom away.

29
Stubb, the second mate, reflects on Ahab's queerness, and he recalls that Ahab's steward reported on Ahab's restless dreams.

30
Ahab throws his pipe over the side.

Holy journeys require ascetic preparation, a stripping away of what is irrelevant, and unholy journeys are apparently no different. Melville was a devoted smoker and had already given us that sacramental scene of Ishmael and Queequeg smoking together ashore. The pipe, standing for serenity and the bonds of our common humanity, is destroyed. If you are going to become a god to kill one, you must cease being a man.

31
Stubb tells Flask his dream.

32
Melville, in a playful mood, lists the various species of whale. The whale, he assures us, is a fish, and the Book of Jonah is his proof.

This chapter suggests some of Melville's anxiety about proper form: "any human thing supposed to be complete, must for that very reason infallibly be faulty." He is clearly talking about his own books, and this one in particular, which is clearly giving him a good deal of trouble.

Early in 1850 Melville started work on the whale book, intending to make it a fairly straightforward adventure story, drawing on his own earlier experiences at sea. In the late summer of that year, however, something happened. He had begun his first close reading of Shakespeare. But the decisive event was his meeting with Nathaniel Hawthorne. Three fragments from the November 17, 1851, letter, written after Hawthorne had praised *Moby-Dick*, suggest the emotional intensity, both sacramental and erotic, of this new friendship, at least from Melville's side.

> . . . your heart beat in my ribs and mine in yours, and both in God's. A sense of unspeakable security is in me this moment, on account of your having understood the book.

* * *

Whence come you, Hawthorne? By what right do you drink from my flagon of life? And when I put it to my lips—lo, they are yours and now mine. I feel that the Godhead is broken up like the bread at the Supper, and that we are the pieces.

* * *

Lord, when shall we be done changing? Ah! it's a long stage, and no inn in sight, and night coming, and the body cold. But with you for a passenger, I am content and can be happy. I shall leave the world, I feel, with more satisfaction for having come to know you. Knowing you persuades me more than the Bible of our immortality.

In the midst of the excitement of this new friendship, *Moby-Dick* gets reconsidered, rewritten, expanded and deepened in every way. Narrative successfully moved into metaphor, and his masterpiece is the result. It is this painful recasting and rewriting process that leads him to complain that all of his books are botches, and to the strange prayer at the end of the chapter, "God keep me from ever completing anything."

33
Melville reflects on those whaling vessels where the authority of the captain is restricted.

At the close of the chapter is the turgid discussion of the relation of intelligence to power that we have already discussed. Ahab is inferior because he seeks power over others. Unlike Plato, with his vision of the philosopher–king, Melville wants to separate intelligence from political power. When the two are combined, tyranny results, and this is the reason power should belong only to the ordinary and inferior if it is to be safely exercised. This recalls the early panegyric to the religion of democracy and the divinity of ordinary man. Ahab is the presence lurking behind this meditation, but readers will be excused if they find themselves thinking about our contemporary political history.

34
The eating routine of the officers and harpooners.

As Ahab's character and quest become clearer, we will come to understand more fully the remark here that Ahab, though "nominally included in the census of Christendom . . . was still an alien to it." This does not mean that Ahab is not a Christian, or that he is an atheist. He has entered on a journey to kill God, or what he takes to be God, and in readiness for that journey he has himself become God, devil, and mad.

35

The procedure of the masthead watch is described.

Another form of Ishmael's piety. Here he confesses to a meditative dreaminess while standing his masthead watch. Platonists—those for whom the visible world is a mere shadow of eternal reality, like Ahab himself—are of no use to the capitalists of the whaling industry who want oil and money, not metaphors and symbols. Ahab may well symbolize a capitalist; he is not himself one.

At the close of this chapter, Melville draws an important connection between this transcendentalist–pantheist–symbolic view of nature and death. It is a connection foreshadowing Ahab's own death, and partly explaining it.

36

Ahab defines the *Pequod*'s journey as the search for Moby-Dick, and he nails a sixteen-dollar gold piece to the mast to be given to the one who first sights the white whale. In a sacramental act, a kind of black mass, Ahab, using the mates and harpooners as acolytes, ratifies the search as he distributes grog to the crew.

Starbuck, both as a Christian suspecting blasphemy and as a capitalist, rejects the symbolic journey, declaring that he shipped aboard to fight whales, not metaphors. Ahab rejects money as motive, setting himself against the economic basis of the whaling industry and of nineteenth-century American industrial expansion. My vengeance, he declares to Starbuck, "will fetch a great premium *here!*" He strikes his heart: this is what drives and defines him; here his madness lies.

Ahab's act of striking his heart introduces a fundamental device in Melville's psychological portrait of his captain—the dualism of head and heart. Here Ahab sets "heart"—goal, madness—over the calculating and economic motives for the voyage. Melville's development of the head/heart distinction is both subtle and important.

It may be useful to contrast Ahab's monomaniac heart with Ishmael's domestic and sensible one. Later, in chapter 94, Ishmael reflects on the intense sperm-squeezing experience with his ship-mates, observing that

> man must eventually lower, or at least shift, his conceit of attainable felicity; not placing it anywhere in the intellect or the fancy; but in the wife, the heart, the bed, the table, the saddle, the fireside, the country. . . .

As fine a definition of what "heart" ought to be, and isn't, in Ahab: wife, bed, table, etc.

When Melville celebrated the heart in his June 1(?), 1851, letter to Hawthorne, it was, of course, Ishmael's, not Ahab's he was thinking of (though it may have been Ahab's too calculating "head" he was rejecting):

> I stand for the heart. To the dogs with the head! I had rather be a fool with a heart, than Jupiter Olympus with his head. The reason the mass of men fear God, and *at bottom dislike Him*, is because they rather distrust His heart, and fancy Him all brain like a watch.

It appears that God and Ahab are dangerous because they are both all brain along with an untrustworthy (mad?) heart.

The head-heart dualism is operating, I think, in the analysis of Ahab's dream in chapter 44. (See the comments on this dream in the note for chapter 4, above.) "Mind" in this analysis seems to include both calculating head and monomaniac heart working in unequal tandem in Ahab awake. "Soul" is Ahab's fragile sanity, eternal but weak, briefly liberated by sleep from mad mind, but under absolute control of that mind in Ahab awake.

It appears the Ahab may be suffering from his mad heart in the conversation with the ship's carpenter in chapter 108. There he asks to be rebuilt, all brain and no heart—asking, in other words, to be remade sane. But Ahab was never to be freed from his tormenting heart. At the end of the voyage (chapter 135), temptations to sanity have been overcome, madness is in full control. The dualism of head and heart collapses, and he becomes wholly heart, wholly mad, wholly Fedallah.

> Ahab never thinks; he only feels, feels, feels; *that's* tingling enough for mortal man! to think's audacity. God only has that right and privilege. Thinking is, or ought to be, a coolness and a calmness; and our poor hearts throb, and our poor brains beat too much for that. And yet, I've sometimes thought my brain was very calm—frozen calm, this old skull cracks so, like a glass in which the contents turn to ice, and shiver it.

One more dualism may help us understand how the head-heart distinction functions in Melville's portrait of Ahab. In chapter 132, we read of the murderous masculine sea (Ahab's sea) is in contrast to the feminine and gracious air. Here the sea seems to parallel the "mind" of the dream, the mad heart yoked to the calculating head, while the air is soul, eternal yet powerless, feminine and true, incapable of resisting the forces of masculinity, sea, and death. A diagram can suggest the interconnections of these images and terms.

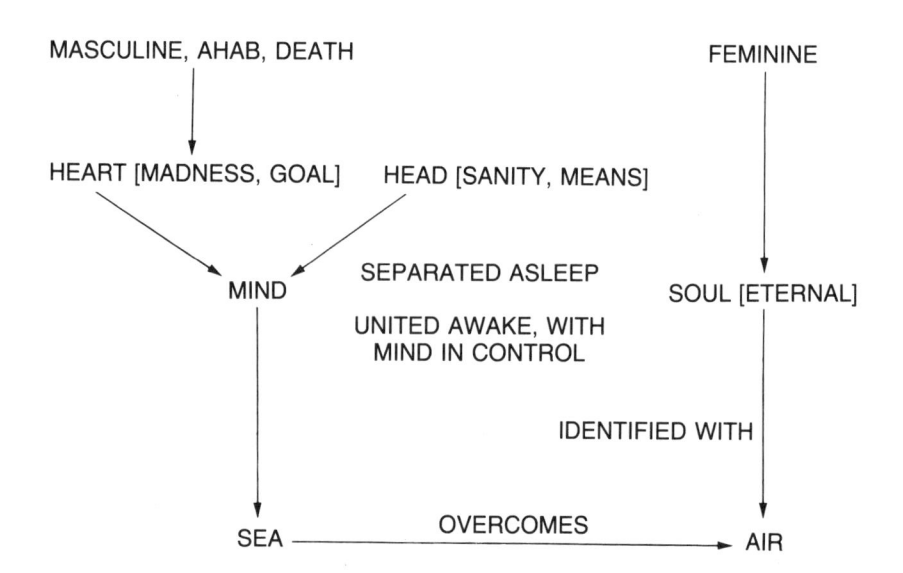

```
MASCULINE, AHAB, DEATH                          FEMININE
           |                                        |
           v                                        |
HEART [MADNESS, GOAL]   HEAD [SANITY, MEANS]        |
            \             /                         |
             \           /                          v
              v         v                        SOUL [ETERNAL]
                MIND         SEPARATED ASLEEP        |
                 |                                   |
                 |         UNITED AWAKE, WITH        |
                 |           MIND IN CONTROL         |
                 |                                   |
                 |                 IDENTIFIED WITH   |
                 v                                   v
                SEA ———————— OVERCOMES ————————→ AIR
```

Returning to Ahab's response to Starbuck's practical criticism of his symbolic journey, the captain takes us to the very center of his understanding of nature, language, and whales.

> Hark ye yet again,—the little lower layer. All visible objects, man, are but as pasteboard masks. But in each event—in the living act, the undoubted deed—there, some unknown but still reasoning thing puts forth the mouldings of its features from behind the unreasoning mask. If man will strike, strike through the mask! How can the prisoner reach outside except by thrusting through the wall? To me, the white whale is that wall, shoved near to me. Sometimes I think there's naught beyond. But 'tis enough. He tasks me; he heaps me; I see in him outrageous strength, with an inscrutable malice sinewing it. That inscrutable thing is chiefly what I hate; and be the white whale agent, or be the white whale principal, I will wreak that hate upon him. Talk not to me of blasphemy, man, I'd strike the sun if it insulted me. For could the sun do that, then could I do the other; since there is ever a sort of fair play herein, jealousy presiding over all creations. But not my master, man, is even that fair play. Who's over me? Truth hath no confines.

There is both metaphysics and epistemology here. Physical things like ropes and bones and whales are really not what they appear to be to the senses. They wear "masks," and we have to get rid of those masks to get at reality.

Ahab is not doing here what biblical scholars used to call "demythologizing." That barbarous word meant that "myth" is the historically conditioned element in our imaginative language that has to be removed in order to find out what is real. For Ahab, myth is the reality and all the rest is irrelevant, whether morality or the Nantucket whaling market.

But "reality" is not utterly passive in this struggle for true knowledge. Reality doesn't just wait there behind the mask, it sends a kind of signal to the inquirer—"some unknown but still reasoning thing puts forth the mouldings of its features from behind the unreasoning mask." Not only does reality make a move toward us, we move as well. We have to strike or thrust through the mask. It is not that we pull the mask off as at the climax of a masked ball; we penetrate. Knowledge in Ahab's sense is masculine-phallic; nature is the passive mother we seek incestuously to possess.[6]

Suddenly, the metaphorical climate changes. The knower or inquirer turns into a prisoner and the mask is a prison wall. A prisoner of what? Of the tyranny of appearances, of the illusion that a piece of nature is nothing but what the senses report? The prisoner must be freed, for the right kind of knowledge.

At last Moby-Dick swims into Ahab's language. Moby-Dick becomes that wall that imprisons, that mask concealing truth from the knower. Moby-Dick is not that truth, he is the superfluity that must be penetrated by the knower, the harpooner. The deeper truth is the only reality.

But, he muses, "Sometimes I think there's naught beyond." No face; nothing on the other side of the prison wall. What does Ahab mean by this despairing skepticism? Is the monomaniac's conceptual system really so shaky? Ahab might mean that empiricism is correct after all, that what the senses say we know is all we know. Or, more likely, Ahab means that the senses do indeed deceive, and there are indeed masks. But the faces covered by the masks are blank or dead. Neither sense nor spirit can be trusted. There is a heaven, let us say, but God is not there. There is a real empty hole in our reality, a positive nothing. Our imperfect knowledge in this world—seeing through a glass darkly—has generally implied a better knowledge in some other world—a knowing face to face. But there is no "other." The implication of a better knowledge is still offered, but it is a lie. (Melville was quite capable himself of this kind of epistemological nihilism, and he never wholly shook himself free from it.)

Ahab interrupts these speculative asides abruptly: "But 'tis enough." He simply refuses to explore the question whether there is anything outside the wall. He turns from theory to "him," to Moby-Dick. "He tasks me"—he loads a dreadful task on me. (These constructed verbs suggest an intense emotional level here.) "He heaps me"—he dumps (something) on me. Ahab sees in Moby-Dick not only strength—anyone can see that—but malice or malevolence of a particular kind. The thing he hates is the inscrutability. There is something of the intellectual's passion in Ahab, hating what he cannot understand. This is right and we all do it, or should. But what we do not all do is to take Ahab's next monomaniac step. We do not decide to destroy what we cannot understand. In a strange sense, the voyage of the *Pequod* is a war against ignorance. Could this be the real meaning of Ishmael's breezy aside that a whale-ship was his Yale College and Harvard?

If Ahab's quest is a war against ignorance, it is also a war against interpretation (theory): "be the white whale agent, or be the white whale principal" I hate Moby-Dick and will destroy him. I really don't care if he is a mask concealing a deeper reality or the deeper reality itself behind the mask. I will ignore and destroy the nervous distinction between *res* and *signum*.

Ahab does not claim to be an initiator of hatred. He is simply returning it to the sender. *Quid pro quo.* Ahab has "decided,"and this is surely where the madness lies, that Moby-Dick hates him and that there is no good reason why he should do so. "I will wreak [inflict] that hate [back] upon him."

Ahab emerges from his "monologue" and we remember that he has been speaking to Starbuck all along. With "talk not to me of blasphemy," he puts words into the mouth of his pious first mate only to deny them. Ahab respects Starbuck's intelligence enough to know that Starbuck can spot blasphemy when he sees it. With this denial of blasphemy the philosophical reflections cease; the explanation of theory and repudiation of theory is set aside, and Ahab turns inward upon himself to self-justification and to a kind of mad theology that brings us close to the heart of his religious significance.

Ahab is not introducing a new idea when he brings up blasphemy. Blasphemy is contempt toward God and contempt toward God has been the hidden theme of Ahab's first address all along. All that anguished talk about masks and walls can readily be translated into talk about God. Starbuck's silent accusation is dead right, and Ahab knows it.

Ahab rejects the accusation of blasphemy because he rejects a key element in the definition—the eternity of God. He begins to reflect on his relation to the cosmos as a whole. "I'd strike the sun if it insulted me." If it can insult, I can surely strike. We are equal. Of course the sun—Apollo, the cosmos, the gods, God—

has insulted him. He lost a leg, didn't he, and he is simply striking back in response, killing the gods and wiping out all metaphysical levels above him. The sun is not Ahab's master because nothing is, or should be, or is to be. No one is above him because no one has a right to be. "Who's over me?" This is part of Ahab's theological significance. There are no gods over Ahab and/or the only gods are Ahab. Gods being defined as that which nothing is over. God is that "being than which none greater can be thought." Ahab is being driven mad, becoming himself divinized, by means of a simple meditation on the ontological argument.

"Truth hath no confines," which is to say, "my actual truth has no upward limit; I stretch all the way to the heavens, usurping the gods, getting rid of any that interfere, becoming God in their place." Starbuck has listened accurately. He calls all this "his heaven-insulting purpose" (36), and he is right.

Yet Ahab is as much Calvinist as nature-divinizing transcendentalist overdosed on the "all feeling." God is tied to tragedy and to woe. Happiness is unworthy, woe is mystical, and when you explore the causes of woe (as Ahab is in fact doing with *his* woe) you are carried back to "the sourceless primogenitures of the gods" who "themselves are not for ever glad" (106). Ahab is not talking about Emerson's god, but Edwards's, that "terrible mixture of the cunning and awful." To Ahab the Calvinist God is simply the cause of all that is, and therefore of his own dismembering injury. Ahab is shaping himself into a divine evil killer of the evil divine not because of his unbelief but because of his faith. He has been fully nourished by the Calvinist doctrine of Providence, the wit and wisdom of the *Institutes* I.16. Moby-Dick ripped his leg off; God is the cause of all things; God and Moby-Dick merge into a single enemy. Both are evil and because they are evil they must be killed; to kill Moby-Dick is to kill the Protestant God. The *Pequod's* search is a religious search; a search for God.

What Ahab is doing is to forge an original and unusual mixture of the best liberalism and the best orthodoxy the nineteenth century could offer: transcendentalism and Puritan Calvinism.

As transcendentalist he divinized one particular piece of nature—a single sperm whale. As Calvinist, reflecting on his woe, pressing back to the primogenitures of the gods, he defined that divinity in terms of the doctrine of Providence. That divinity was alive and evil and worthy of destruction.

Whales are not simply whales for Ahab, partly because he is mad, partly because he is a transcendentalist (and Melville permits us to connect the two). The only acknowledgement that whales can be whales is when Ahab decides that the crew needs an occasional non-symbolic killing to keep their skills and morale intact. Ahab's white whale has nothing to do with capitalism, or profit, or oil. What is it then—God? It is whatever stands higher than Ahab, reminding him of his dependence. (Romantic theology, beginning with Schleiermacher, thought it had discovered a direct causal connection between the experience of dependence and God.) Moby-Dick stands for the world Ahab cannot master; not so much God himself as the maddening reminder that he is not God. To fight what is greater than he is Ahab must become divine. *Nemo contra Deum sed Deus ipse*— no one (can be) against God but God Himself—: this phrase from the novel just after *Moby-Dick*, *Pierre*, perfectly expresses the self-divinizing logic of Ahab. A God is killed in *Moby-Dick*; it is the Ahab–God. And we should never forget that the divine being whose traditional function is to undermine God has always been named the devil. Here is surely an important explanation for the identification of Ahab with fire.

Melville may have begun *Moby-Dick* intending to make Ahab a conventional romantic hero, resisting the world like a character from Byron or Carlyle. But the author is drawn more and more into the captain's depths and madness, and Milton's Satan becomes a more significant source. Melville could not help but admire and fear Ahab, and his readers have followed suit. The God beyond Ahab must be killed, and so with Ahab in control there is "little external to constrain us," as Ishmael remarks. For the new religious era, the old god is to be killed: with the new one in ascendance, there must be new sacraments and a new priesthood. Ahab binds his crew to him, with only Starbuck in ineffectual dissent, with a black mass: rum rather than wine, harpoon cups for chalices, death rather than life as the message.

Some observers find a structural break at the close of this chapter, saying that the Ishmael or land section goes from 1–23, while 24–36 is devoted to the meaning of the voyage.

This leaves a large central section, Chapters 37–131, on whaling and the voyage itself, which can be further broken down:

—up to the first lowering (37–48)
—up to the encounter with the *Jeroboam* (49–71)
—through the straits of Sunda and into the Java Sea (72–87)
—up to the typhoon and the corpusants (88–119)
—up to the meeting with the *Delight* (120–131)

Chapters 132–135 are devoted to the chase and to the conclusion.

37
Ahab meditates in his cabin.

The demonic Ahab is succeeded by another. Troubled, almost gentle, deeply aware of his own condition, he says of himself, "Gifted with the high perception, I lack the low, enjoying power, damned . . . in the midst of Paradise." Damned, demonic, madness maddened. How mad are you when you know you are mad?

38
A despondent Starbuck movingly prays to the God Ahab has dethroned, admitting Ahab's power over him.

39
Stubb's answer to all problems is laughter.

40
The crew sings and talks at midnight on deck.

This portrait of the crew shows us what we already know, that Melville loves these men on whom the new democratic god has come to rest. But there is a problem. How can these "mariners, renegades and castaways" be the bearers of the new God for the new age when they are, at the same time, the convinced followers of the demonic Ahab? At the end of the chapter the black Pip prays to the white God to have mercy on him. That prayer will shortly be rejected.

> 41
> Ishmael, back briefly as the narrator voice, recounts the legends and tales concerning Moby-Dick: his ubiquity, his "mystic modes," his immortality, his "seeming malice," and, according to reports, his "unexampled, intelligent malignity."

We have already seen that Ishmael has been attracted to Ahab's symbolic view of nature, particularly when he is standing the masthead watch. We need not be surprised, at the outset of this important chapter, to find him admitting that he had become committed to his captain's mad quest. Quest for whom or for what? Melville tells us, as directly as he ever will, in this chapter.

Two themes dominate Ishmael's reported tales about Moby-Dick, the supernatural and the terrible: "half-formed foetal suggestions of supernatural agencies, which eventually invested Moby-Dick with new terrors unborrowed from anything that visibly appears." Note that all this information is carefully described as "reports," and we are meant to be uncertain about whether or not they describe the white whale as he is in himself. He is, sailors say, terrifying, ubiquitous, and immortal. Psalm 139, where God is both omniscient and omnipresent, may be in Melville's mind as he weaves Moby-Dick and divinity together. When Melville talks about the whale's intelligent malignity, we can suppose that he is making a statement about his attitude to the omnipotent God of the Christians.

In one of Melville's very greatest pieces of writing, Ahab locates the devil lurking at the heart of Calvin's God, and affirms his own fidelity to it.

> Ahab had cherished a wild vindictiveness against the whale, all the more fell for that in his frantic morbidness he at last came to identify with him,

not only all his bodily woes, but all his intellectual and spiritual exasperations. The White Whale swam before him as the monomaniac incarnation of all those malicious agencies which some deep men feel eating in them, till they are left living on with half a heart and half a lung. That intangible malignity which has been from the beginning; to whose dominion even the modern Christians ascribe one-half of the worlds; which the ancient Ophites of the east reverenced in their statue devil;— Ahab did not fall down and worship it like them; but deliriously transferring its idea to the abhorred white whale, he pitted himself, all mutilated, against it. All that most maddens and torments; all that stirs up the lees of things; all truth with malice in it; all that cracks the sinews and cakes the brain, all the subtle demonisms of life and thought; all evil, to crazy Ahab, were visibly personified, and made practically assailable in Moby-Dick. He piles upon the whale's white hump the sum of all the general rage and hate felt by his whole race from Adam down; and then, as if this chest had been a mortar, he burst his hot heart's shell upon it.

It is Ishmael who is offering this diagnosis of Ahab's theological insanity. Behind the external "wild vindictiveness" is the inner "frantic morbidness" which leads Ahab to ascribe to Moby-Dick not only the loss of his leg, but "all his intellectual and spiritual exasperations." When you make something the cause of all your distress, you are making it the cause of all that happens to you, and it has become your Calvinist divinity.

But all this is inverted transcendentalism as well. Transcendentalism because natural objects, in this case whales or a whale, are said to stand for something deeper than themselves. But it is bad or inverted transcendentalism because nature does not redeem (it almost did once—when Ahab wept into the sea), as it is supposed to do in all romanticisms, but it curses and wounds and destroys. The nineteenth century American invented transcendentalism so he could lose his Christian faith comfortably and get on with the intellectual and imaginative work that needed to be done. Mad Ahab has the worst of both worlds.

In Ahabic transferrence, Moby-Dick is transformed into an incarnation of all the suffering experienced by one profound American man, but Ahab's satanism is not devil-worship, however much his rum-filled harpoon chalices may remind us of a black mass. His satanism is not liturgical but ethical; it leads to slaughter. Ahab has a kind of piety to him, as becomes a god. Evil is there to be killed, the demons must be exorcised. This is Ahab's theological logic. God is the one behind every moment of Ahab's time, both the loss of the leg itself to Moby-Dick and the castration-wound caused by the artificial leg in Nantucket. Ahab is in effect collapsing the distinction between God and the devil: naming God the devil. Divinity is therefore transferred or ascribed to Moby-Dick, and Ahab is vowing in this place to kill the evil Christian God. (Better than killing Christians, but of course Ahab did that as well.) All evil is from Moby-Dick, so all evil is due him; Ahab's hate is piled upon the one from whom all things come, and on that One he "burst his hot heart's shell upon it." As a result of that artillery blast, there remained no heart in Ahab.

The sailors' stories had turned Moby-Dick into a god. Ahab's own story turned that superstitious sailor-god into the devil, and Ahab turned himself into God in order to kill the devil-God that he says hates him. If you would kill the God of Calvin, of Protestantism, of Christianity (Melville makes no nice denominational distinctions), deemed evil by virtue of your meditations on Providence, you must become God to kill him. You must deny all other transcendence; nothing must be allowed to exist above you; no sun; no quadrant must point to that sun. The *Pequod's* voyage is one of the great mystical pilgrimages in literature. The story of one man's attempt to kill the Christian God. Ahab did not pull it off; Melville nearly did.

Ahab's project should not be confused with atheism or rebellious unbelief. It is more like faith raised to the breaking point. When you divinize yourself in order to wipe out all other claimants to divinity, there remains nothing transcending you to judge the evil you have done. You are free to perform all the teleological suspensions of the ethical you choose. Again and again, Ahab reads himself as God. "Ahab is for ever, man"; he is proud as a Greek god, a suffering god, owner of sacramental power able to baptize the new harpoon in the devil's name.

"There is one God that is Lord over the earth, and one Captain that is Lord over the Pequod."

To Starbuck, pious but no transcendentalist, the whale is but a "dumb brute." To Ahab, the whale Starbuck sees is but one of nature's masks, and he must press beyond and beneath for understanding. This symbolic imagination, often honored as man's most civilizing gift, is here read as something darker than Plato or Calvin or Byron or Emerson ever imagined. Perhaps we can see why poets are said to be dangerous.

In many ways, Ahab surpasses his mediocre mates in humanity. When he is on stage, we watch only him. Yet he is both evil and mad: "all my means [head] are sane, my motive and my object [heart] mad." At the chapter's end, Ishmael's ambivalence hovers between Starbuck's weak protests and Ahab's mad and death-ridden certainty: he is totally committed to the search, yet he could see "naught in that brute but the deadliest ill."

42

Ishmael tells us how he has come to view the white whale. It is the whiteness that appalls him, he says, and this chapter is an unforgettable meditation on the color white.

The effect of this meditation is to fix in our minds the triangular interconnection between evil–white–the Christian God. White is the absence of color, not nature, but nature's opposite—appalling. In opposition to Emerson, and Ahab, and to Ishmael's own half-way attraction to transcendentalism, we find here one of Melville's darkest sentences: "Though in many of its aspects this visible world seems formed in love, the invisible spheres were formed in fright." A brutal axe severs the connection between nature and God, the Puritan's nature as well as the Deist's. Whatever order one may think one sees in the natural world cannot obscure the radical disorder in the world of spirit.

This is no simple nineteenth-century unbelief; no confession, as in Matthew Arnold's "Dover Beach," of the waning of the sea of faith and the need to turn to human love. Melville really believes in the existence of the invisible world formed in fright, in the mad God who needs to be killed. He is here closer to Nietzsche, or to Ivan Karamazov, than to the gentle Victorian honest-doubters.

The "dark" vision of a hostile, colorless nature at the end of the chapter anticipates the impact Darwinian thought will have on the literary imagination a few years after the writing of *Moby-Dick*.

During a night-watch, a sailor hears some mysterious sounds below deck. (See the beginning of chapter 21 and the end of chapter 47.)

44

Ahab's heart and head once more, though here the dualism is between soul and mind. (See the analysis of Ahab's dream in note to chapter 4 above.) Awake, his rational faculties are impressive and unimpaired. Asleep, however, his nails bloody his palms and in his dreams the rational order of his working world falls apart.

45

More historical notes on whales and whaling. This kind of factual material, Melville playfully adds, will keep the reader from confusing *Moby-Dick* with "a hideous and intolerable allegory."

46

How Ahab manages to control his crew and to keep them from rebellion.

In this chapter, Ahab expresses a view of human nature utterly different from that optimistic outburst we read in chapter 26. For Ahab, human nature—at least that of his crew—is sordid, and sordid men need the hope of money to be kept in line.

47

Queequeg and Ishmael weave a sword-mat and Melville weaves a metaphor.

Throughout his entire life, Melville was entranced and mystified by the theological problems of freedom and necessity. (Calvinism, even when it recedes, leaves indelible deposits.) These problems were as fascinating to Melville as they were to his contemporary, Abraham Lincoln (whom Melville once met in a White House receiving line). America, land of the free; Christianity, land of necessity. How to bring them together?

The mat-weaving metaphor is a rather obvious meditation on this problem. The significant incident of the chapter comes at the very end. When a whale is sighted by Tashtego, the ball of cord, symbolizing free will, is dropped by Ishmael. To search for whales is to give up your freedom. Ishmael has given his freedom to Ahab's search. When you give your freedom away, to a person or to a god, do you give up your humanity? Twenty years after this time, in his copy of a book of Matthew Arnold's poetry, Melville was to write: "What in thunder did the Gods create us for then? If not for bliss, for hate? If so, devil take the Gods."

48

> The three mates, with their harpooners, lower to engage the whale, and they are joined by Ahab's secret crew, and their harpooner, Fedallah. Queequeg, in Starbuck's boat, gets one shot at the whale, but the whale capsizes them and they do not find their way back to the ship until the next morning.

Fedallah was a Parsee; a worshipper, like Ahab, of fire: religiously a Zoroastrian, with its radical dualistic scheme of light against darkness, goodness against evil. The non-white Fedallah seems to serve as Ahab's evil angel, while the black cabin-boy Pip is his good angel. Fedallah is not so much the tempter as that part of Ahab that has already submitted to diabolical temptation.

On of my favorite pieces of Melville prose comes in this chapter:

> Not the raw recruit, marching from the bosom of his wife into the fever heat of his first battle; not the dead man's ghost encountering the first unknown phantom in the other world;—neither of these can feel stranger and stronger emotions than the man does, who for the first time finds himself pulling into the charmed, churned circle of the hunted sperm whale.

This is Melville's candid celebration of the sheer physical excitement of whaling. He seems to hold, like our contemporaries Hemingway and Mailer, that man is definitively tested only in extreme physical engagements. Ahab's moral offense is that in spiritualizing whaling he has denied its concrete physical reality. The bread and wine are no longer bread and wine; they are nothing but body and blood.

49
After having his boat overturned by a whale and spending a wet night in the boat, Ishmael decides that perhaps life is nothing more than a practical joke. He decides to make a will, and that makes him feel better.

Another chapter in the tale of Ishmael's piety. No more pious belief in immortality, no more dreamy reveries on the masthead (for a while, at any rate). Let us transcend both piety and melancholy, he decides, and adopt "this free and easy sort of congenial, desperado philosophy." How deeply Melville must have longed for this kind of spiritual carelessness, and how far he was from ever attaining it!

50
The crew become accustomed to the overt presence of Ahab's boat crew, except that Fedallah remains something of a mystery.

51
A mysterious silver jet of water is sighted several times from the *Pequod*, and it gives some a feeling of being treacherously beckoned forward by something dangerous. The *Pequod* goes through some rough weather off the Cape of Good Hope.

Is this jet or "spirit-spout" symbolic of something? After the publication of *Moby-Dick*, Mrs. Hawthorne wrote to Melville commenting on the possible symbolism of this chapter. Melville responded that he did not recall having anything particularly symbolic in mind, but there might be something to her impression. Writers love to say this sort of thing to their critics, and sometimes they even mean it.

52
The *Pequod* passes the *Albatross*, long away from port. As if making a

horrified response to the *Pequod*'s question about the white whale, the *Albatross*'s captain drops his speaking trumpet in the water before he can reply.

The *Albatross* is the first of nine ships encountered by the *Pequod* on her voyage. Critics have sometimes made a lot of the symbolic character of these encounters: each ship standing, they say, for a different approach to whaling, or to the meaning of existence, or to God. This may be worth something, though I can live without it.

53
Gam, a particular form of meeting at sea between two whaling vessels, is defined.

54
A self-contained short story which appeared independently in several magazines at the time of *Moby-Dick*'s publication.

This may not have any particular function within the novel itself, though it has been suggested that Melville intended to contrast Steelkilt's courageous resistance to Radney's cruelty with Starbuck's timidity.

We have already noted how a passage from a later work can illuminate an earlier. This chapter has an interesting example of the reverse, an early passage illuminating a later. Here, from the narrator of "The Town-Ho's Story," is an exact description of the motivation of John Claggart in Melville's late *Billy Budd*.

> Now, as you well know, it is not seldom the case in this conventional world of ours—watery or otherwise; that when a person placed in command over his fellowmen finds one of them to be very significantly his superior in general pride of manhood, straightway against that man he conceives an unconquerable dislike and bitterness; and if he have a chance he will pull down and pulverize that subaltern's tower, and make a little heap of dust of it.

55–57
Three chapters discussing various published portraits of whales.

Toward the end of Chapter 57, there is another confession of faith from the religiously variable Ishmael, a form of his earlier decision to take life as a joke.

> Long exile from Christendom and civilization inevitably restores a man to that condition in which God placed him, *i.e.*, what is called savagery. Your true whale-hunter is as much a savage as an Iroquois. I myself am a savage; owning no allegiance but to the King of the Cannibals; and ready at any moment to rebel against him.

We know from *Typee* that Melville had been both happy and miserable among the "savages" on his Pacific island. How elegantly Melvillean is the final clause, with its suggestion that not only civilized but uncivilized gods must be rebelled against.

58
A description of yellow brit leads to a meditation on the violence and evil of the sea.

There is no way of making a straightforward list of symbolic equivalents for the characters and objects in this novel. Melville is deceptive on these matters and intends to be. On the very first page of the novel Ishmael told us that land and cities are death-dealing and evil, while water heals and redeems. Yet in this marvellous short chapter on the sea, look what has happened to Ishmael's first redeemer. The sea is now foe, fiend, savage tigress, masterless, designed to insult and murder man, so proud of his technology and skill. But against this "universal cannibalism of the sea," there is a human antidote. It is, of all things, land.

> For as this appalling ocean surrounds the verdant land, so in the soul of man there lies one insular Tahiti, full of peace and joy, but encompassed by all the horrors of the half-known life. God keep thee! Push not off from that isle, thou canst never return.

How deeply Melville longed for this domestic, landlocked joy! Ishmael began by pushing off from two islands, Manhattan and Nantucket, and Melville himself was always pushing off, failing to find what he sought and failing to content himself with what he found when he returned.

59
Daggoo mistakes a giant squid for the white whale.

60
The rope in the whale-boat is carefully described and Melville gets a rather lugubrious metaphor from it.

61
The first whale of the voyage is taken by Stubb.

Ishmael's adopted cynicism fails him at the start of this chapter. He is on watch again on the masthead and he reverts to his earlier mysticism. His soul leaves his body (as Ahab's did in the dream) just as the mystics say it can. He nearly loses his grip and falls, but wakes from the sea-induced trance just in time. Ishmael discovers that even the gentle sea can kill.

62
Melville describes the standard procedure for the harpooner's use of the dart, and proposes an improvement in the routine.

Anyone in anxious or relieved flight from the work ethic will find comfort in the final lines of this chapter:

> To insure the greatest efficiency in the dart, the harpooners of this world must start to their feet from out of idleness, and not from out of toil.

63
Placement of the harpoons in the whale boat is discussed.

64
After he has killed his whale and settled down to eat a steak cut from its tail, Stubb rather cruelly persuades the old black cook Fleece to preach a sermon to the sharks, gnawing at the whale's carcass alongside the ship.

This encounter between Stubb and Fleece is no model for inter-racial community. Why do we have a sermon here? Is it to suggest that all Christian sermons are as hopelessly irrelevant as Fleece's—urging gluttonous sharks to desist from their gluttony? Are we not to conclude, then, that Father Mapple's sermon, for all of its literary splendor, is ultimately just as irrelevant as old Fleece's?

65

The whale's edibility is discussed.

Melville gets around to cannibalism again, and he insists that cannibals will do better at the last judgment than will those over-civilized gourmands who gorge themselves on pâté.

66

An unforgettable portrait of a group of disemboweled and wounded sharks, swimming in circles, eating their own intestines.

The image of the circle is a persistent one in *Moby-Dick*, and you could probably produce a complete interpretation based entirely on these circular images: vortices, whirlpools, coils. You could do it, but a lot of the book's fun would be left out. The point of this scene is not the circles, but Queequeg's theological conclusion: "But de god wat made shark must be one dam Ingin." Nature is not orderly or nice, and the god who made sharks isn't very nice either. Perhaps Melville is trying to exorcise whatever lingering affection for the primitivist view of nature he may still possess. I would not be surprised if Albany's eschatological vision of evil in *King Lear* was in Melville's mind as he wrote these words.

> If that the heavens do not their visible spirits
> Send quickly down to tame these vile offenses,
> It will come,
> Humanity must perforce prey on itself,
> Like monsters of the deep. (IV.ii.46–50a)

67

A hook is inserted into the captured whale, and the blubber is removed.

68
The blubber, as skin, is further described.

Chapters that begin technological often end up mystical, and I have already tried to persuade the reader not to skip what appears to be technical detail about whales and whaling. Melville is very good at pulling a metaphor out of a piece of nature or technology, and he often does it at the end of the chapter. Here the reader is invited to imitate—not Jesus, as in Christianity—the whale. Retain your solitary individuality; live in the world without being of it; find your own private inner Tahiti and remain there. If you do imitate the whale, there will be no human community, no democracy, no Queequeg–Ishmael marriage. You will be ever alone, the eternal Isolato. Melville never found effective relief from his desperate sense of isolation from both family and nation. A few shipmates, and Hawthorne, and probably no one else, were able to break through his solitariness.

69
The beheaded whale is released from the side of the ship and floats slowly away.

The reader will find some of Melville's most splendid writing in the paragraph beginning "The vast tackles have now done their duty." Note the shift in tone from the horror of death to peaceful, joyous calm.

Suddenly, a somewhat forced joke against orthodoxy appears. What is orthodoxy in this image? Thinking that something is there when it isn't? It may be that Melville really did wish that God wasn't "there." But He was, alas, an evil trickster, haunting not ignoring him. He was never to know the comfort of either belief or unbelief.

70
The whale's head, defined and described, is hoisted alongside the ship, and Ahab addresses it.

How different is Ahab's sea from Ishmael's. Ishmael is lulled by the undulating surface. Ahab, addressing the whale's head, sees the sea in terms of what it contains—dead ships and dead men.

> "Speak, thou vast and venerable head," muttered Ahab, "which, though ungarnished with a beard, yet here and there lookest hoary with mosses; speak, mighty head, and tell us the secret thing that is in thee. Of all divers, thou hast dived the deepest. That head upon which the upper sun now gleams, has moved amid this world's foundations. Where unrecorded names and navies rust and untold hopes and anchors rot; where in her murderous hold this frigate earth is ballasted with bones of millions of the drowned; there, in that awful water-land, there was thy most familiar home. Thou hast been where bell or diver never went; hast slept by many a sailor's side, where sleepless mothers would give their lives to lay them down. Thou saw'st the locked lovers when leaping from their flaming ship; heart to heart they sank beneath the exulting wave; true to each other, when heaven seemed false to them. Thou saw'st the murdered mate when tossed by pirates from the midnight deck; for hours he fell into the deeper midnight of the insatiate maw; and his murderers still sailed on unharmed—while swift lightnings shivered the neighboring ship that would have borne a righteous husband to outstretched, longing arms. O head! thou hast seen enough to split the planets and make an infidel of Abraham, and not one syllable is thine!"

Later in the novel is another description of the terror of the sea bottom. In chapter 93, little Pip is driven mad after a night floating alone in the water. He saw, or imagined, something under the water that destroyed his cheerful sanity.

Melville wrote in a letter, several years before *Moby-Dick*: "I love all men who *dive*. Any fish [Ishmael?] can swim near the surface...." Ahab as one who saw the tragedy beneath the smooth surfaces of things was the Ahab Melville could not help admiring.

Ahab's purest theoretical expression of his transcendentalism comes at the end of this chapter.

> O Nature, and O soul of man! how far beyond all utterance are your linked analogies! not the smallest atom stirs or lives in matter, but has its cunning duplicate in mind.

71
The *Pequod* meets the *Jeroboam*.

On board the *Jeroboam* is a mad sailor of the Shaker community named, appropriately, Gabriel. The other Gabriel was an angel, and the function of angels has always been to bring true messages from God, which this Gabriel does. Gabriel has met Moby-Dick before and he believes him to be "the Shaker God incarnated." Gabriel is mad, but angels never lie, and he predicts Ahab's fate.

72
How Queequeg, standing on the back of the whale alongside, and roped to Ishmael on deck, inserts the first hook into the captured whale.

Ishmael and Queequeg are again symbolically yoked. Melville reflects on the relationship and the reflections are strange. In one sense, he appears to be celebrating such trusting interdependence; yet he is also clearly uneasy with it. Trust another, and he may let you down. Needing and mistrusting human community; this is the meaning of the monkey-rope meditation.

73
Stubb and Flask together kill a Right Whale. Flask reminds Stubb of the tradition that a ship with a Sperm Whale's head on the starboard side and a Right Whale's head on the port can never capsize. The two mates talk about Fedallah.

74
A careful description of the head of the Sperm Whale.

Here is a striking example of Melville's descriptive prose at its best.

> A curious and most puzzling question might be started concerning this visual matter as touching the Leviathan. But I must be content with a hint. So long as a man's eyes are open in the light, the act of seeing is involuntary; that is, he cannot then help mechanically seeing whatever objects are before him. Nevertheless, any one's experience will teach him, that though he can take in an undiscriminating sweep of things at one glance, it is quite impossible for him, attentively, and completely, to examine any two things—however large or however small—at one and the same instant of time; never mind if they lie side by side and touch

each other. But if you now come to separate these two objects, and surround each by a circle of profound darkness; then, in order to see one of them, in such a manner as to bring your mind to bear on it, the other will be utterly excluded from your contemporary consciousness. How is it, then, with the whale? True, both his eyes, in themselves, must simultaneously act; but is his brain so much more comprehensive, combining, and subtle than man's, that he can at the same moment of time attentively examine two distinct prospects, one on one side of him, and the other in an exactly opposite direction? If he can, then it is as marvellous a thing in him, as if a man were able simultaneously to go through the demonstrations of two distinct problems in Euclid. Nor, strictly investigated, is there any incongruity in this comparison.

The Melville reader learns to be wary of such artless information. This is neither bravura, pedantry, nor inability to excise the irrelevant. Melville is directly attacking Ahab's projection of evil onto the white whale by arguing, with almost a zoologist's precision, that the vacillation, apparent timidity, and erratic motion of the Sperm Whale—all that behavior deemed malicious by Ahab—are all in fact determined by the placement of the eyes.

On the smallness of the eye, Ishmael moralizes in a familiar vein. "Why then do you try to 'enlarge' your mind? Subtilize it." Another sign of Ishmael–Melville as Isolato, anti-wanderer, longing for a secure island in the midst of ocean chaos, preferring hearth to noble adventure. A contemporary equivalent of Ishmael's advice: "Why try to expand your consciousness? Reduce it."

75
A careful description of the head of the Right Whale concluding with an awkward philosophic mediation.

76
The frontal part of the Sperm Whale's head described.

From this carefully written chapter one is tempted to conclude that Melville is now identifying himself with the Sperm Whale. He sees in the whale a balance between power and life, work and love, aggression and libido, that he covets, yet never finds, for himself. It is conventionally, and rightly, said, that Melville is sometimes Ishmael and sometimes Ahab in this novel. Here, for a moment, he seems also to be the novel's hero, Moby-Dick himself.

77

A description of that portion of the head containing the spermaceti.

78

Tashtego is involved in removing the spermaceti from the head. He falls into the head, and Queequeg rescues him.

Once more Queequeg becomes a savior. On the boat from New Bedford to Nantucket, he saved the life of a man who had insulted him. Here he obstetrically delivers Tashtego from inside the body of the whale. Note the chapter's final sentence: "How many, think ye, have likewise fallen into Plato's honey head, and sweetly perished there?" Why Plato? Because for Plato, as for Emerson, the transcendentalists, and Ahab, the visible world is a deceptive and unreal shadow of the real, eternal world of forms lying above and beyond. Who else nearly perished in that honey head? Why, Ishmael himself, standing watch on the mast head, mystically dreaming over the water, nearly losing hold and falling to his death. Ahab, committed to nature as a pasteboard mask, will soon die in that honey head, bringing all but Ishmael down with him.

79

A phrenological description of the Sperm Whale's head.

The Sperm Whale, and therefore Moby-Dick, as the oldest and most erratic of the species, is here identified with "the Deity and the dread powers," with both God and the devil. The genius of the Sperm Whale is said to lie in his "pyramidical silence." A Melvillean connection between God and pyramids ought not to go unnoticed. Six years after *Moby-Dick*, Melville visited the great pyramids of Egypt, and was deeply moved. He wrote in his journal:

Reading Moby-Dick 57

I shudder at the idea of ancient Egyptians. It was in these pyramids that was conceived the idea of Jehovah. Terrible mixture of the cunning and awful. Moses learned in all the lore of the Egyptians. The Idea of Jehovah born here . . . gradual nervousness and final giddiness and terror.

At the close of the chapter, that familiar place where things seem regularly to happen, Melville advises any cultured nation wishing to enthrone the old chthonic gods in the "now egotistical sky" to consider the Sperm Whale's candidacy for divinity. Why does he call our contemporary skies egotistical? Perhaps because no God is now there, only man? Perhaps because the God that is there is such an untamed egotist.

80
The brain described.

81
The *Pequod* meets the *Virgin*, barren of oil. Crews from both ships lower for a whale, and the *Pequod* makes the kill. But the whale, alongside, begins to sink and has to be cut away.

From his attacks on missionaries in *Typee* to his portrait of the pleasant but compromised chaplain in *Billy Budd* (including some nice bishop-baiting a few pages further on in *Moby-Dick* chapter 83), Melville found it hard to resist the needling of organized Christianity. The defender of whaling yet observes that the whale must die, even be murdered, in order "to illuminate the solemn churches that preach unconditional inoffensiveness by all to all."

82
Some mythological references to whaling.

"There are some enterprises," Melville opens this chapter, "in which a careful disorderliness is true method." His methodological anxiety again, as if he'd been arguing with some literary critic. He is talking here about writing about whaling, but he is also once again apologizing for, and defending, the disorderly structure of this novel.

83
The story of Jonah as considered by whalemen.

84
How to pitchpole a harpoon.

85
The whale's spout, described and analyzed.

There is a special poignancy in the comment here about the whale's inability to speak. "Seldom have I known any profound being that had anything to say to this world, unless forced to stammer out something by way of getting a living." The romantic Melville: fiercely self-confident, yet gradually aware of his isolation from his nation and readers. Hence the touching irony of the sentence that follows. "Oh! happy that the world is such an excellent listener!"

At the close of the chapter is another Ishmaelian confession of faith, not a little obscure. It seems to contain that familiar and unresolved mixture of longing for domestic tranquillity and for a mystic union with nature that marks both Ishmael and probably his creator.

> Doubts of all things earthly, and intuitions of some things heavenly; this combination makes neither believer nor infidel, but makes a man who regards them both with equal eye.

86
The whale's tail and some metaphors.

There is a curious identification of power and beauty here, and this leads to a reflection on the beauty and power of God. But knowing Melville's deep distrust of God as both powerful and evil, we are not prepared for this word of praise for the merger of power and beauty. This takes Melville into deeper, and odder, waters. God may be power, he says, and Jesus—rightly portrayed by Renaissance painters—may be love, but his love is in a form "hermaphroditical . . . negative, feminine," all submission and endurance. Melville's continuing fascination with this weak but loving Jesus is reflected in his later long poem *Clarel*, and may well have played a part in his portrait of Billy Budd. A contemporary theological investigator might do worse than to follow up Melville's hint that the relation between the first two persons of the Trinity can be construed as the relation between masculine and feminine.

At the end of the chapter, the connection between gods and whales is again driven home. You can see the back parts of the whale, but you cannot see the face. Indeed, the whale has no face, but Melville does not say whether this makes him like or unlike God. See Exodus 33:23.

87
Approaching the straits of Sunda, the *Pequod* finds itself virtually surrounded by Sperm Whales, chasing and being chased.

At the chapter's close is one of Melville's most striking images, circular of course. A wide circle of male whales is swimming around Ishmael's boat, and at the center of that circle, next to the boat, is another circle of whales, almost Dantean in its sense of beatitude (*Paradiso*, canto 28), composed of nursing mothers and their young. The whale, it seems, is all innocence so long as man never intervenes. It is man, like mad Ahab, who interrupts this peace by imposing his own diabolism on nature. The experience of the double circle makes Ishmael reflective. The mad, evil world may circle around the "tornadoed Atlantic of my being," but "deep down and deep inland there I still bathe me in eternal mildness of joy." Ishmael, it seems, is becoming consistent in his metaphorical use of land and sea.

88
Two kinds of Sperm Whale schools: one with a group of females and one male; the other, all young males.

Melville makes a point about gender. When a male whale is harpooned, his male companions flee. When a female is caught, her female friends hover near.

89
A legal chapter in which loose-fish and fast-fish are defined and modestly metaphorized.

Is not Ahab a fast-fish, impaled and captured by his own heroic madness, bound in fatal search to an evil God? And Ishmael is finally a loose-fish; literally at the end, as he finally becomes free of Ahab's ideology and spell.

90
A peculiar English law concerning whales captured on the coast.

91
The *Pequod* meets the French *Rose-bud* which has taken two whales, one constipated. Stubb, with the help of an English-speaking crew member of the *Rose-bud*, persuades the stupid French captain to release the whales. Stubb finds, as expected, a generous supply of the precious ambergris in the digestive system of the constipated whale.

92
Ambergris is defined.

93
Pip, Ahab's black cabin-boy, has once before jumped overboard while rowing a whale boat. At that time Stubb warned him that if he did such a thing again he would not stop to pick him up. Pip did jump again, out of fear as before, and he is left alone in the water for an extended time until he is rescued. Here is Melville's haunting description of the effect of the experience on poor Pip.

The sea had jeeringly kept his finite body up, but drowned the infinite of his soul. Not drowned entirely, though. Rather carried down alive to wondrous depths, where strange shapes of the unwarped primal world glided to and fro before his passive eyes; and the misermerman, Wisdom, revealed his hoarded heaps; and among the joyous, heartless, ever-juvenile eternities, Pip saw the multitudinous, God-omnipresent, coral insects, that out of the firmament of waters heaved the colossal orbs. He saw God's foot upon the treadle of the loom, and spoke it; and therefore his shipmates called him mad. So man's insanity is heaven's sense; and wandering from all mortal reason, man comes at last to that celestial thought, which, to reason, is absurd and frantic; and weal or woe, feels then uncompromised, indifferent as his God.

The experience has driven Pip mad: "the sea had . . . drowned the infinite of his soul," like Ishmael at the mast-head or Ahab waking from sleep. Pip has seen something, not just *on* the water, but *in* it. He has descended, either actually or figuratively, into the depths and there has "seen" the terrible omnipotence of God, that doctrine that so haunted and infuriated Melville. "He saw God's foot upon the treadle of the loom, and spoke it." He saw, in other words, that God was indeed in control of the evil world, and he said so. Reflecting Paul in 1 Corinthians 1, Melville concludes that "man's insanity is heaven's sense." Not Ahab's insanity, but Pip's. Melville own angry religious location half-way between belief and unbelief is expressed, I think, in this touching story of Pip's vision.

Pip, strange brother of Fedallah (one dark and good, the other dark and evil), becomes the second of Ahab's alter egos. Pip sees the truth about the terrible power of God and it drives him mad. Fedallah is not mad, but fire-worshipping and demonic. Both are in Ahab as he prepares for the final stage of his quest. This chapter partly explains what Melville meant when he wrote to Hawthorne about *Moby-Dick*: "I have written a wicked book, and feel spotless as the lamb."[7]

94
Ishmael joins his shipmates around a large vat of sperm, squeezing the lumpy substance into a smooth liquid. We also have some odd definitions: white-horse, plum-pudding, slobgollion, gurry, and nippers.

The sperm-squeezing scene is striking: loving, funny, and certainly sexual. It leads Ishmael to yet another domestic vision. Gone is the tendency to mystic rapture, the genial skepticism, the sturdy defenses of whaling. Here whaling serves not to produce oil and heat, but metaphors for something else, for that good life as far from gods and whales and sea as possible.

95
A sailor processes the whale's penis.

96
The try-works is the name of the system on the open deck by which the

blubber is boiled down. On this voyage, it is first brought into use at night.

With the furnaces in full operation at night, the *Pequod* becomes fire and hell, a perfect symbol of Ahab's character and will. Ishmael, brooding at the tiller, has a momentary vision of a directionless ship, driving toward death. Disorder and death, this is what fire—and the worship of fire—does to men and to ships.

97
A note on the use of whale-oil lamps on the ship's forecastle.

98
On cleaning up the ship after a whale has been completely processed.

99
The main characters of the novel pass, one by one, before the doubloon on the mast and reveal their thoughts or lack of them: Ahab, Starbuck, Stubb, Flask, the Manxman, Queequeg, Fedallah, and finally, Pip.

The doubloon as Rorschach ink blot; a static but vivid device for character analysis. Ahab, castrated, sees only phallic images on the coin. Pip looks at it, sees nothing. Pure subjectivity; verbs, no nouns; nothing is outside him; the self/world distinction has been obliterated. Pip's madness is pure; Ahab's is mixed, impure. Pip says, in effect, "there is nothing outside me." Ahab says "there must be nothing outside or above me, and if there is I'll kill it."

100
The *Pequod* meets the *Samuel Enderby*. Ahab discovers that the captain lost his arm to Moby-Dick the season before.

Perhaps Melville's own interpretation of the white whale is placed on the lips of the hard-drinking, clear-sighted British doctor on the *Enderby*: "what you take for the White Whale's malice," he says to Ahab, "is only his awkwardness."

101
Ishmael recalls a later visit of his to the *Enderby* during which he ate and

drank exceptionally well. This leads him to some humorous reflections on Dutch whaling vessels and their reputation for good food and drink.

How difficult it is for Melville to suppress the vein of touching bitterness that crops up from time to time. At the chapter's end: "if you can get nothing better out of the world, get a good dinner out of it, at least."

102
An imaginative description of the Sperm Whale's skeleton which Ishmael presumably visited, assembled on land, on an island called Tranque (non-existent), in the Arsacides group (existent).

103
Some measurements of the skeleton.

104
Fossil evidence concerning the whale is assembled.

105
The question is raised as to whether the whale could ever become extinct.

The answer given is "no," and Melville is probably right in terms of the existent technology. The real dangers of extinction emerged with the use of automatic weapons.

106
After his return from the *Enderby*, Ahab weakens his whale-bone leg, and decides to have another made.

Here we learn something about Ahab and God that we have not met before. We know how Ahab has been divinizing himself, clearing out all above him. We know the god he is seeking to kill, and we will soon meet the sun-fire god that has transformed him into Apollo. Here is Ahab's sorrowful god. Not the one who has wounded him, or the one who will be wounded by him, but the one who shares his wound.

Ahab lost a leg to Moby-Dick on an earlier voyage. Just before the *Pequod* left Nantucket on the current voyage, we now learn,

Ahab fell so that his bone leg nearly castrated him. This double castration is part of Ahab's reflection on misery: how woe and misery perpetuate themselves, yet how behind some kinds of suffering and woe there stands a mystic significance, "an archangelic grandeur." The gods themselves, thinks Ahab, "are not forever glad." They are born when we begin to seek our sorrows' origin. There ought to be meaning to our suffering, Ahab–Melville is saying. Christianity has always said so. But Christianity lies.

It appears that Ahab's engagement with God and the gods is fully as complex as that of Ishmael. Indeed, Ahab's massive suffering will be given a redemptive character before this journey is over.

107
The ship's carpenter, who is to fashion Ahab's new leg, is described.

We have already suggested that the voyage of the *Pequod* is both political and theological, having to do with a search for America and a search for a trustworthy divinity. Both themes are reflected in a remarkable passage at the beginning of this chapter: "take high abstracted man alone," man, theologically perceived, Puritan man, probably,

> and he seems a wonder, a grandeur, and a woe. But from the same point, take mankind in mass,

—man as misused in the American industrial system of the day—

> and for the most part, they seem a mob of unnecessary duplicates, both contemporary and hereditary.

The reader will think back to chapter 26 with its tribute to the crew and to the great democratic God. The distinction there between detestable man in groups and ideal man reminds us of the distinction here.

In Melville's description of the carpenter's character, observe his almost angry emphasis on stolidity, heartlessness, unintelligence. This seems to be a strange and fascinating attack on an American type rarely criticized in either literature or life: the amateur inventor, the tinkerer, the American "good with his hands."

108
Ahab and the carpenter converse while the leg is being made.

Ahab, half in earnest, asks the carpenter to remake all of him: fifty feet tall, legs rooted in one place, lots of brains, no heart. Everything Ahab wanted, and just the sort of man Melville had written Hawthorne he didn't care for, and just the sort Melville thought God was, too much head, not enough heart.

Ahab, disliking his dependence on the carpenter, curses "that mortal inter-indebtedness" that qualifies his radical freedom, just as Ishmael had wondered about mutual dependence in the monkey-rope scene. Melville deeply longed, we have already observed, for a loving human community. He knew it spasmodically, rarely, only in fragments. For the most part, until just the very end, he lived the loneliest of lives. Ahab longs for freedom here, defined as having nothing above you. Freedom so defined can easily lead to revolution or to the solitary authenticity of existentialism. It cannot lead to ethics.

109
Ahab and Starbuck argue, and Starbuck stands up to Ahab's petulant loss of temper.

Ahab's longing for freedom, that rejection of everything above him, continues as he responds passionately to Starbuck's criticism: "There is one God that is Lord over the earth, and one Captain that is Lord over the *Pequod*. . . ." On the water, Ahab is to be the only god; beneath the water, of course, may lurk another.

110
Queequeg is seized with a fever, and he asks for a coffin to be made for him. Then he rallies, deciding it is not yet time for him to die. He proceeds to decorate his coffin, now his sea-chest, with copies of his own

tattoo marks. The coffin becomes Queequeg, preparing for the novel's last page.

111
The *Pequod* enters the Pacific, its final ocean.

Melville's lyrical meditation on the Pacific Ocean will warm the hearts of all lovers of that superb ocean among his readers. Notice the poetic fervor of this passage, and how, at the end, the sea becomes divine. Narcissus first; now Pan.

> There is, one knows not what sweet mystery about this sea, whose gently awful stirrings seem to speak of some hidden soul beneath; like those fabled undulations of the Ephesian sod over the buried Evangelist St. John. And meet it is, that over these sea-pastures, wide-rolling watery prairies and Potters' Fields of all four continents, the waves should rise and fall, and ebb and flow unceasingly; for here, millions of mixed shades and shadows, drowned dreams, somnambulisms, reveries; all that we call lives and souls, lie dreaming, dreaming, still; tossing like slumberers in their beds; the ever-rolling waves but made so by their restlessness.
>
> To any meditative Magian rover, this serene Pacific, once beheld, must ever after be the sea of his adoption. It rolls the midmost waters of the world, the Indian ocean and Atlantic being but its arms. The same waves wash the moles of the new-built Californian towns, but yesterday planted by the recentest race of man, and lave the faded but still gorgeous skirts of Asiatic lands, older than Abraham; while all between float milky-ways of coral isles, and low-lying, endless, unknown Archipelagoes, and impenetrable Japans. Thus this mysterious, divine Pacific zones the world's whole bulk about; makes all coasts one bay to it; seems the tide-beating heart of earth. Lifted by those eternal swells, you needs must own the seductive god, bowing your head to Pan.

The climax of this move toward the divinization of the sea—a central theme in *Moby-Dick*—comes in a line from a poem by Melville written in the last year of his life (1891) called "Pebbles": "Healed of my hurt, I laud the inhuman Sea—". Forty years after *Moby-Dick*, Melville finally found a god he didn't have to hate, from whom he did not need to flee.

112
The blacksmith's story is told; how he became a drunkard, lost his wife and children, and went to sea.

The place of death in the blacksmith's life leads to one of Melville's most beautiful meditations. *Moby-Dick* began with a suicidal Ishmael and it will end with a mass death scene. Death has never been far from the surface of our meditations on the ocean, on Ahab, or Queequeg. Here death is tied both to landlessness and to the sea.

> Death is only a launching into the region of the strange Untried; it is but the first salutation to the possibilities of the immense Remote, the Wild, the Watery, the Unshored; therefore, to the death-longing eyes of such men, who still have left in them some interior compunctions against suicide, does the . . . ocean alluringly spread forth his whole plain of unimaginable, taking terrors . . . and from the hearts of infinite Pacifics, the thousand mermaids sing to them—'Come hither, broken-hearted; here is another life without the guilt of intermediate death; here are wonders supernatural, without dying for them . . . come hither, till we marry thee!'

Of course the Lorelei are singing here, but it may not be too eccentric to discern a faint hint of Jesus' powerful words in Matthew 11:28: "Come to me, all who labor and are heavy laden, and I will give you rest." May it not be that the ocean mermaids function here as a Melvillean divinity, offering at last that gospel he could believe in—a call to the divinized sea, to guiltlessness and rest, based not upon life but death?

> 113
> Ahab talks to the blacksmith, who forges him a new harpoon. After it is tempered in the blood of the three harpooners, Ahab takes the finished harpoon into his cabin, and at the same time a mournful laugh from Pip is heard.

After the baptism in blood, Ahab cries out the sacramental words, "Ego non baptizo te in nomine patris, sed in nomine diaboli!" I baptise thee not in the name of the Father but in the name of the devil. The double devil: the devil Ahab has become, and the devil he has madly made of Moby-Dick. Melville wrote to Hawthorne on June 29, 1851: "This is the book's motto (the secret one), Ego non baptiso te in nomine—but make out the rest yourself."

114
Ishmael, Ahab, Starbuck, and Stubb on the sea.

Ishmael is beguiled again by the ocean's tranquillity, and the mystic mood—previously banished by his decision to become a genial skeptic—returns, tempting him to forget the remorseless fang that lurks beneath the ocean's velvet paw.

Even Ahab is captivated by the quiet Japanese waters, and Melville's own voice can be heard in the captain's meditation.

> Would to God these blessed calms would last. . . . There is no steady unretracing progress in this life; we do not advance through fixed gradations, and at the last one pause:—through infancy's unconscious spell, boyhood's thoughtless faith, adolescence' doubt (the common doom), then skepticism, then disbelief, resting at last in Manhood's pondering repose of If. But once gone through, we trace the round again; and are infants, boys, and men, and Ifs eternally. Where lies the final harbor, whence we unmoor no more? . . . Where is the foundling's father hidden? Our souls are like those orphans whose unwedded mothers die in bearing them: the secret of our paternity lies in their grave, and we must there to learn it.

Then Starbuck, naive Christian, courageous yet somehow weak, gazes at the same sea and finds no mystery and no evil: "Let faith oust fact; let fancy oust memory; I look deep down and do believe." Starbuck's faith, without memory or fact, had once been Melville's. He hated both himself and that faith because it had been proved false and he had been proved a fool.

This is as good a place as any to bring to the reader's attention an important passage from the June 1(?), 1851, letter to Hawthorne. Here Melville records his partial attraction to, and ultimate rejection of, the transcendental view of nature, so central to any interpretation of Ahab.

> In reading some of Goethe's sayings, so worshipped by his votaries, I came across this, 'Live in the all.' That is to say, your separate identity is but a wretched one,—good; but get out of yourself, spread and expand yourself, and bring to yourself the tinglings of life that are felt in the flowers and the woods, that are felt in the planets Saturn and Venus, and the Fixed Stars. What nonsense! Here is a fellow with a raging tooth-

ache. 'My dear boy,' Goethe says to him, 'You are sorely afflicted with that tooth; but you must live in the all, and then you will be happy!' As with all great genius, there is an immense deal of flummery in Goethe, and in proportion to my own contact with him, a monstrous deal of it in me. . . . This 'all' feeling, though, there is some truth in. You must often have felt it, lying on the grass on a warm summer's day. Your legs seem to send out shoots into the earth. Your hair feels like leaves upon your head. This is the *all* feeling. But what plays the mischief with the truth is that men will insist upon the universal application of a temporary feeling or opinion.

115
The *Pequod* meets the *Bachelor*.

The *Bachelor* is the only happy ship the *Pequod* meets and it is, of course, full of sperm.

116

Shortly after his apostrophe to the gentleness of the sea, Ahab looks on a dying whale turning to the sun, and returns in meditation to his truest comrade—sea, the one full of power and evil.

117

Fedallah, speaking for the first and only time, interprets Ahab's dream and makes some soothing predictions about his death.

Melville's study of Shakespeare at this time explains the reflection of *Macbeth* in this scene.

118

Ahab takes a final sight of the sun, then destroys the quadrant by throwing it to the deck.

When Ahab destroys the quadrant, he is not only rejecting science, but the very idea of order and degree. The quadrant can only tell Ahab where he is, but what he really wants to know is where he will be and where Moby-Dick is. The final offense of the quadrant, that "paltry thing that feebly pointest on high," is that it reminds him of that fire which is above him, of God and his dependence, of everything that he hates.

119
A typhoon strikes the *Pequod*, and the electrical storm brings on the corpusants—bright tips of fire at the end of the yard-arms. Ahab delivers his "fire-sermon," and holds the frightened crew to their original oath of obedience.

120
Ahab and Starbuck exchange words during the storm.

121
Stubb and Flask, during the storm.

The typhoon leads Stubb to wonder whether the world is anchored anywhere. Thirty years after *Moby-Dick*, Friedrich Nietzsche perceived that one consequence of the experience of the death of God is the perception of the free-floating earth, unchained from the sun.[8]

122
Tashtego decides he prefers rum to thunder.

123
Starbuck pauses outside Ahab's cabin door, wondering whether he ought to feel responsible for restraining or killing Ahab. Like Hamlet, watching Claudius trying to pray, Starbuck cannot act.

124
The typhoon has desensitized the compass needle, and Ahab, partly to impress the mates and crew, makes and magnetizes a new needle.

At the beginning of the chapter, after the rite of self-purification in the fire-sermon, Ahab becomes Apollo, God of the sun, when he calls the *Pequod* the "sea-chariot of the sun." After the magnetizing of the new needle, he further divinizes himself as the "lord over the level loadstone."

125
The log and line, a traditional way of determining a ship's rate of speed, is tested and found to be worthless.

In this chapter it is Ahab, committed in his own way to the death of God, who perceives that "the skewer seems loosening out of the middle of the world." Pip, mad with a holy madness, stands beside Ahab and seems for a moment to have the power to soften his master's unholy madness. "Thou touchest my inmost center," Ahab tells Pip, and he clasps Pip's hand, black and white together, as the song was to say a hundred years later.

There has always been madness holy and destructive, sacred and profane. Here Ahab, suggesting Lear with his Fool, cries out of that part of his madness not yet fully corrupt:

> Lo! ye believers in gods all goodness, and in man all ill,

Melville clearly means Calvinists—

> lo you! see the omniscient gods oblivious of suffering man; and man, though idiotic, and knowing not what he does,

both mad Pip and mad Ahab—

> yet full of the sweet things of love and gratitude. Come! I feel prouder leading thee by thy black hand, than though I grasped an Emperor's!

126
The *Pequod* sails near some rocks, and a mysterious wailing is heard. Perhaps it is "newly drowned men in the sea," perhaps it is seals. Then a sailor falls from the masthead into the water. The life-buoy is thrown after him and it sinks, along with the sailor, into the sea. Queequeg's unused coffin is brought out to be waterproofed to serve as an alternate life-buoy.

127
Ahab and the carpenter talk while the carpenter works on the coffin.

The coffin makes Ahab reflective. But he is still all head and no heart, in that sense all that Melville himself distrusts. Ahab, convinced transcendentalist, still sees nature itself as unreal, real only in what it signifies. "Oh! how immaterial are all materials! What things real are there, but imponderable thoughts?" Melville cannot be wholly opposed to this view of nature, for it is at the heart of the imaginative power of this book. But in the hands and mind of such as Ahab, Melville clearly is aware that this view of nature and language and meaning leads inexorably to madness and death.

128
The *Pequod* meets the *Rachel*, which reports having seen Moby-Dick the day before. Ahab is so elated that he coldly refuses the Captain's urgent request to join in a search for his young son lost at sea in a whale boat.

129
Ahab sadly tells Pip that he must not follow him around any more.

"There is that in thee, poor lad, which I feel too curing to my malady." In the New Testament, the demoniacs, perceiving Jesus' healing power, tried to avoid him, for they too felt him too curing to their malady (Mark 5:7). Three things, during this final stage, show some power to break through Ahab's insanity: Pip, the tranquil sea, and Starbuck's eyes.

130
Ahab, separated from Pip, is now seen constantly with Fedallah. A special hoist is rigged so Ahab may stand his own watch aloft, and once while he is aloft, a sea-hawk swoops down, takes off Ahab's hat and drops it in the sea.

Ahab is once again stripped for action: the pipe, the quadrant, and the hat. The "spiral" fall of the heat into the water prefigures both the spiral fall of the *Pequod* and the fall into the sea of Ahab himself.

131
The *Pequod* meets the ship *Delight*, battered by Moby-Dick, with five crewmen lost.

We have already observed that "delight" was the theme of the conclusion to Mapple's magnificent sermon (chapter 9). "O Father!", Mapple said, expounding delight, "chiefly known to me by Thy rod—mortal or immortal, here I die." Yes, delight is what God gives his faithful, and the good ship *Delight* finally tells us what this delight truly means: destruction and death.

132
Ahab, on a striking clear day, remembers his children and drops a tear into the sea. He speaks of his home to Starbuck, and asks his first mate to stay aboard the ship when the rest lower for Moby-Dick.

The chapter begins with the contrast between the feminine air and the murderous, masculine sea. It is this murderous sea that Ahab has become united with. In the fire-sermon, he had declared the fire to be his father, and had claimed that he knew not his mother. Doubly castrated, he had defeminized himself and submitted himself utterly to the murderously masculine. Apollo, sun, fire, sea—he is one with them all. In the feminine air he could no longer live. He can be truly Ahab only on, then finally in, the sea.

Just before Moby-Dick is sighted, in a strange sane calm before the final storm, Ahab—moved by his love of Pip—is beguiled by the enchanted air and is attentive even to Starbuck's pleas. But he abruptly breaks out of his reverie, confessing his unfreedom and union with God. No will of his own; no heart, all head; no feminine humanity obscuring his goal: "mother I know not."

> Is it I, God, or who, that lifts this arm? But if the great sun move not of himself; but is an errand-boy in heaven; nor one single star can revolve, but by some invisible power; how then can this one small heart beat; this one small brain think thoughts; unless God does that beating, does that thinking, does that living, and not I.

Utterly biblical, utterly Protestant. And this is how Ahab sounds just before the slaughter he causes. "Ahab is for ever Ahab, man. The whole act's immutably decreed. . . . I am the Fates' lieutenant; I act under orders" (chapter 134). Ahab is Melville's most terrible word about what faith in the Christian God can lead to, especially when it is combined with theological reflection. Becoming God to kill God becomes madness, suicide, and murder. This is a *Moby-Dick* that can illuminate that terrible and marvellous sigh that Melville uttered to Hawthorne concerning the wickedness of his book.

133
Ahab is the first to sight Moby-Dick; all the boats but Starbuck's are lowered. Moby-Dick quickly overturns Ahab's boat, breaking it in two, but Ahab and his crew are thrown free and picked up by Stubb. At the end of the day, the *Pequod* is still chasing the whale.

When Moby-Dick first appears, Melville allows us to see the whale as he really is, not as sailor's tales tell of him, not as Ahab has seen him in his madness. He divinely swims, he is truly god—a suffering god, and he manifests a "gentle joyousness—a mighty mildness of repose." The "grand god revealed himself . . . and went out of sight," as gods are wont to do.

Ishmael himself has been torn between power and love, God and Jesus, vigorous action on the sea and domestic rest on land, skepticism and mysticism—choosing now one, now the other. Now the white whale finally surfaces in "mighty mildness," in both power and love equally, and Ishmael's dualisms are collapsed. The true Moby-Dick contains them all, and this may be why some have insisted that he is, after all, the only convincing hero of the book. If there is in him some "malicious intelligence," it is not his own; it is solely ascribed to him by Ahabic madness.

How many gods can Ahab become? How many gods do we need to capture him? He is God, Satan, Apollo, and as all of them thoroughly evil. Yet look what Melville can add at this critical moment of climax.

> But this intensity of his physical prostration did but so much the more abbreviate it. In an instant's compass, great hearts sometimes condense to one deep pang, the sum total of those shallow pains kindly diffused through feebler men's whole lives. And so, such hearts, though summary in each one suffering; still, if the gods decree it, in their life-time aggregate a whole age of woe, wholly made up of instantaneous intensities; for even in their pointless centres, those noble natures contain the entire circumferences of inferior souls.

Ahab at the end, the divinely evil pursuer of the divine whale, turns briefly into a kind of Christ whose intensity of suffering sums up and includes the little sufferings of lesser men, binding all men together. Ahab prepares an atonement no one has asked for, an atonement of death. Atonement is, after all, a making one, an at-one-ment, and the community of the drowned is being called into being. We are not, after all, completely unprepared for Ahab as a Christ. He was prepared for, as in Old Testament messianism, by a prophet named Elijah; he wept, like Jesus, over his ocean–Jerusalem; his palms were bloodied as he slept his troubled sleep. And in a moment (chapter 135), Ahab will "give up the spear" and die as Jesus on the cross "gave up the ghost" and died (Luke 23:46, King James Version).

> 134
> On the second day of the chase, Moby-Dick capsizes and destroys all three of the whaleboats that have lowered for him.

Fedallah is lost, later to be seen dead and bound by whale-lines to the back of Moby-Dick. Fedallah is no longer needed; he has fully entered into Ahab possessed and Ahab has become him, the evil god, eternal, predestinating, who can look on a human face and see—nothing.

> Starbuck, of late I've felt strangely moved to thee; ever since that hour we both saw—thou know'st what, in one another's eyes. But in the matter of the whale, be the front of thy face to me as the palm of this hand—a lipless, unfeatured blank. Ahab is forever Ahab, man. The whole act's immutably decreed. 'Twas rehearsed by thee and me a billion years before this ocean rolled. Fool! I am the Fates' lieutenant; I act under orders.

> 135 and epilogue
> Ahab and Starbuck briefly speak, and the three boats are lowered even before Moby-Dick is sighted. The boats of Stubb and Flask are destroyed by the whale, and Ahab orders the crews back to the *Pequod*. Moby-Dick destroys the *Pequod*, and turns to attack Ahab's boat. Ahab at last releases his harpoon at Moby-Dick, but the line wraps around the captain's neck and pulls him to his death. The capsized crew from the water watches in horror as the *Pequod* and all aboard her sink, and they too (except one) are finally pulled down in the vortex created by the sinking ship.

The morning of the third day dawns. Ahab seems to experience the morning world as at the beginning of creation, "a new-made world" he calls it. Or is this third day the day of resurrection? This voyage began, after all, on Christmas. Where or when did it end? At some new Eden, or a new Flood with Ishmael as the Noah to start over again? Or on Easter?

Ahab defines his mind as frozen, himself as pure feeling. Only God has the right to think. All head and no heart before, he is now changed, converted. Even now, at the end, Melville cannot distance himself too greatly from Ahab; he had always preferred heart to head.

In Psalm 139, it is God who seeks man. Starbuck has his theology straight. "Oh! Ahab," he cries, "Moby-Dick seeks thee not. It is thou, that madly seekest him!" Moby-Dick cannot be the evil god Ahab thinks him to be, for he is seeking no one. "Ahab," Starbuck in effect declares, "thou hast become the evil god, seeking, seeking. . . ."

The Melvillean alternative to Ahab's mad theological egotism is not orthodoxy, atheism, or the divinity of man. It is a religious, post-Christian vision of human solidarity. We saw it first in a touching friendship between a white seaman and a cannibal harpooner. It was expressed somewhat rhetorically in the paean to democratic equality (chapter 26). In a moment it will be finally presented in that last picture of Ishmael clinging to his comrade Queequeg's coffin.

Ishmael, bearer of this vision, is "the third man" flung out of Ahab's whale boat, outside the mighty vortex that pulls the rest of the crew, and the ship itself, to the bottom. Even a bird of heaven, entangled in the mast-head flag, must be dragged, with the ship and men, into the deep.

Ahab's transcendentalism required him to see a whale as something more than a whale. So, many were killed and he himself died of this symbolism. Ishmael, finally deconverted from Ahabic mad faith, saw at the end that whales were but whales. So he lived, saved by Queequeg, who had earlier made himself one with his coffin.

A reading of *Moby-Dick* needs one more thing. *Moby-Dick* must, at all costs, be deprived of any hint of a happy ending in which evil at last is defeated. This at least one owes to Herman

Melville. There are two ways to do this. We could say that Ahab did not die and never will. "Ahab is forever Ahab." Is there not a "little lower layer" according to which he does not die? It might go this way. Ahab becomes one with the only "nature" he could acknowledge, Moby-Dick and his surrounding sea. His alter egos, Pip, Fedallah, Starbuck, do indeed die. But Moby-Dick lives and Ahab lives too, bound to the white whale by rope, by blind faith, in mystical union. The novel begins with a group of men separating themselves from land, and ends with one man uniting himself with the sea. It begins with Christmas, where Christians start from, and ends with mystical union where Christians sometimes end.

Or, we could go about it another way. Let us suppose that Ishmael remained in the whaling business, that he became a harpooner and finally a first mate. One day, in Nantucket, a ship owner offered him his own ship. Ishmael accepted. "I think I'll call the ship the *Ahab*. I wonder if that white whale is still...."

II

The Conversions of Michelangelo

A theological portrait of Michelangelo is both difficult and dangerous. The artistic and literary material is, of course, abundant, but it is not as easy as it seems to read off Christianity or neo-platonism from the paintings, sculpture, or poetry. For instance, here are two examples of the wrong way to go. The first, an elegant piece of neo-platonizing, comes from Charles de Tolnay.

> The yearning for the metaphysical heights remains all his long life the directing force of his being. It appeared under different aspects, first as Platonism and later as Christianity. But it is always the same detachment from the world, the same ardor for absolute truth, the same desire to reach to the "upper regions" where the essence of existence is revealed.[1]

There is a strong whiff of German romanticism here, and de Tolnay apparently holds (with Ficino) that neo-platonism and Christianity are but different forms of the same longing. But it is doubtful that Michelangelo himself held to this identity, for we shall see the two systems merging, then splitting apart, in both the life and work of the artist. But de Tolnay has at least the right ingredients for the theological stew.

Kenneth Clark's theologizing is both charming and wild.

> *The Conversion of St. Paul* is an explosion, the breaking up of a world, and at the centre of this explosion is a figure which must be one of the most moving inventions in the whole of art: the blinded Paul lying on the ground in the arms of his attendant. . . . The actual head of St. Paul conveys most movingly the pain of spiritual sight, with its antecedent blindness, and Michelangelo has given it added poignancy by making it an idealized self-portrait. This self-identification has a profound meaning for him. The conversion of St. Paul is the supreme example of Grace.

Now, the problem of Grace—could a sinner be saved simply by the power of God—was at the centre Luther's theology, and it was Michelangelo's circle of friends who were most troubled by the problem, and who had, in fact, come very close to the position of the Protestants. If Michelangelo did not entirely share their belief, it was because his profound pessimism would not allow him to accept so comforting a doctrine.[2]

What is Lord Clark trying to say? Since Michelangelo's Paul is a self-portrait, we can assume (can we?) that Paul's ideas are of some interest to him. But there is a problem because Michelangelo was a pessimist and justification by faith is optimistic. But "pessimism" and "optimism" just will not do here. Michelangelo has his dark and pessimistic moments, but he has other colors as well. And it does not make any sense to call Pauline justification a comforting doctrine, and thus inaccessible to pessimists. One might even argue that the creator of this optimistic ideology was in fact a pessimist ("O wretched man that I am . . ."). Or, more securely, it should be noted that the doctrine is in fact not comforting at all. It requires a radical and complete confession of sin, with all confidence in works, law, and goodness set aside.

When two such masters stumble, the rest of us are bidden to be careful.

Michelangelo's work has traditionally been divided into three periods. The first, going up to 1530, includes the early love poems, the Rome Pietà, and the ceiling. The second, from the early 1530's, begins with Michelangelo's involvement with the "Spirituali"—the Catholic–humanist reform movement with Vittoria Colonna at the center—and includes the Sistine Last Judgment and the poems addressed to Vittoria and Tommaso de' Cavalieri. The final period covers Michelangelo's last twenty years, from 1545 to his death, during which he moves beyond the Renaissance mixture of Plato and Christ to a radically de-platonized Christological faith in which the student of his work is virtually invited to "participate in the sufferings of God at the hands of a godless world." This is the world of the final Pietàs and the last drawings of Mary and her son.

We ought to imagine the young Michelangelo being fed by three streams in his early years. First, there was his inherited Christian piety, always intense, always serious. Second, the Florentine artistic tradition, beginning in the early fourteenth century with Cimabue and Giotto. His early drawings after Giotto and Masaccio remind us vividly of Vasari's definition of the High Renaissance style: "the appeal and vigor of living flesh," celebrating the grandeur and dignity of man through bodies "exquisitely graceful and full of movement." Exactly what we see on the Sistine Ceiling, through the whole of what we are calling the first stage.

A third stream, and perhaps the most decisive for our theological concern, comes from that brief period in his late teens, 1490–1492, when Michelangelo lived in that glorious neo-platonic circle in Florence assembled around Lorenzo de'Medici. Here, his traditional piety becomes laced by deep and heady draughts of Florentine neo-platonism. Michelangelo's intellectual and spiritual existence (and, to a lesser degree, his artistic existence as well) for the next seventy-five years was to be defined by that mixture from the Medici garden—for good or ill, for clarification or confusion. All we really know is that the theological Michelangelo begins with that Medici mix, and ends somewhere else.

Among those that the young Michelangelo lived with for those two or three years before Columbus landed on the Bahamas were: Landino, the great Dante commentator; Marsilio Ficino and Pico della Mirandola, the Christian neo-platonists decisive in shaping the character of the Florentine movement; and a handful of future popes, all eating at the same table. Here, at this decisive point in both his artistic and spiritual life, he absorbed the central presupposition of Florentine neo-platonism, that paganism and Christianity were but different manifestations of the same universal truth. A pre-supposition probably false and both helpful and troublesome to him in his later years.

Neo-platonism, unlike classical Christianity, saw man as basically good, and redemption coming less from God's grace than from human intelligence enhancing the practice of virtue.

Life is not a journey from sin to grace (the fundamental theme, I will argue, of the upper nine panels on the ceiling), but a journey of the soul, progressively freed by contemplation from its imprisoning body, all the way to death where the final body–soul split is achieved. Ficino, especially, saw the pleasures of the senses as gravely hindering the soul's ascent through higher and higher degrees of knowledge and love until, at last, it comes to union and identification with God. I wish to emphasize that for Florentine neo-platonism the human body was a problem, a menace, a necessary evil to be transcended. It will not be surprising to discover that this conviction may have made more sense for Michelangelo's life than for his work.

As a way of underscoring the influence of these brief years at the Palazzo Medici, it will be interesting to look at what is perhaps the ancient text most decisively shaping Renaissance thought in Florence at the close of the fifteenth century. It is the climax of Socrates' (though placed in the mouth of his beloved mentor, Diotima) great speech on love from Plato's *Symposium*.

> "The man who would pursue the right way to this goal must begin, when he is young, by applying himself to the contemplation of physical beauty, and, if he is properly directed by his guide, he will first fall in love with one particular beautiful person and beget noble sentiments in partnership with him. Later he will observe that physical beauty in any person is closely akin to physical beauty in any other, and that, if he is to make beauty of outward form the object of his quest, it is great folly not to acknowledge that the beauty exhibited in all bodies is one and the same; when he has reached this conclusion he will become a lover of all physical beauty, and will relax the intensity of his passion for one particular person, because he will realize that such a passion is beneath him and of small account. The next stage is for him to reckon beauty of soul more valuable than beauty of body; the result will be that, when he encounters a virtuous soul in a body which has little of the bloom of beauty, he will be content to love and cherish it and to bring forth such notions as may serve to make young people better; in this way he will be compelled to contemplate beauty as it exists in activities and institutions, and to recognize that here too all beauty is akin, so that he will be led to consider physical beauty taken as a whole a poor thing in comparison. . . .
>
> "The man who has been guided thus far in the mysteries of love, and

who has directed his thoughts towards examples of beauty in due and orderly succession, will suddenly have revealed to him as he approaches the end of his initiation a beauty whose nature is marvellous indeed, the final goal, Socrates, of all his previous efforts. This beauty is first of all eternal; it neither comes into being nor passes away, neither waxes nor wanes; next, it is not beautiful in part and ugly in part, nor beautiful at one time and ugly at another, nor beautiful in this relation and ugly in that, nor beautiful here and ugly there, as varying according to its beholders; nor again will this beauty appear to him like the beauty of a face or hands or anything else corporeal, or like the beauty of a thought or a science, or like beauty which has its seat in something other than itself, be it a living thing or the earth or the sky or anything else whatever; he will see it as absolute, existing alone with itself, unique, eternal, and all other beautiful things as partaking of it, yet in such a manner that, while they come into being and pass away, it neither undergoes any increase or diminution nor suffers any change.

"When a man, starting from this sensible world and making his way upward by a right use of his feeling of love for boys, begins to catch sight of that beauty, he is very near his goal. This is the right way of approaching or being initiated into the mysteries of love, to begin with examples of beauty in this world, and using them as steps to ascend continually with that absolute beauty as one's aim, from one instance of physical beauty to two and from two to all, then from physical beauty to moral beauty, and from moral beauty to the beauty of knowledge, until from knowledge of various kinds one arrives at the supreme knowledge whose sole object is that absolute beauty, and knows at last what a absolute beauty is."

Diotima may be the most valuable key to unlock Michelangelo's neo-platonic gate. Instead of homosexual narcissism in which like loves only like, Diotima celebrates a selfless love of beauty. Possession of another's body is inadequate. Beyond the mere body is beauty itself, as love of *eros* ascends from that beauty to the good and finally to the divine. Michelangelo came to the Medici palace a Christian, and to that was added this heady neo-platonic brew.

We are not surprised, therefore, to observe that his earliest works seem to fall into pairs, one manifesting the neo-platonic–pagan side of his young mind, the other showing the Christian. There is the celebration of the body in the Battle Relief (1491–1492), and there is the unforgettable Madonna of the Steps (*c.* 1491). This Mary is more than a traditional Christian icon. He has made her his own, and he is already showing us something of his inner self. She is deeply self-absorbed, showing no rapture toward God and no concern for the child, as she already appears to anticipate the tragic future of the one seeming to emerge from her loins. This Mary is no Tuscan wife, and the child is no blessing savior. This is a solemn Mary offering no consoling touch; rejecting, stony, detached, even as she nurses. The sleeping child is just as eerie. The twisted right arm suggests death as much as sleep, and we can confirm our suspicions by noting the same left-arm twist in the dead Jesus of the Florence Pietà, many years later.

This first Madonna tempts us to offer a sympathetic ear to the psychoanalytical interpreters of Michelangelo's work who call attention to the mother–son theme throughout the artist's whole career. The most recent of these studies, and the most convincing, says this about the early Madonna.

> She represents the fused image of Michelangelo's wet-nurse and natural mother, both of whom were forever lost to him. The yearning to recapture the lost sense of well-being in a symbiotic union with the breast remained an intense moving force within Michelangelo. . . . However, to yield to this regressive yearning was also to risk death—both in the union with the dead mothering one and in the unleashing of the impounded rage connected with the sense of abandonment so early in life.[3]

Michelangelo was a Christian before he encountered neo-platonism, and he continued to be a Christian after he abandoned the youthful Florentine optimism.[4] It is important to recall that neo-platonism bequeathed a profoundly conflicted message about the human body. There was the pagan side that celebrated man's glorious physical humanity; and there was the shadow side, both platonic and Christian in origin, that distrusted and feared the body, inviting love to flee the body for the soul, to move from the passing beauties of particulars to the love of beauty itself.[5]

Before we look at the neo-platonism and Christianity in the early poetry, it may be useful to remember that Michelangelo could be both funny and sensual in writing about a woman.

The Conversions of Michelangelo

> You have a face more beautiful than a turnip,
> Sweeter than mustard; it appears the snail
> Has walked on it, it shines so; like a parsnip
> The whiteness of your teeth is, and like treacle
> The color of your eyes; surely the Pope
> To such as this must be susceptible,
> Whiter and blonder than a leek your hair;
> So I shall die if I don't get your favor.
>
> I think your beauty much more beautiful
> Than ever in a church a painted man,
> And your mouth is just like a pocketful
> Of beans, it seems to me, and so is mine.
> Your eyebrows seem dyed in a crucible,
> And more than a Syrian bow they twine.
> Your cheeks are red and white when you sift flour,
> Like fresh cheese and poppies mixed together.
>
> And when I look upon you and each breast,
> I think they're like two melons in a satchel,
> And then I am like straw, and start to flash,
> Although I'm bent and broken by the shovel.
> Think, if my lovely cup I still possessed,
> I'd follow you past others like a beagle,
> And if I thought that getting it was possible,
> Here and today I'd do something incredible.[6]

The young poet, obedient to the neo-platonic signals, ascends from the beauty of the beloved to God.

> What sets my love alive is not my heart,
> There's no heart in the love I love you by,
> It cannot stay where there's mortality
> With all its falsehood, nor in vicious thought.
>
> Love, when the soul quit God, made you be light
> And brilliancy, and me a steady eye,
> So my great longing cannot fail to see
> Him in what's mortal in you, to our hurt.
>
> As heat from fire, likewise my admiration
> Cannot be parted from eternal beauty,
> Praising Him most like it who is its cause.
>
> Since in your eyes you carry all of Heaven,
> I, to return there where I loved you early,
> Hurry back, burning, underneath your brows.
>
> (Gilbert #32)

It is not heart that makes this ascent, nor is it thought, body, or emotion. It is love, neo-platonic *eros*, fallen from its original divinity, that seeks its return: finally, the beloved *is* God.

But conventional Catholic theology can inform these early verses as well. Here is a straight scholastic interpretation of the artist's craft.

> If my rough hammer in hard stones can form
> A human semblance, one and then another,
> Set moving by the agent who is holder,
> Watcher and guide, its course is not its own.
>
> But that divine One, staying in Heaven at home,
> Gives others beauty, more to itself, self-mover;
> If hammers can't be made without a hammer,
> From that one living all the others come.
>
> And since a blow will have the greatest force
> As at the forge it's lifted up the highest,
> This above mine to Heaven has run and flown.
>
> Wherefore with me, unfinished, all is lost.
> Unless the divine workshop will assist
> In making it; on earth it was alone.
>
> (Gilbert #44)

There is no prevenient grace from this God. He remains in heaven, ever the unmoved Aristotelian mover. But he is involved in Michelangelo's sculptural projects. Without the unmoved mover, the sculptor confesses he cannot complete his work. (The vexing problem of the unfinished nature of so many of Michelangelo's statues may achieve a partial solution here: I cannot finish "unless the divine workshop will assist.")

Even in the early years of his life, Michelangelo is deeply critical of the corruption of his beloved pre-Reformation church. He never became a Protestant, but in mid-life he would move gently toward some of the ideas of that movement. Here is an early attack on church corruption.

> They make a sword or helmet from a chalice,
> And sell the blood of Christ here by the load,
> And cross and thorn become a shield, a blade,

And even Christ is being stripped of patience.

He should not come again into this province;
Up to the very stars his blood would spread.
Now that in Rome his skin is being sold,
And they have closed the way to every goodness.

If ever I wished that riches were cut off
What's happening here has changed all that in me;
The Cloak can do as Gorgon did in Atlas.

Yet if high Heaven favors poverty,
But other goals cut off our other life,
What is there in our state that can restore us?
(Gilbert #10)

Some writers have been tempted to speak about Michelangelo's "conversion" to Christianity, late in life, as if it were the emergence of something new. But Michelangelo was never outside Christianity. In his late teens he was an intelligent late fifteenth-century Renaissance–Christian–neo-platonist. His works, we have observed, reflected that amalgam. The late "conversion" is better described as a move from the early amalgam (a classical Catholic faith plus a learned neo-platonism that believed itself to be the same thing as Christianity) forged in the Medici gardens to a late-in-life radical, Christological, de-platonized Christianity: beyond beautiful bodies, beyond beauty itself, beyond pagan and Renaissance. The journey we will be tracking is the journey from the Medici gardens, through the Medici chapel to those late anti-platonist drawings and Pietàs. Michelangelo's spiritual journey is within, not to Christianity. He has shifts, not conversions.

An exact portrait of the early piety is difficult, in part because it is not easy to define his relation to the Dominican firebrand who took over the governance of Florence at the close of the fifteenth century, Savonarola. Some have attempted to identify the monk's influence on the Madonna of the Steps, since in one of his sermons he had declared that "the Virgin was illuminated even more than the other prophets by the prophetic light and that is why she knew in advance that the Child was to suffer his

Passion as a human being." But the prophetic Virgin was an iconographic tradition well before the fifteenth century. Condivi, possibly writing from the artist's own dictation, tells us that Michelangelo read the Bible under Savonarola's influence, that he studied the writings of the friar "for whom he has always had great affection and whose voice still lives in his memory."

But this is a long way from establishing a Savonarolan "influence." It may be that Michelangelo heard some of those 1494 sermons predicting the violent downfall of Florence, and it may even be that his strange 1494 flight from Florence was caused by the fears inspired by those sermons. But he could never have taken to the monk's views on art. Savonarola rejected what he called "pagan nudity" and insisted—like those seventeenth-century Pietists Bach objected to—that art could be justified only by its moral and religious lessons. Michelangelo could have had nothing but contempt for such philistine moralism. Condivi's words may enshrine a myth the artist wanted, later in life, to perpetuate.

The early art, rather than possible sermons listened to, provides safer clues to the shape of that inherited Christianity that Michelangelo brought to the teen-age neo-platonic years.

The Doni Madonna (1503–1504) is striking for a number of reasons. It is apparently Michelangelo's first painting, and it is a portrait of a vigorous peasant Mary, physically involved with her child. His wet-nurse, some have suggested, not his own rejecting mother who died when he was six. Even though it is often stated that Michelangelo cared little for theology, there is here some theological sophistication. The three distances—the background, the middle ground, and the foreground—stand for the three stages in the salvation drama. The lollygagging boys in the background, not sinners but ignorant of salvation, stand for life before the law—*ante legem*—while in the foreground are the mother and child, life *sub gratia*. In the middle (*sub lege*) we find two mediators between the time before the law and the time after the law: Joseph who may be serving as one kind of bridge between *sub lege* and *sub gratia*, and the infant John the Baptist whose direct, rapt gaze bridges the gulf between law and grace,

Old and New Testaments. The Doni Madonna, John Addington Symonds has written,

> ranks among the great pictures of the world. Once seen, it will never be forgotten: it tyrannises and dominates the imagination by its titanic power of drawing.[7]

Before we turn to the final examples of the first stage, the paintings on the Sistine ceiling, notice should be taken of the strange and moving sculpture of St. Matthew done in Florence in 1504–1508 at a time of great personal distress. The combination of contorted muscular action and inhibition or bondage reminds us of the portrait of God on the ceiling in the Separation of Light from Darkness. What a strange portrait of an inspired evangelist. He doesn't look the least inspired; he looks doomed. Michelangelo at this time had fled from Rome to Florence, bitterly arguing money matters with Julius II (the letters suggest that money was a perpetual worry throughout the whole of his long life), angry and distressed. Is it significant that this embodiment of anguish should be a former tax-collector?

Turning to the Sistine chapel, we find the same pattern of the salvation-drama that we found in the Doni Madonna. The chapel wall on the right, facing the altar, had a series of paintings of Moses, man under the law. On the left was the life of Christ, the realm of grace. It was thus necessary that the new ceiling should represent that part of the total drama as yet untended: man before the law, *ante legem*, between creation and the giving of the Law on Sinai. In an eloquent passage, de Tolnay has praised the achievement of the ceiling.

> The philosophic and religious beliefs of Humanism found in it its most perfect artistic embodiment: the conception of earthly beauty as a manifestation of the divine idea, the belief in the inner *renovatio* of the human soul which is of divine nature, and the belief of the possibility of its return to God (*deificatio*). Yet it is not a mere illustrative translation in imagery of a given philosophic system, but a philosophy in itself—a creative synthesis in visual symbols of the transcendent idealism. This creative synthesis is much clearer and much more consistent than those found in the works of contemporary philosophers and poets. Writers like

Landino, Ficino, and Pico were unable to express their thoughts in unequivocal language and to arrive at a coherent synthesis. The fine arts should be considered the primary language of thought in the sixteenth century.

The Sistine Ceiling is the greatest *Summa* of the life-ideals of Humanism, the perfect compendium of the artistic, philosophic and religious tendencies of the time, a veritable *Divina Commedia* of the Renaissance—as unique and as representative as Dante's poetry was for his age.[8]

He is right about the significance, though we need not be so certain that he is right about the interpretation. His is a classic and lucid expression of the neo-platonic reading of the ceiling. It tells the story of the soul's deification, the liberation of the soul from the bodily prison to dwell forever in union with God. I find this unconvincing; it is not what the body means in these paintings, and it does not accurately describe what the ceiling has to say about man's relation to God. The neo-platonizers depend on a theory of vertical symbolism: below, the lunettes and spandrels show ordinary humanity, the *genii*, those without the gift of the spirit. At the next higher level rest the prophets and the sibyls; human, yet possessing supernatural faculties to see into the future and to point forward to divinity. At the top, is divinity itself.

I will argue that this misses completely the real drama that is unfolding at the ceiling's top. For some reason, perhaps because he wishes the aging Michelangelo to experience a "conversion" from neo-platonism to Christianity, de Tolnay needs to see in the ceiling more neo-platonism than there is, and less biblical faith. I suspect that in the nine central panels of the ceiling a deep fissure is beginning to emerge between the pagan and Christian elements in Michelangelo's Florentine neo-platonic inheritance. It is a fissure that will finally become a canyon.

In those nine central panels, we do not discern neo-platonic ambivalence about the body. The ceiling is not about flight from the body, or deification, or loss of self in the divine. It is an attack on the neo-platonic myth of the identity of paganism and Christianity. It is about Creation, that anti-platonic, biblical affirmation of the goodness of the body. And it is about the radical separateness of self from God, not an ultimate merger.

There is a spiritual journey in the nine central panels, but it is not a journey from an evil body to an final loss of self in the divine; it is a simple biblical journey from sin to grace, from the drunkeness of Noah, just above as sinners enter the chapel, to the tumultuous and transcendent power of the Creator over the altar, at the end of the sinner's journey. This is good solid Catholic, even clerical, piety, for the original screen separating the *presbyterium*, the clergy, the old men, at the altar end from the sinning laity at the other end originally stood between the Temptation-Expulsion (laity equals sin?) and the Creation of Eve (clergy possesses God and the means of grace). The four paintings above the layman's space are all about sin; the five brooding over the clergy are all about God. No layman has any rights beyond the *presbyterium* screen; no access of his own to God.

The deepest theological message of the nine ceiling panels is not neo-platonic at all. It lies in the astonishing series of five portraits of God the Creator, "beginning" not with the actual order of creation in the book of Genesis, but beginning in the order defined by the sinners' move toward the altar, with the Creation of Eve. Then the Creation of Adam, the Separation of Land from Water, the Creation of the Sun and Moon, and the Separation of Light from Darkness.

In the Creation of Eve, God draws Eve from Adam's side. He is a praying shaman, while she is pious and, for the moment, obedient. The Old Testament reference is Genesis 2:21–22.

In the Creation of Adam (Genesis 2:7), God is no longer an aged magician, he is a vigorous and busy athlete offering his own manifest power to the curved, waiting, androgynous, and apparently still undersexed, male. The divine left arm is as active as the famous right—nestled against it is Eve, waiting to be made and looking, not without some dread, at what she may be up against. The left hand rests on the shoulder of a lovely child, reminding us that the man in the process of being made will not be forever docile. He will sin, and his heirs will some day need redemption through that child, and Eve will become a second Eve, a Mary. Liebert describes this familiar painting.

> No image in Western art has commanded the awe and popular response of this vision of an anthropomorphic God who, with transcendent grace and power, soars to the apogee of his celestial journey. He bestows his compassionate grace and tender procreative gesture upon Adam, whose concave and receptive form languidly reaches out for the mysterious infusion of physical strength and spiritual purity already latent in him. The miraculous event-to-be exists outside of time, against the barren brown-blue of the earth, thereby placing in relief the feeling of devotion between the two. Beholders of this image cannot help but respond with a sense of rediscovering and reexperiencing some lost moment of their own innocence in the buried past, when there could be complete trust in an all-caring, omnipotent parent.[9]

The journeying sinner moves forward toward the altar and backwards into mythic time; from sin, to the Creations of Eve and Adam, to the very beginnings of all things. Along that journey, Michelangelo's portraits of God take on a more and more mysterious air, becoming more interesting, more intense, more frightening.

In the final three paintings, altar-wards from the Creation of Adam, "Michelangelo was so possessed by his desire to reveal the essence of the Creator that he neglected the material object of creation."[10] These last three panels are not about creation at all, they are only "about" the Creator. Here is no divine "all" to lose oneself in, no God to unite with. Here is pure power making a gulf between sinner and divinity, and one's response is terror and awe. This is not the God of the neo-platonic synthesis in the Florentine garden. This is the God of the Bible, the God of Michelangelo's emerging faith, whom one cannot see and live. This ceiling is not wholly neo-platonism; it is also the death of neo-platonism.

It is hard to see what is going on in the Separation of Land from Water. The title is Vasari's and the reference is to Genesis 1:9, the third day of creation. Condivi calls this panel the creation of the fish of the sea; Genesis 1:20, fifth day. It could just as well be Genesis 1:6–8, the firmament separating the upper and lower waters; or even Genesis 1:2, where "the Spirit of God was moving over the face of the waters," even before creation began. This God lunges at us out of some darkness, hovering over what looks like a piece of water. There is no earth, only God in his solitary divinity; eyes half-closed, reflecting.

The double portrait in the Creation of the Sun and Moon (Genesis 1:14-16, fourth day, for sun and moon; some would add plants, Genesis 1:11, third day) shows a God all fire and intensity. After the sun and moon are done, he turns across our line of sight and moves away, making a few plants with his outstretched right hand, almost as an afterthought. Michelangelo may well have had in mind Exodus 33:23, where God says to Moses "you shall see my back, but my face shall not be seen."

The climax of the ceiling's theological journey comes with the unforgettable Separation of Light from Darkness (Genesis 1:18b, fourth day, Fig. 1) Here God appears to be creating himself, or seeking to break out from the primeval chaos, or to sink back into it. He has no context, and there is no action we can name. His figure is not even differentiated sexually, for he seems to possess maternal breasts. This portrait denies the simple identity of masculinity and power in order to show something deeper and wiser than power (not love, that would be twentieth-century sentimentality)—God as life, the source of life, maternal, dynamic, tortured, twisting, terrifying—the true and decisive summation of the four divine portraits that have come before.

It is only fair to give the other side equal time. Here is de Tolnay in all his neo-platonic passion on the final panel.

> In the *Separation of Light and Darkness*-the last fresco of the series-God seems to extricate Himself from primitive chaos in a swimming movement. Confused formless clouds swarm in space. An instinctive impulse urges Him to seek an escape from this gloom. He evolves from the folds of His mantle which describes whirlwinds around His figure. His body is convulsively twisted, His outstretching arms grope with probing gestures in the welter which surrounds Him (it is the same gesture for liberation that Michelangelo will use later in his drawings of the Resurrected Christ); His eyes are closed as in blindness. . . . This is a spirit seeking itself.
>
> In this image of the autocreation of God from chaos, Michelangelo

Figure 1. Michelangelo, The Separation of Light from Darkness, Sistine Chapel ceiling, fresco, Vatican.

surpassed an iconographic tradition more than a thousand years old. Up to that time God was represented as a transcendent being existing from eternity, a being Who creates the universe as He would a plaything. Michelangelo, on the contrary, integrated Jehovah with the concept of the ancients by revealing for the first time in an image how God created Himself. As in ancient cosmogonies of Hesiod and of Lucian, in the beginning there was chaos, and from the chaos was born the gods themselves. Cosmogony here contains theogony as its organic part.

In the previous histories God appears as a plastic figure creating around itself the effect of space; here He is a flat "shadow" gliding swiftly through chaotic space. His body seems to be the condensation of a cloud-like substance, soft, immaterial and formless. No more undulating outlines are given; the forms are simplified (this is especially noticeable in the arms and hands). God is assimilated to the nature of clouds, from which, nevertheless, He tries to disentangle Himself. The idea is again renewed of the ancient cosmogonies (the theory of the Ionian School), according to which there was in the beginning only a primitive substance called $\upsilon\lambda\acute{\eta}$ which by condensation composed celestial bodies. At the same time this vision anticipates by its dynamism the modern conception of the genesis of the universe as expressed in the theory of Laplace.[11]

But we really do not need Thales to read the Separation of Light from Darkness. Where de Tolnay stumbles, I think, is where he has Michelangelo glorifying himself at the same time he glorifies God.[12] I simply do not think the paintings permit that reading. There is no longing here; no *eros*, and, incidentally, no *agape*. This is the naked biblical God of Exodus 3:14—"I will bring to pass what I will bring to pass"—or of Isaiah 6, whose face is shielded by angel wings, before whom one does not "aspire" or seek "deification," but only confesses one's uncleanness. Michelangelo's God does not come out of the whirlwind, He *is* the whirlwind. A hundred years later, an old king, looking perhaps something like this God, will face an early seventeenth-century world in which there are only whirlwinds, and no gods of any kind, not pagan, not neo-platonic, not Christian.

> Blow, winds, and crack your cheeks. Rage, blow.
> You cataracts and hurricanoes, spout
> Till you have drenched our steeples, drowned the cocks.
> You sulph'rous and thought-executing fires,

> Vaunt-couriers of oak-cleaving thunderbolts,
> Singe my white head. And thou, all-shaking thunder,
> Strike flat the thick rotundity o' th' world,
> Crack Nature's moulds, all germains still at once
> That makes ingrateful man. (*King Lear*, III.ii.1–9)

At the close of what we are calling Michelangelo's first stage, we have tried to read the Sistine ceiling as a document of the High Renaissance, to be sure, but as less neo-platonic and more classically Christian than some observers allow. The body is glorified on the ceiling. This is Renaissance optimism, or the Christian doctrine of the good creation, but it is not Ficino. But man, even with his splendid body, is still very much the sinner standing in need of grace.

There is, of course, another Renaissance convention about human nature alongside the optimistic one, as every reader of *Hamlet* knows. There is indeed "What a piece of work is man"—in part, this is the ceiling. There is also "this quintessence of dust." We do not have to wait for the Medici Chapel to look at Michelangelo's melancholy preoccupation with death. He was death-haunted for at least half of his nearly ninety years. The Dying Slave, from the time of the Sistine ceiling, is an example of this near-obsession. What are we to make of the strange abandon of this young man? Is this sexual exhaustion, and if so, is guilt or pleasure predominating? Is he waking from a troubled sleep, or falling asleep, or shaking off a terrible nightmare? Ths passive and powerful abandon of this beautiful young man is haunting and terrible. Michelangelo may even have briefly let us inside his own mind, something he very rarely does. Here, as with the Medici Chapel to come, is the darker undercurrent of the Renaissance. Here, with the Dying Slave, all is a dream. Sometime between 1510 and 1530, at the close of what we are calling the first stage, Michelangelo began to feel old before his time. Our second stage will be about death, but also about love and faith. We will meet the figures in that gloomy chapel in Florence, in the Last Judgment, and, in the real world, Tommaso de' Cavalieri and Vittoria Colonna.

When you have been working at the height of your powers, the consequent plunge into the depths can often be intense. Michelangelo expressed on that ceiling in Rome not the deification of a bodiless soul or even an ascent to God, but his own encounter with the biblical God. His reaction was one of awe and terror, and the brooding meditation on death, and death unsupported by either faith or hope, that is the Medici Chapel in Florence is the artist's theological response to the experience of the ceiling.

Leo X, preparing to bungle the negotiations with Luther, assigned Michelangelo to Florence to get him out of Rome and out of his hair. They were in fact good friends, but Michelangelo was hardly easy to get along with. He worked on the Medici statues throughout the 1520's. Thoughts of God turn into thoughts of death, and a new style seems to appear. Renaissance vigor seems spent, and in that chapel we can sense the subtle shift from High Renaissance to Mannerism. All is melancholy and suffering; resigned, dreamy reflection. Now, at forty-five, Michelangelo began to complain about being an old man, and he was but half through with his life.

Some have suggested that the reclining pairs on the two tombs are designed to split the sepulcher open so the immortal souls can pop up to heaven. But Michelangelo must have known that these minor Medicis were hardly worthy of eternal blessedness. The chapel does not need to be neo-platonized, any more than the Sistine ceiling does. This room is not about platonic immortality at all; it is about transcience and about Michelangelo's fears that nothing may lie beyond the death of the body. He himself observed that the statues of Night and Day stand for "time, which consumes all"—even the soul? Both the young dukes are dead, isolated, and blind: their eyes are carved without pupils. Night and Day speak to Guiliano, Michelangelo wrote: "With our speedy course, we have led Duke Guiliano to his death." The dukes are not only dead, they are worried. They stare across the chapel trying vainly to catch the Virgin's eye, while she blandly ignores them (Fig. 2). As with the Madonna of the Steps the mother offers no support to the child. Her right arm hangs inactive, while the infant vainly searches for the covered breast. Her legs are crossed; everything suggests rejection. Mary attends neither to the worried dukes across the room nor to her child.

But is it really a child? When we look carefully at the muscular back we see not so much an infant seeking milk but a lover seeking penetration. Is this not a Christ seeking to possess Mary, the veritable bride of Christ, to consummate the Holy Marriage? No wonder her legs are crossed. In a haunting 1544 madrigal, Michelangelo tells us something about his artistic anxieties and draws a stunning comparison between the hard, rejecting mother and the hard, rejecting stone he is trying to work.

> As, in hard stone, a man at times will make
> Everyone else's image his own likeness,
> I make it pale with weakness
> Frequently, just as I am made by her,
> And always seem to take
> Myself for model, planning to do her.
> The stone where I portray her
> Resembles her, I might
> Well say, because it is so hard and sharp;
> Destroyed and mocked by her,
> I'd know, at any rate,
> Nothing but my own burdened limbs to sculpt.
> And yet if art can keep
> Beauty through time only if she endure,
> It will delight me, so I'll make her fair.
> (Gilbert #240)

The four reclining figures on the Medici tombs determine the dark, almost despairing, religious atmosphere of the chapel. Night is asleep, perhaps trying not to wake, perhaps dreaming unhappily. Her well-used and beautiful body seems cramped and uncomfortable. Creatures from her nightmares afflict her: the owl, a satyr-mask with goat teeth (which is supposed to stand for sensuality). Sleep is death in this room; all the figures are defeated, powerless in the face of their mortality. When Night was opened to the public, a poet piously wrote:

> The Night thou seest here, posed gracefully
> In act of slumber, was by an angel wrought

Figure 2. Michelangelo, Madonna Medici Chapel, marble, Florence, San Lorenzo.

> Out of this stone; sleeping, with life she's fraught:
> Wake her, incredulous wight, she'll speak to thee.

Reading this journalistic gush, Michelangelo replied, in effect, "That is not it at all / That is not what I meant at all." And he wrote a counter-quatrain:

> Dear is my sleep, but better to be mere stone,
> So long as ruin and dishonor reign;
> To hear naught, to feel naught, is my great gain;
> Then wake me not; speak in an undertone.

Day is a powerful man in the prime of life. The face may be concealed and unfinished because Michelangelo wished to obscure the obvious fact that this is a self-portrait. The top figure in the Florence Pietà, designed for his own tomb and explicitly a self-portrait, looks just like Day. He is powerful, contorted, tense, glaring at us with an uncontrollable rage and contempt. He is afraid to die, to be dead; of judgment and of nothingness.

Dusk is another middle-aged man, but not at all angry. He seems almost comfortable on the uncomfortable tomb. He has given up the struggle and his hands are limp and passive as he seems to reflect back on a worthless life.

Dawn reminds us how wrong are those who tell us that Michelangelo was unable to portray the body of a woman with sensuous appeal.[13] He surely has done so with Dawn. She is awakening, and the bent left leg suggests that she is about to turn over or arise. She seems to dread the transition from sleep to waking. Hopelessness is written on both body and face, and some sort of cry emerges from her parted lips. The ribbon below her breasts binds her to the bed. What does she fear? The torments of a restless sleep? Life itself? The body?[14] Or is she afraid of waking from the sleep of death to discover on the other side that there is nothing—or worse? We will meet Michelangelo's fear of damnation again.

Throughout the 1520s, Michelangelo's inherited Christianity (beginning to split from the neo-platonism that had become

Figure 3. Michelangelo, The Temptation and Expulsion from Paradise (detail), Sistine Chapel ceiling, fresco, Vatican.

yoked to it in the Medici gardens) appears to give him little peace or joy. The somber mood of the Medici Chapel is, however, decisively broken when he meets in Rome, around 1531–1532, a young man who was to transform his life, and who drew from him the first real experience of human love he had ever known.

Tommaso de'Cavalieri was a twenty-three year old Roman aristocrat when Michelangelo, aged fifty-seven, met him. He was exceptionally handsome, intelligent, thoroughly heterosexual, and he continued to be a loyal friend throughout Michelangelo's long life. There is no doubt that Michelangelo "loved" Tommaso, and that this love became a central fact of his existence.

Florentine neo-platonism offers us a language and a culture through which we can understand such a love. (Even though I have attempted to mitigate the influence of neo-platonism on the Sistine ceiling and the Medici Chapel, I am not insensible to the fact that it was most important in Michelangelo's personal life.) But it is an ambiguous language: it is easy (neo-platonism itself) and impossible (the Christian part of the mixture) to ascend to God. The body and the senses are both good and dangerously imperfect and evil, needing to be transfigured into spirit. This ambiguity is surely inevitable when one tries to mix what cannot be mixed: Athens and Jerusalem. It is surprising to find that neo-platonism worked as well as it did for Michelangelo when we compare its optimism with those darker shadows of the Christian understanding of unworthiness and sin which were so characteristic of the artist.[15]

Yet for all its theological optimism, neo-platonism was an other-worldly, escapist creed that rejected the appetites as a madness plunging the human spirit into the imprisoning body. But Michelangelo never could despise the body; it was his primary subject. Even his melancholy demanded a plastic form. Those evil bodies on the Florentine sepulchers are quite beautiful. The physical must be transcended (the neo-platonists said so) and must be celebrated (Michelangelo's own presupposition). Why then was he so drawn to neo-platonism, and why did it take such a long time to lose its hold on him? Perhaps there is a way out. The body was, after all, the proper beginning on the journey to beauty and God, but it was only a beginning. Neo-platonism initiated Michelangelo into a life-long war between spirit and matter that required a material form. He had to find some way of both using and transcending the material world at the same time. His artistic torment was always a theological one as well. How strange it is that neither Savonarola (with his moralism), nor neo-platonism, nor Vittoria Colonna, could ever freely allow Michelangelo to be an artist. This must be why he so often had to unmake what he was making.

Now Michelangelo clearly loved Tommaso, but this is how the neo-platonic sublimation system worked. True love can be only initially, and not primarily, love for the beautiful form. It is only content when it becomes love for the divine idea of beauty that contemplation of the form leads to. From Tommaso to beauty to God, with no stops along the way. But, for Michelangelo as Christian (the part that did not mix with the neo-platonism), Tommaso could only seem an idol, a false god, a replacement of the true. That Christian God of the ceiling, shaking loose from neo-platonic entanglements, filled Michelangelo with terror, fear of death, and guilt over his homosexual impulses. But the real Tommaso gave him pleasure, and he delighted in what he called their "chaste love." He was an intensely emotional, highly sexed man who almost certainly died a virgin.[16] A passage in one of Giannotti's *Dialogues* may be a trustworthy fragment of self-description on Michelangelo's part. He had been spending the day with friends, and was asked if he would go on with them to dinner. No, he said, I cannot; the emotional exhaustion would be too great.

> I am a man more inclined than anyone who ever lived to care for people. Whenever I see anyone possessed of some gift which shows him to be more apt in the performance or expression of anything than others, I become, perforce, enamored of him, and am constrained to abandon myself to him in such a way that I am no longer my own, but wholly his.

Emotional, deeply drawn to Tommaso; neo-platonism partly worked and partly did not work as a system of sublimation.

Christianity was there as a donor of guilt. All this must be kept in mind as we look at the poetry addressed to Tommaso.

There is an interesting early love poem (before Tommaso) where Michelangelo expresses his fears over the woman's capacity to "kill," that is, to send him to hell for enjoying her favors.

> So eager is this my lady, and so swift,
> That she, at the same time that she would kill,
> Promises me with her eyes all joy, and still
> Can keep inside the wound the cruel knife.
> Thus both my death and life,
> Opposed, I feel within my soul concurrent
> During one little moment.
> But still the fatal torment
> Mercy can threaten, lengthening the pains,
> For evil harms much more than joy sustains.
> 									(Gilbert #122)

A striking brief study of repression, joy, and forgiveness. As Freud has reminded our century, civilization needs all the strategies of repression it can get. In the 1530s, this is what neo-platonism did for Michelangelo. It shaped, guided, controlled his sensual, sexual, spiritual, and unconsummated love for Tommaso.[17]

In the first sonnet directed to Tommaso, the artist rejects any homosexual interpretation of their love, whatever the homosexual crowd may say,

> If the immortal wish, the lift and goad
> Of others' thoughts, let mine show openly,
> It could perhaps even now induce to pity
> The house of love's inexorable lord.
>
> But since the soul, by the decree of God,
> Has long life, while the body dies so quickly,
> Its value and its praise our sense can barely
> Describe, being things that it can barely read.
>
> Therefore, alas, how will the chaste wish
> That burns my inward heart ever be heard
> By those who always see themselves in others?

> For me the precious passing day is crushed
> With my lord, who gives heed to such a falsehood:
> In fact, the unbelievers are the liars.
>
> (Gilbert #56)

In what is perhaps the most intense of the love poems, the love is still chaste, but it is further described as a flame that both consumes the self and stops time.[18] "Dear Lord" and "sweet Lord" hint at a deeper dimension to his love: Tommaso is both friend and Lord. Note the contrast between the insistence on the "chaste fire" and the "unworthy ready arms" in the last line.

> Since through the eyes the heart's seen in the face,
> I have no other way so evident
> To show my flame; let this then be sufficient,
> O my dear Lord, to ask you now for grace.
>
> Perhaps your spirit, gazing at this chaste
> Fire that consumes me, will, more than I credit,
> Have trust, and be with me speedy and lenient,
> As grace abounds for him who well entreats.
>
> O happy that day, if this is true!
> Then at one instant in their ancient road
> The hours will be stopped, time, sun, the days,
>
> That I may have, though it is not my due,
> My so much desired, my so sweet lord,
> In my unworthy ready arms for always.
>
> (Gilbert #70)

The poet underlines the non-physical nature of his chaste love by defining the union of lover and beloved in terms of soul, not body.

> If a chaste love, if an excelling kindness,
> If sharing by two lovers of one fortune,
> Hard lot for one the other one's concern,
> Two hearts led by one spirit and one wish,
>
> And if two bodies have one soul, grown deathless,
> That, with like wings, lifts both of them to Heaven,
> If love's one stroke and golden dart can burn
> And separate the vitals of two breasts,

> Neither loving himself, but each one each,
> With one delight and taste, such sympathy
> That both would wish to have single end,
>
> If thousand thousands would not be one inch
> To love so knotted, such fidelity—
> And mere affront can shatter and unbind?
>
> (Gilbert #57)

Michelangelo can mix neo-platonic and Christian analysis in a profoundly subtle way in this sonnet on his love for and union with Tommaso. Tommaso, at the end, becomes like the God of the Old Testament whom one cannot see and live. The poet seems to be saying that if he treats Tommaso the way neo-platonism advises, he turns him into an idolatrous god-substitute, prohibited by Christianity. His great love is already, in this first year of their relationship, the source of subtle and agonizing conflicts.

> You know that I know, my Lord, you know
> I have come to enjoy you closer by;
> You know I know you know that it is I,
> So why put off our greetings longer now?
>
> If the hope you have given me is true,
> And true the good desire that's granted me,
> Let the wall set between us fall away,
> For there is double power in secret woe.
>
> If I in you love only, dear my Lord,
> What you love most in you, do not be angry;
> The one's enamored of the other spirit.
>
> What in your beautiful face I have wished and learned
> Human intelligence can grasp but badly,
> He is required to die who wants to see it.
>
> (Gilbert #58)

But the neo-platonic language is still serviceable for defining the love as chaste, spiritual, beyond the comprehension of the vulgar crowd.

> I see within your beautiful face, my Lord
> What in this life we hardly can attest;

> Your soul already, still clothed in its flesh,
> Repeatedly has risen with it to God.
>
> The evil, foolish and invidious mob
> May point, and charge to others its own taste,
> And yet no less my faith, my honest wish,
> My love and my keen longing leave me glad.
>
> All beauty that we see here must be likened
> To the merciful Fountain whence we all derive,
> More than anything else, by men with insight.
>
> We have no other fruit, no other token
> Of Heaven on earth; one true to you in love
> May rise above to God, and make death sweet.
> (Gilbert #81)

In the final two stanzas, particularly in the phrase "merciful Fountain," Michelangelo appears to be trying to transform the passive neo-platonic idea of divine beauty into the active God of Christianity. (Neo-platonizing Christianity always has trouble with grace; Augustine had to turn off his neo-platonic batteries when he took on the Pelagians.) But the transformation fails and God ends up utterly passive, waiting for the ascending soul to arrive to have its immortality assured.

To me the most moving of the love poems to Tommaso is Gilbert #258. It is a candid defense of man's love for man as superior to any other form, and it is also a splendid and valiant attempt to hold neo-platonism and Christianity together. In the first stanza, neo-platonic love, described as "violent passion," is defended as—of all things—preparation for prevenient grace, that "holy dart."

> Violent passion for tremendous beauty
> Is not perforce a bitter mortal error,
> If it can leave the heart melted thereafter,
> So that a holy dart can pierce it quickly.

The ascent of the soul from the evil ("too scanty") world is the subject of the second stanza.

> Not hindering high flight to such vain fury,
> Love wakens, rouses, puts the wings in feather,

> As a first step, so that the soul will soar
> And rise to its maker, finding this too scanty.

In the final two stanzas, the poet compares two kinds of love.

> The love for what I speak of reaches higher;
> Woman's too much unlike, no heart by rights
> Ought to grow hot for her, if wise and male.
>
> One draws to Heaven and to earth the other,
> One in the soul, one living in the sense
> Drawing its bow on what is base and vile.

Man's love for man permits one to ascend to God, while man's love for woman can only descend to earth. Heterosexual love is a love that demands a physical expression; homosexual love can have no physical expression. It is all soul, all spirit. A perfect defense of homosexual love as best and as chaste. Yet notice how Michelangelo can dare to express this "chaste love" in very physical terms in Gilbert #87. The intensity and beauty of his love for Tommaso is perhaps best expressed in this sonnet, which has been called one of the finest lyric poems of the sixteenth century.

> I with your beautiful eyes see gentle light,
> While mine are so blind I never can;
> With your feet, on my back can bear a burden,
> While mine are crippled, and have no such habit;
>
> Having no feathers, on your wings my flight,
> By your keen wits forever drawn toward Heaven,
> As you decide it I am flushed and wan,
> Cold in the sun, at the cold solstice hot.
>
> My wishes are within your will alone,
> Within your heart are my ideas shaped,
> When you have taken breath, then I can speak.
>
> It seems that I am like the lonely moon,
> Which our eyes fail to see in Heaven, except
> The fraction of it that the sun may strike.

In the early 1530's, at the time when Michelangelo met Tommaso, he was fifty-seven years old. His father and favorite brother had both recently died; republican Florence was destroyed, and he was exiled from his beloved home town. The superb poetry for Tommaso wrestles with this decisive point in his spiritual and physical life, as the poet tries to define this new love: for himself, for Tommaso, and for the observing and vulgar world. Both the neo-platonic and the Christian systems are brought to the task of definition.

The solution appears from a most unexpected source—from a woman. In 1536, when he was sixty-one and she forty-six, Michelangelo met the one significant woman in his life, Victoria Colonna, the Marchesa di Pescara. The ten years between their meeting and her death were the most decisive years for Michelangelo's final relation to the Christian faith. By the early 1530's, the Papacy's attempt to form a secular state in Italy had failed, the Reformation was distressing the Roman hierarchy, and Rome was cruelly sacked by troops that included violent Lutheran mercenaries. The serene social underpinnings of the High Renaissance were wiped away, and Italy experienced a sense of deep uncertainty and foreboding. So did Michelangelo. He'd become dissatisfied with any homosexual solution to the frustrations of his existence. Neo-platonism was failing; and guilt, both from his Christian faith and from his own character and integrity, came to oppress him. During the time of Vittoria's guidance and friendship, neo-platonism recedes, as growing older does naturally for his powerful sexual impulses what neo-platonism had been doing imperfectly. Vittoria became his guide in his cultural distress and guilt-laden Christian–pagan synthesis to a unique, purer Christocentric Christianity, neither Protestant nor Tridentine Catholic. Condivi spoke movingly of his love for Vittoria.

> He loved the Marchesa of Pescara deeply and was inspired by her divine spirit. She returned his love. He has in his possession many letters from her, full of the purest, most virtuous love such as could only spring from a pure and noble heart. He on his side then began to address numerous sonnets to her, full of *esprit* and sweet desire. Many were the times she would leave Viterbo, or some other place to which she had gone to relax or to pass the summer, just in order to see him in Rome. So deeply in

love was he with her that I recall his saying that nothing caused him greater anguish than that, when he visited her as she lay dying, he had not kissed her forehead or her cheek as he had kissed her hand. Her death left him benumbed and drove him at times to distraction.

Vittoria Colonna's contribution to Michelangelo's theological search was to provide a connection to the religious movement known as "Italian Reform" or the "Spirituali." After Savonarola's death, some of his followers continued to struggle for the reform of the Catholic Church. This group eventually gathered around the young Spaniard Juan Valdes (1509–1541), who left Spain for Rome in 1531 and who lived the rest of his short life after 1534 in Naples.

Valdes fled Spain as the Inquisition began, labelled a Lutheran heretic, which he was not. The Swiss Reformers initially called Valdes an "Anabaptist", trusting too much in Spirit, not enough in Word. But Valdes turned out some elegant commentaries on the Pauline letters, and Calvin and Beza were later to praise him for his contribution to what was to become the Reformation in Italy. Valdes was a mystic, and something of a humanist–rationalist in the Erasmian tradition, with a powerful sense of the war between flesh and spirit, which would be a delight both to the pious (and apparently unattractive) widow and to her beloved disciple. For all this, Valdes had a deep and abiding belief in the radical grace of God, without human cooperation or the need for good works. It appears that the significant influence on Valdes came from Pedro Alcaraz and the movement (1511–1524) known as the "Alumbrados," or enlightened ones. This was a popular lay movement, Catholic but critical of the Church, that was crushed by the Inquisition. Hence Valdes' flight to Italy in 1531.

The "Spirituali" group was influenced by the Northern Reformation, but in its inception it was loyal to the Church. Its central tenet was a belief in justification by faith alone without the need for good works as a condition of salvation. It further emphasized the completeness and adequacy of Christ's sacrificial death as meriting that free forgiveness of sinners. It should be noted that "justification by faith"—a phrase today virtually impossible to bring to life—did not mean, in the sixteenth century or in any century, that man is justified or forgiven if he only has faith, whether you define faith as belief or as trust. This would make forgiveness conditional upon some sort of belief or attitude, while the justification that the Lutherans, the Calvinists, the Anabaptists, and the "Spirituali" proclaimed was utterly without condition. You cannot *do* anything to make forgiveness happen. Not even repentance will guarantee it. Justification by faith is a picture of a forgiving God descending the ladder between God and man to the bitter depths where man is found unable to perform a single act of virtue or belief. The whole system of relics, of indulgences, of penance is quietly ignored by the idea of justification that Vittoria and her friends shared with the Protestants. If the Catholic tradition has always perceived grace primarily as power, and the Protestant tradition has always preferred grace as pardon, the "Spirituali" were probably on the Protestant side of the fence. But they believed the Church could be changed. Their ideas were circulated in a small book called *Del beneficio di Gesu Cristo crocifisso verso i Cristiani*, written by one Fra Benedetto da Mantova. Here is the passage on justification:

> The justice of Christ is sufficient to make us the children of grace, without any good works on our part; these cannot be good unless we previously make ourselves good and just by faith before executing them, as St. Augustine maintains.

(Incidentally, this particular passage would upset Luther, and probably even the late, anti-Pelagian Augustine, neither of whom would care much for the rather sloppy formulation of Fra Benedetto: "make ourselves good and just by faith." Too much here of what we can do unaided, and a very weak sense in the whole passage of the prevenient and continuing grace of God.)

This circle provided Michelangelo with a liberal, humanistic, educated Catholicism which never left him, but which, with the beginning of the Counter-Reformation in 1542, the Church repudiated. In the face of the Church's conservative turn, the Spirituali collapsed. Some members, like Cardinal Pole, joined the Protestants. Michelangelo stayed with the tradition, even after the movement vanished, and his reputation guaranteed him immunity from the Counter-Reformation death squads. Some of Vittoria's circle were put to death as heretics. She herself, ever sensitive to where the power lay, went along with the Counter-Reformation and the Inquisition. She repudiated her friends who turned Protestant, and even managed to hand over to the Holy Office some incriminating letters from a former colleague on trial for heresy. "Saints do not intercede," she is reported to have said, managing bad theology and moral cowardice in four words (three, to be exact).

The poetry addressed to, and therefore influenced by, Vittoria Colonna almost invariably casts the poet as suppliant, begging for understanding, love, even forgiveness. An almost Protestant sense of sin suffuses one sonnet; no one can possibly deserve grace, and grace comes, not from God, but from Vittoria!

> So that I might at least be less unworthy,
> Lady, of your huge high beneficence,
> To balance it, my poor wits at first
> Took to plying my own wholeheartedly.
>
> But then, seeing in me no potency
> To clear the way to grasp that goal exists,
> My evil fault for its forgiveness asks,
> And the sin makes me wiser constantly.
>
> And well I see how anyone would stray
> Who thought my flimsy, transient work could equal
> The grace pouring from you, which is divine.
>
> For wit and art and memory give way;
> In a thousand attempts none who is mortal
> Can pay for Heaven's gift out of his own.
>
> (Gilbert #157)

In a madrigal for Vittoria, the opening lines show us Michelangelo, the neo-platonist, tired of his body, with the soul longing for release. The poet even confesses his envy of the dead, presumably because they have no physical bodies. He is deeply distressed, but at the end the neo-platonic climate abruptly changes, and we enter the Christian world. He longs for the "pitying arms" of Christ to reach out and remake him. Are we to infer a connection, in this song for Vittoria, between her arms and Christ's?

> What kind of biting file
> Makes your tired carcass shrivel and decrease,
> Sick soul, forever? When will time release
> You from it, back to where you were in Heaven,
> Earlier bright and joyful,
> Your dangerous and mortal veil thrown down?
> Although I change my skin
> For short years toward the end,
> I cannot change old ways to which I'm used,
> That with more age push and compel me more.
> To you, Love, I must own
> My envy of the dead.
> I am frightened and confused,
> Such, for myself, my soul's convulsive fear.
> Lord, in the final hour,
> Stretch out thy pitying arms to me, take me
> Out of me, make me one that pleases Thee.
> (Gilbert #159)

Sometimes, it is true, she is merely the teacher, source of theological counsel.

> My short time left; let me not live so blindly.
> Tell me, high sacred Lady,
> Whether in Heaven less honor is bestowed
> On humble sin than on the sovereign good.
> (Gilbert #160)

This is a question about justification, and the correct answer, for the Spirituali circle, is "no." But Vittoria and God are sometimes conflated.

> In your face I aspire
> To what I am pledged from Heaven,
> And in your beautiful eyes, full of all safety.
> (Gilbert #161)

Or, more candidly (and notice the confusion about Vittoria's gender):

> A man, a god rather, inside a woman,
> Through here mouth has his speech
> And this has made me such
> I'll never again be mine after I listen.
> (Gilbert #233)

She can be both the judgment and mercy of God.

> ... to be reborn from you,
> High worthy Lady, a thing high and perfect;
> If you in mercy trim my surplus down
> And build my little, what is my fierce fire due
> As penance, when you punish and correct?
> (Gilbert #234)

Here is perhaps the most important of all the religious poems. It is the poet's summary of the influence of Vittoria, written seven years after her death.

> My course of life already has attained,
> Through stormy seas, and in a flimsy vessel,
> The common port, at which we land to tell
> All conduct's cause and warrant, good or bad,
>
> So that the passionate fantasy, which made
> Of art a monarch for me and an idol,
> Was laden down with sin, now I know well,
> Like what all men against their will desired.
>
> What will become, now, of my amorous thoughts,
> Once gay and vain, as toward two deaths I move,
> One known for sure, the other ominous?
>
> There's no painting or sculpture now that quiets
> The soul that's pointed toward that holy Love
> That on the cross opened Its arms to take us.
> (Gilbert #285)

He speaks of moving toward two deaths. The first death, the "one known for sure," is the death of Christ. Vittoria mediated this death to him. The second death, the ominous one, may be in part the poet's own death. But it is more likely to refer to the death of art as capable of bearing salvation. It was Vittoria, in her evangelical fervor, who mediated this second death to her friend. She wrote: "Most honoured Master Michelangelo, your art has brought you such fame that you would perhaps never have believed that this fame could fade with time or through any other cause. But the heavenly light has shone into your heart and shown you that, however long earthly glory may last, it is doomed to suffer a second death."

Since fame and art were incapable of meeting his deepest needs, she seems to argue, he is advised to return to the first death, the death of Christ, whose arms reach out to him, just as Vittoria's had.

In the two drawings that we know Michelangelo presented to Vittoria, the association of her theological influence with the death of Christ is established beyond doubt. The first drawing is a 1539 *Crucifix*, done just as he was completing the Last Judgment. Christ is alive, his body twisted by suffering, eyes open, seeming to challenge God himself: "My God, my God, why hast thou forsaken me?" The torments experienced by those about to be judged in the final judgment are here experienced by Christ himself. The belief of the Spirituali in the centrality and adequacy of the atoning death is simply set forth.

The other drawing presented to Vittoria is a Pietà, but a strange one. The dead Jesus awkwardly slumps back between his mother's legs, as angels try to keep the body from sliding to the ground. The cross is inscribed with a haunting line from Dante, as if spoken by Mary: "they do not think there (on earth) how much blood it costs." Whose blood? Jesus', of course; he is dead. But also Mary's. Her spread thighs remind us that she is not only weeping and praying, she is giving birth. The early fathers loved (rather too intensely?) to dwell on the parallels between those two open enclosures of the divine: the inviolate womb of Mary which knew no male organ, but only a male child; and the tomb of Joseph of Arimathea which knew Jesus briefly, and then was empty. Mary here is giving birth, and giving up her son to death and to resurrection. She is also praying. Her hands are letting go of the body of her son and moving together for prayer. Dante's words, inscribed on the cross, are spoken by

Beatrice (*Paradiso*, XXIX.91) and they refer to the false interpretations of the Bible by those who have forgotten what it costs the church (in blood) to achieve true interpretation. Mary is, finally, the church. No wonder de Tolnay could call this drawing a "diagram of a doctrine."

In the pictures and poems to Vittoria, Michelangelo surrenders himself to the crucified Jesus rather than to the love of a living man. This surrender Vittoria achieved for him. Perhaps only a woman, and an asexual and maternal one at that, could have effectively turned Michelangelo's inner life from sexual passion for Tommaso, repressed by neo-platonism, to the cross of Christ. The rejecting mother theme and the search for a post-platonic theology come together in the Colonna Pietà. The son meets the mother who no longer rejects him. But he is dead. In this drawing, as in the final sculptured Pietàs, Vittoria as Mary as the non-repudiating mother finally brings the son, the artist, to the foot of the cross. In the first Pietà, the Roman one, Mary lives in her own world, looking only at the son, and we are kept outside. In the Colonna Pietà, the viewer is almost abruptly addressed and invited to meditate on the saving death.

When Michelangelo began to work on the Sistine wall in 1536, just before he met Vittoria, it was a time of turbulence for both the artist and the Church. Paul III established the Jesuit order in 1540. The Council of Trent began its deliberations in 1545, and its final report would contain some grumbling about the nudity in these very frescoes. Indeed, with Trent, the Church was demolishing the theological and spiritual platform on which Michelangelo, with Vittoria's help, was learning to stand. To look at the Last Judgment on the Sistine altar wall is to see an artist afraid of his unworthiness, afraid and angry in the presence of a Christ whose nature he cannot understand.

There is a great contrast between the ceiling and the wall. The bodies on the wall have none of the physical beauty of those on the ceiling. They are more abstract, less sensuous, "heavy and lumpish, with thick limbs, lacking in grace."[19] The world of this Last Judgment has no sense of real space, no perspective, and the effect of this is to upset us, to throw us off balance. We can begin to understand the influence of Vittoria's idea of the second death, the death of art, the loss of interest in beauty as a way to the divine.

> The work expresses a bitter effort on the part of Michelangelo to renounce the culture in which he lived. His discontent was not simply a criticism of the prevailing artistic climate, the sorry state of Christendom, or the new tyrannical rule of the Medici in Florence. That is, it was not merely a judgment or the external world. It also represented a bitterness of a more inner-directed nature—perhaps over the failure of his platonic homosexual adaptation, which had focused on Tommaso, to achieve the magical goal of suspending time, with its unrelenting process of aging.[20]

And, of course, this fresco is about Michelangelo's fear of damnation. The scene is from Matthew 24:30–31: the coming of the Son of Man at the end of time. The judgment itself has not yet begun. There are no blessed, no damned; only anticipations, including the artist's own.

No one has read the theological nuances of the Last Judgment with more care and perception than Professor Leo Steinberg.[21] His reading is in fact a set of disturbing, perhaps unanswerable, questions. Here (Fig. 4) we find a beardless athlete, not the traditional west wall judge at all. Mary huddles close to her son, and whatever she is doing there, she is not interceding for anyone. Some of the holy virgins are nude (or were, until Tridentine moralism covered them up), some are overweight. Angels are shockingly wingless, and the presence of the mythical Charon on the boat and the mythical Minos in the right-hand corner (being sodomized by the snake in the original, apparently) suggests that perhaps more than just this corner is myth rather than history.

Everything depends, Steinberg argues, on what you believe Christ to be doing. This can hardly be determined with certainty. What is his position: standing, sitting, rising, striding? What is his intention? The face is not angry at all, it is impassive, imperturbable, blank. What do the gestures of the arms say? Are they working together, or at cross purposes? Is one arm judgment, the other mercy, or both, or neither? Could mercy be

Figure 4. Michelangelo, Last Judgment (detail), Sistine Chapel, fresco, Vatican.

being offered to all, so that Mary's intercession is superfluous? Michelangelo's sorry and terrified face on St. Bartholomew's skin places the artist and his anxiety about salvation at the very center of the fresco. Am I damned? Is there damnation for anyone?

One of Steinberg's most striking and convincing suggestions comes at this point. Purgatory has no place in this painting, and even hell is hard to find. There is that hole in the center at the bottom of the picture, but it is either empty or severely underpopulated. Could it be that Michelangelo has decided to solve the problem of his own anxiety about eternal damnation by proposing that no one is to be eternally damned? We do not have universalism here, the salvation of all. But this picture can be read as suggesting what is technically called "conditional immortality." God's will is the salvation of some, and the non-saved or rejected pass out of existence. This comes from Matthew 10:28b: "rather fear him who can destroy both soul and body in hell." We know that the leader of the Spirituali group, Juan Valdes, rejected the idea of eternal punishment, and such rejections were in the air of sixteenth-century Italy. One Petrus Pomponatius merely suggested that the immortality of the soul was not demonstrable (a shocking indifference to Plato for the Italian Renaissance!), and he got himself condemned by the Fifth Lateran Council of 1512–1517 and by a 1513 bull from the hand of Leo X.

Steinberg loves to draw straight lines through the fresco and to argue from them. One of his magic diagonals begins with the self-portrait on the skin, rising northwest through the wound on Christ's side, to the point on the cross where the head rested, to the vault of heaven, and thus to salvation. But the same line extended southeast down from the face on Bartholomew's skin takes us to the famous young man fearing the worst right down to the groin of Minos, henchman of Satan, clearly enjoying his unusual sexual adventure.

What is it that we see in the fresco's central drama: the skin, the saint, the mother, and the Son of Man? Is Christ looking at the Michelangelo face, and if so, is it a look of blessing? It is hard to define the direction of the gaze, but it seems clear that that howling face is not experiencing blessedness or forgiveness. What should we make of Bartholomew's hostile gesture? Is he pointing the knife at Christ, as if to say, "Why are you sending me to hell, after martyrdom and all I've done for you." Or is the knife directed to Mary? If so, this suggests that Bartholomew is not only carrying Michelangelo's skin, but he *is* Michelangelo, enraged against the judging Christ and Christianity, or against Mary, his abandoning mother, or both.

The Last Judgment is Michelangelo's cry: "What shall I do to be saved?" No restful assurance is given:

> The artist's presence at the focal point of the action usurps Christ's immediate attention. Christ's glance and suspended gesture, whether to damn or save, direct themselves pointblank at the rag stamped with Michelangelo's features. And the line that descends from the Judge through the martyred Apostle to the artist's distorted face becomes the main artery of the design. A verdict is about to be handed down, and the first arraigned is the wretched likeness of Michelangelo's self. The whole cosmic drama collapses upon his destiny. Not because the artist thinks himself foremost amongst mankind, but because the Last Judgment conceived as more than a fable, and more than a warning to others, is real and serious only to the extent that the man who tells of it knows himself to be the first on trial.[22]

The painting of the Last Judgment found Michelangelo at the most tormented period of his life. Tommaso and Vittoria are decisive influences. Neo-platonism and homosexual desires are waning, and Christianity brings both guilt and anxiety as his hopes for a reformed Catholic Church collapse. In the 1540's the problem and the solution are both present in Michelangelo's art and life. The massive Last Judgment is almost totally problem. That is perhaps why it moves us so, we who are so wary of "solutions." The solution for Michelangelo will lie in the development of some of the themes in the presentation drawings to Vittoria Colonna. Our study of the third stage will be a study of the expansion of these themes, as we observe Michelangelo's final return to Christ—but to the crucified, not the formidable

The Conversions of Michelangelo

judge, and to the mother of the crucified as the final non-rejecting mother.

> After so long and intense an involvement with the material substance as well as the idea of a statue, to bring this active relationship to an end held the prospect of evoking echoes of his early, profound separation anxieties. Moreover, the figure that emerged from the husk of marble could never really be the object of his unconscious search. It was simply what it was—lifeless and unresponsive to him. Therefore, more often than not, Michelangelo avoided the pain associated with that stark end. He turned instead to the next project, and the next, and finally, in the last fifteen years of his life, to one theme, the union of Son and Mother in the Pietàs.[23]

We have already looked at the 1554 sonnet in which Michelangelo rejected art as salvation (the second death) and turned—recalling the abiding influence of Vittoria—to the first death, the cross. The early Medici garden mix of Christianity and neoplatonism continued to lose its hold, complaints about illness and aging become more and more frequent in the letters, and fear of both death and damnation come to dominate the last two decades of Michelangelo's life. Anxiety about salvation is anxiety about the character of Christ: is he the powerful and ambiguous athlete of the Sistine wall, or is he the open-eyed, crucified savior of the Colonna drawing, crying out against God? The final years of the artist's life work these questions out, particularly in the final two Pietàs and the last drawings.

The Florence Pietà or Deposition (1547–1555) was originally designed by Michelangelo for his own tomb. Christ's body slumps heavily toward the ground, supported by Mary and a hooded grieving figure, either Nicodemus or Joseph of Arimathea, who looks just like Michelangelo. It is this upper figure, the sculptor himself, who gently brings the son and mother together. She no longer rejects, no longer refuses to touch. Finally she is able to hold him, her eyes closed in rapture and sorrow. Mary Magdalene, on our left, looks aside, as if blinded by the ecstatic three-fold union. Michelangelo, mother, the dead Christ, together at the end. Resignation and peace. No more proud anger, as with the David; no weariness as with the Dusk; or self-pity and fear on Bartholomew's skin and on Peter's face in the Pauline chapel. All these are self-portraits. Here, in the Deposition, Christ is no longer the enemy and the mother no longer rejects.

Many of the late drawings continue this theme of son, mother, Son. In a drawing in the Louvre (1550–1555), Jesus has just died. Mary on the left and John on the right accept with gestures of deep grief. In a pencil drawing at Windsor, Mary and John stand trembling, as John raises his hands in terror or surrender. Perhaps one of the seven last words is being suggested: "Behold your mother" (John 19:27). Whose mother?

In a chalk sketch from the British Museum, Christ's head is bowed as Mary and John draw close to the cross in union with their Lord. John embraces the cross with his right arm, and Mary seems to shudder, in a kind of ecstasy, as she presses her cheek to her dead son's thigh. All are bound together by the grace offered by the outstretched arms.

Of a London drawing dating from around 1560, Frederick Hartt has written:

> The Figure hangs in utter loneliness. . . . The aged hand shakes, the contours shift and change, form and atmosphere can scarcely be distinguished from one another, substance is shadowy and melts, yet in these broken chords the ultimate shape and the ultimate meaning come through with overpowering clarity. Never in Christian art has Christ's sacrifice received a more exalted expression.[24]

This drawing is the climax, the perfection of the crucifixion series.

But the series, and particularly this London drawing, must be set alongside another mystical and mysterious drawing, a mother and child, from the British Museum. Is this Mary and her child, or just any mother and child, or all? Is she nude? At last, she is enclosing the child with a full embrace. Michelangelo seems now to be at peace, and he makes us so.

Michelangelo may have started on his last sculpture as early as 1555, but we know he was still working on it six days before his death (Fig. 5). It went through many revisions over the ten year period, but those details need not concern us here. What is before us in the Rondanini Pietà is a simple, inevitable, necessary extension of the works just preceding it. A slender, unfinished Christ is fully merged with an unfinished Mary. She seems to bend over him, not so much supporting him or keeping him from sliding down, as simply embracing him in a gesture of ecstatic love. She rests on him, while he seeks support from her with his arms. De Tolnay's words on this final Pietà are unforgettable.

> In this work the master superseded at last the Renaissance principles of causality and the representation of the rationally possible. What he achieved is an image contradicting the law of gravity and yet speaking with utmost immediacy to the heart of the beholder. The result surpasses the earlier art of Michelangelo; even the Florentine Pietà remained within the Renaissance rationalistic conception. It can be compared rather with a few late works of Rembrandt (like the Prodigal Son in Leningrad, Hermitage) where the renunciation of ideal realism and rationalism also leads, not to abstraction (Mannerism), but to a more profound and more concrete language of the spirit. A fully articulated body would here only detract from the essential: the inner gesture. The soul speaks more directly through the rough-hewn marble where the forms are merely suggested. As in the Florentine Pietà the roughness of the surfaces of the marble block softens the contrast of light and shade and helps to diffuse the light so that the group seems to glow from within.
> This final message of Michelangelo conveys a glimpse of an ultimate peace after the life-struggle.
> Although surprisingly different from any earlier work of Michelangelo, this Pietà should not be interpreted as a complete deviation from the master's lifelong aims. It is true that instead of the heroic struggle of fully developed perfect bodies, here we have broken powerless beings existing only by divine mercy-and mirroring Michelangelo's own physical and spiritual state. Nevertheless it can be considered from a certain point of view the culmination of his art: always his work had transcended the pure formal harmony of the High Renaissance and instead had conveyed an existential message of the spirit. But until now he tried to reconcile his spiritual striving with the normative forms, the rational structure of the High Renaissance conception. Only in the Pietà Rondanini did he definitely sacrifice the Renaissance conception art, to be truer to himself and to express the inner gesture of the soul alone.[25]

124　　*The Conversions of Michelangelo*

Figure 5. Michelangelo, Rondanini Pietà, marble, Castello Sforzesco, Milan

One feels, before this last shattered fragment, now in the Sforza Castle in Milan, that Michelangelo finally succeeded in liberating himself from Florentine neo-platonism, as important as that had been to him. His journey ends with the skeletal remains of the two things he most longed for, mother and Christ.

He died in Rome on February 18, 1564 (five weeks before Shakespeare's birth), almost ninety. Tommaso was at his bedside. He made a death-bed will: soul to God, body to earth, possessions to relatives. Then, Vasari notes, "he told his friends that, as he died, they should recall to him the sufferings of Jesus Christ." His tomb, devoid of any artistic distinction, is in the Santa Croce church in Florence.

III

Shakespearean Death

> When Shakespeare's King Richard invites his faithful remnant to sit upon the ground and "tell sad stories of the death of kings," he is invoking the concept of tragedy inherited by the Renaissance from the Middle Ages. A tragedy was the sad story of the death of a king or someone comparably eminent. Death was the nexus—as it was not in Greek tragedy. The first adjustment the modern reader must make in achieving rapport with our older literature is to accept death as a fitting subject for contemplation. We tend to think of death as something in rather poor taste, its traces to be genteelly disguised and its inevitability to be put out of the mind.
>
> <div align="right">Alfred Harbage, <i>William Shakespeare, A Reader's Guide</i>, The Noonday Press, New York, 1963, p. 299.</div>

Concerning death and mortality, Shakespeare stood at the crossroads of a collapsing religious consensus, a new worldliness, and a new uncertainty. Up to the end of the twelfth century, north-European man neither glorifies nor fears death. He is somber and realistic before his end; he makes ready, believing that after death there is rest until judgment. Sometime in the fourteenth century this atmosphere changes. We do not know exactly why. It may have been the mendicant preachers or the even more vivid lessons of the plague. (Between 1347 and 1350, twenty-five million die of the plague—one-third of Europe's population.) In any case, we can watch the old serenity fade away. In its place comes a new despising of this life and a concentration on death as something to be feared. A more complicated eschatology now stresses the moment of death and the soul's subsequent adventures. (Purgatory is not officially affirmed until 1278). The last judgment becomes an afterthought. Blessed souls not requiring Purgatory rest in what came to be called Abraham's bosom; they wake at the last day, take on their new bodies, and continue in blessedness.

With Purgatory and this new eschatological geography, the to-be-damned soul goes at once to the fires of hell, starts on the eternal torment, and all the final judgment adds is a body and a resultant increase in discomfort. Neither for the blessed nor for the damned does the final judgment seem to make much difference after the fourteenth century. (Recall the curious absence of Purgatory and apparent emptiness of hell in Michelangelo's Sistine Last Judgment.) This shift from the last day to the last days directs an intense spotlight on the death-bed and the precise moment of death. This is something new in medieval death. How we die becomes even more important than how we have lived; dying well is virtually blessedness itself. Redemption and eschatology merge, and both get completed on the death-bed. Otherworldliness takes command; we now find discourses on the torments of the damned, on the decomposition of the corpse, on the vanity of life. Huizinga called this new death consciousness mere aristocratic ennui without religious significance, while Ariès wisely discerned behind the other-worldly morbidity a deep love of life and an affection for people and things.[1]

From the fourteenth century to Shakespeare's day this mixture persists. John Calvin can despise this world as passionately as a Bernard or an Augustine. What the sixteenth-century intellectual revolutions add is not only a bit more worldliness but a substantial eschatological uncertainty. The Protestants were obliged to abolish Purgatory, that geographical linch-pin of the dying penitential system, but they lost a shrewd religious compromise that offered real assurance to those too honest to believe themselves ready for immediate heaven and too decent for eternal flames. The eschatology of Luther—always the archaist—goes back to the pre-Purgatorial twelfth century: at death, soul and body both sleep until the last days. For Calvin, the body rests after death, but the soul proceeds at once to eternal damnation (remember all those Puritan sermons?) or to imperfect, because bodiless, blessedness, to await, in both cases, the new bodies of the last day. The world into which Shakespeare was born knew this late-medieval death anxiety, along with the new Renaissance worldliness and the new Protestant uncertainty.

Shakespeare himself makes use of many traditional medieval conventions concerning death. The Dance of Death, probably two hundred years old by Shakespeare's time, is the most dominant: death as skeleton or jester; ugly, rotten, equipped with scythe, grim in his arrest, carrying off rich and poor alike. Shakespeare expands this convention when he portrays death as sexual aggressor, overpowering the dying. Both Antony and Lear declare that they will die like bridegrooms, while Claudio—before his anxiety-attack—boasts that he will hug death as a bride. Death deflowers Juliet, her father declares, while Arthur's mother in *King John* comes to something like orgasm as she anticipates death's embrace.

> Death, death; O, amiable, lively death!
> Thou odoriferous stench! Sound rottenness!
> Arise forth from the couch of lasting night,
> Thou hate and terror to prosperity,
> And I will kiss thy detestable bones,
> And put my eyeballs in thy vaulty brows,
> And ring these fingers with thy household worms,
> And stop this gap of breath with fulsome dust,
> And be a carrion monster like thyself.
> Come, grin on me, and I will think thou smil'st
> And buss thee as thy wife. Misery's love.
> O, come to me!
> (III.iv.25–36)[2]

Death as a lover suggests another medieval convention that Shakespeare makes use of: darkness as that middle term between death and love that illumines both. Death itself is a darkness, our fear of it is related to our fear of darkness, and, of course—in *Macbeth* and *Othello*—death is the blowing out of the candle, that act that precedes the act of love.

Shakespeare's soldiers, whether Christian or pagan, generally love honor more than they fear death. Julius Caesar is a good Stoic, if a trifle pompous, when he declares:

> Cowards die many times before their deaths;
> The valiant never taste of death but once.
> Of all the wonders that I yet have heard,
> It seems to me most strange that men should fear,
> Seeing that death, a necessary end,
> Will come when it will come.
> (II.ii.32–37)

Falstaff, of course, rejects both honor and the pious assurance that he owes God a death.[3] Superb in his cowardice, he breaks the causal link between honor and death, insisting that he is not ready either to die or to accept honor as justification for killing or getting killed.

Shakespeare is decisively post-medieval in one sense. When he looks for a power that transcends death, it is poetic and human, not Christian (with the exception of the pious Sonnet 146). He can parody the idea of the messianic banquet at the end of *Hamlet*, where death takes the place of God as the host. In *King John* he attacks the very linch-pin of Christian theology, the idea of redemptive death: "No certain life is achieved by others' death" (IV.ii.105). In Clarence's dream in *Richard III* there is a visionary description of death by drowning, combining both beauty and decay, a vision anticipating Ariel's song.

> Methoughts I saw a thousand fearful wracks;
> A thousand men that fishes gnawed upon;
> Wedges of gold, great anchors, heaps of pearl,
> Inestimable stones, unvaluéd jewels,
> All scatt'red in the bottom of the sea:
> Some lay in dead men's skulls, and in the holes
> Where eyes did once inhabit, there were crept
> (As 'twere in scorn of eyes) reflecting gems,
> That wooed the slimy bottom of the deep
> And mocked the dead bones that lay scatt'red by.
> (I.iv.24–33)

I

Shakespeare on love and death is more than darkness and candles. Love arms against death-anxiety in the sonnets; love causes death in *Romeo and Juliet* and *Othello*; love becomes the meaning of heaven in the erotic theology of *Antony and Cleopatra*.

In the first seventeen sonnets the poet urges a friend to marry and to breed as protection against aging and fear of death.

> From fairest creatures we desire increase,
> That thereby beauty's rose might never die,
> But as the riper should by time decease,
> His tender heir might bear his memory.
> But thou contracted to thine own bright eyes,
> Feed'st thy light's flame with self-substantial fuel,
> Making a famine where abundance lies,
> Thyself thy foe, to thy sweet self too cruel.
> Thou that art now the world's fresh ornament,
> And only herald to the gaudy spring,
> Within thine own bud buriest thy content,
> And tender churl mak'st waste in niggarding.
>   Pity the world, or else this glutton be,
>   To eat the world's due, by the grave and thee.
>   (Sonnet 1)

There is here the conventional wisdom that we all die, and the slightly less conventional wisdom that in reproducing ourselves we live on in posterity. And:

> But if thou live remember'd not to be,
> Die single and thine image dies with thee.
>   (Sonnet 3)

"Image" in mirror and in memory, and potential image in offspring. To refuse to reproduce is to be self-willed, and to allow death total dominion (Sonnet 6).

In Sonnets 11 and 12 the poet is most explicit about his advice to breed and most insistent that reproduction is the only sure protection against death.

> As fast as thou shalt wane, so fast thou grow'st
> In one of thine, from that which thou departest.
>   (Sonnet 11)

Complex and precise. "Waning" is detumescence after intercourse, and "growing" is the growth of the fertilized egg. "In one of thine" suggests both "in your child" and "in your wife's womb," while "from that which thou departest" points both to the withdrawal of the penis and the release of the sperm. Breeding is death's best antidote.

> And nothing 'gainst Time's scythe can make defence,
> Save breed, to brave him when he takes thee hence.
> (Sonnet 12)

Without a child there is only "folly, age, and cold decay" (Sonnet 11); with one, there is immortality and the world will mourn your death less (Sonnet 9).

These early sonnets have another secular immortality, the immortality of art.

> When I consider everything that grows
> Holds in perfection but a little moment,
> That this huge stage presenteth naught but shows
> Whereon the stars in secret influence comment;
> When I perceive that men as plants increase,
> Cheered and check'd even by the self-same sky,
> Vaunt in their youthful sap, at height decrease,
> And wear their brave state out of memory;
> Then the conceit of this inconstant stay
> Sets you most rich in youth before my sight,
> Where wasteful Time debateth with Decay,
> To change your day of youth to sullied night;
>   And all in war with Time for love of you,
>   As he takes from you, I engraft you new.
> (Sonnet 15)

Throughout the rest of the sequence, the poet returns to this double hope: his victory over death is assured by his love and its fruit, and by the poetic record of that love. It is love, not God, that keeps the despondent poet from suicide. In Sonnet 66 he cries out for restful death, but finally decides against it.

> Tired with all these, for restful death I cry,
> As, to behold desert a beggar born,

And needy nothing trimmed in jollity,
And purest faith unhappily forsworn,
And gilded honor shamefully misplaced,
And maiden virtue rudely strumpeted,
And right perfection wrongfully disgraced,
And strength by limping sway disabled,
And art made tongued-tied by authority,
And folly, doctorlike, controlling skill,
And simple truth miscalled simplicity,
And captive good attending captain ill.
   Tired with all these, from these would I be gone,
   Save that, to die, I leave my love alone.

Fear of death as fear of pre-deceasing the beloved keeps suicide at bay.

Death is the snuffing out of the candle, and so is love: "the deed of darkness"; at night "desire sees best of all"; "Lovers can see to do their amorous rites / By their own beauties." Five of the six deaths in the three plays embodying the love-death theme—*Romeo and Juliet, Othello, Antony and Cleopatra*—are suicides, not always a sin in Shakespearean England. Juliet's suicide imitates the sexual consummation of her marriage. Her body sheathes the dagger as it had sheathed Romeo on their wedding night. This sexualized death has been carefully prepared for. Romeo, before the party, senses "untimely death," and later sees marriage as protection against "love-devouring death." In bed the morning after the wedding night, love and death have already become one.

Let me be ta'en, let me be put to death.
I am content, so thou wilt have it so.
I'll say yon grey is not the morning's eye,
'Tis but the pale reflex of Cynthia's brow;
Nor that is not the lark whose notes do beat
The vaulty heaven so high above our heads.
I have more care to stay than will to go.
Come, death, and welcome! Juliet wills it so.
How is't, my soul? Let's talk; it is not day.
                    (III.v.17–25)

In the tomb, Romeo looks upon Juliet, believing her dead, and thinks of the Dance of Death. So intact is her beauty, he imagines that Death must desire her. He decides to remain with her, in death, to keep his rival away.

> Why art thou yet so fair? Shall I believe
> That unsubstantial Death is amorous.
> And that the lean abhorrèd monster keeps
> Thee here in dark to be his paramour?
> For fear of that I still will stay with thee
> And never from this pallet of dim night
> Depart again. . . .
>   Eyes, look your last!
> Arms, take your last embrace! and, lips, O you
> The doors of breath, seal with a righteous kiss
> A dateless bargain to engrossing death!
> Come, bitter conduct; come, unsavory guide!
> Thou desperate pilot, now at once run on
> The dashing rocks thy seasick weary bark!
> Here's to my love! [*Drinks*] O true apothecary!
> Thy drugs are quick. Thus with a kiss I die.
>   (V.iii.102–108, 112–120)

Othello also closes with a kiss of death. It is Othello's love as much as jealousy that transforms him into a murderer and a suicide. What he loved in Desdemona was a perfection so impossible that it became simple for Iago to tarnish it. Her goodness was the reason for his love, the reason for her death, and the net that killed them both. At the beginning of the final scene, the bedroom candle is Desdemona's life. The Moslem Othello does not have an eschatology that allows immortality for his Christian wife.

> Put out the light, and then put out the light.
> If I quench thee, thou flaming minister,
> I can again thy former light restore,
> Should I repent me; but once put out thy light,
> Thou cunning'st pattern of excelling nature,
> I know not where is that Promethean heat
> That can thy light relume. When I have plucked the rose,
> I cannot give it vital growth again;
> It needs must wither.
>   (V.ii.7–15)

Desdemona has invited the death she cannot understand. Her loving nature demands justice for Cassio, and Othello's mistrust is deepened. Not even Othello's murderous attack cancels her love. Who has done it, Emilia asks the dying Desdemona, and she replies, "nobody; I myself." Exactly. Her love for Othello, her wish, even as she dies by his hand, to protect him from murder's guilt, suggests a martyrdom almost excessive, a love too encompassing. Both died because both loved too well; their loves were idealizing, absolute, and dangerous. Love caused the deaths, yet her love for him does not die, and in the last kiss his love returns. Each dies with love fully intact.

In the opening scene of *Antony and Cleopatra*, the lovers speak of their love as immeasurable, and Antony spills into eschatological language. "Then must thou needs find out new heaven, new earth." Here is something new: beyond the identity of love and death—an erotic eschatology. The state of death is not only like love, it is like orgasm.

Cynical Enobarbus perceives the connection between sensuousness and death in Cleopatra.

> Cleopatra, catching but the least noise of this, dies
> instantly; I have seen her die twenty times upon far poorer
> moment. I do think there is mettle in death, which
> commits some loving act upon her, she hath such a celerity
> in dying.
> (I.ii.137–141)[4]

The resolution of the love–death pattern begins after Antony's defeat at Actium when he says:

> I'll make death love me, for I will contend
> Even with his pestilent scythe.
> (III.xiii.193–194)

At the close of the fourth act, Cleopatra is determined on suicide, denying that it is a sin. She will "make death proud to take us" (IV.xv. 91), anticipating her own death without uncertainty or horror. It is a death deeply desirable and restful, bringing an end to all accident and change. It is a rare Shakespearean death; it is mystical, and it is erotic. Death indeed does take her, and her own death brings the eschatology of the play to a climax. She prepares her body for death as she would prepare it, as she had prepared it, for a lover.

> Give me my robe, put on my crown, I have
> Immortal longings in me. Now no more
> The juice of Egypt's grape shall moist this lip.
> Yare, yare, good Iras; quick. Methinks I hear
> Antony call: I see him rouse himself
> To praise my noble act. I hear him mock
> The luck of Caesar, which the gods give men
> To excuse their after wrath. Husband, I come:
> Now to that name my courage prove my title!
> I am fire, and air; my other elements
> I give to baser life. So, have you done?
> Come then, and take the last warmth of my lips.
> Farewell, kind Charmian, Iras, long farewell.
> [*Kisses them. Iras falls and dies.*]
> Have I the aspic in my lips? Dost fall?
> If thou and nature can so gently part,
> The stroke of death is as a lover's pinch,
> Which hurts, and is desired. Dost thou lie still?
> If thus thou vanishest, thou tell'st the world
> It is not worth leave-taking. . . .
>   This proves me base:
> If she first meet the curlèd Antony,
> He'll make demand of her, and spend that kiss
> Which is my heaven to have. Come, thou mortal wretch,
>   [*To an asp, which she applies to her breast.*]
> With thy sharp teeth this knot intrinsicate
> Of life at once untie. Poor venomous fool,
> Be angry, and dispatch. O, couldst thou speak,
> That I might hear thee call great Caesar ass
> Unpolicied!. . .
>   Peace, peace!
> Dost thou not see my baby at my breast,
> That sucks the nurse asleep?
>   (V.ii.279–297, 299–307, 307–309)

Once again, Shakespearean death is the seducer whose stroke is foreplay, the lover's pinch. Then the poison asp, her final lover, is invited to apply its mouth to her breast. Cleopatra's final words suggest ecstasy, as death and sexual delight become one.

> As sweet as balm, as soft as air, as gentle—
> O Antony! Nay, I will take thee too. . . .
> What should I stay—
> (V.ii.309–311)

II

> Tragedy is not about the fact that all men are mortal (though perhaps it is about the fact mortals go to any length to avoid that knowledge). . . . A tragedy is about a *particular* death, or set of deaths, and specifically about a death which is neither natural or accidental.[5]

Death has a decisive presence in the opening scene of *King Lear*. When we ask why Lear does what he does—the division of the kingdom and the love-test—we find an old king and a father not merely dying but afraid of dying. Old kings worry about succession, especially if they propose to pass the crown irregularly to a youngest child; fathers uneasily approach the end of life anxious to be loved. Lear says that he wishes to prevent strife and "unburdened crawl toward death."

Freud's reading of the play brings death abruptly into this scene. Cordelia's "nothing" and her silence remind Freud that dumbness in dreams is a representation of death. Cordelia is Death before she dies and Lear, Freud notes, "is not only an old man; he is a dying man."[6]

The first act initiates another death theme, one tied to paternity and birth. Lear, in his rage, begins by admitting paternity but denying paternal care, through removing his "father's heart" from Cordelia, to open denial of paternity: "We have no such daughter," and "better thou hadst not been born." His own struggle with death seems connected both to his wish for the destruction of his children and to the denial of himself as their father. In the discussion about the knights (I.iv), Lear's anger with Goneril drives him to ask: "Are you our daughter?", and then to call her "degenerate bastard." He prays for her sterility.

This is not simply sex-nausea, or a generalized hatred of women; it is an attack on procreation, the very creation of life. It is a death-wish for all the world. The "no life" at the play's end is present at the beginning.

With Lear on the heath (III.ii), the violence of his language has broadened. No longer are particular women to cease breeding; nature itself is required to spill its semen so that no "ingrateful man" may ever be made again. This is an apocalyptic vision of the end of life on earth. If he is to die, he decrees that no other life be allowed.

Edgar's project of curing his father's despair (if that is what he is doing) is successful, and Gloucester accepts his mortality.

> Henceforth I'll bear
> Affliction till it do cry out itself
> "Enough, enough, and die."
> (IV.vi.75–77)

But the mad king is not so acquiescent. The "let copulation thrive" speech is more than an attack on female sexuality. It contains his conviction, or hope, that woman—for all her appetite—should be impotent.

> Behold yond simpering dame,
> Whose face between her forks presages snow;
> That minces virtue, and does shake the head
> To hear of pleasure's name.

Woman's appearance, face, suggests frigidity between the legs.

> The fitchew, nor the soilèd horse goes to't
> With a more riotous appetite.
> Down from the waist they are Centaurs,
> Though women all above:
> But to the girdle do the gods inherit,
> Beneath is all the fiend's.
> (IV.vi.117–120, 121–126)

Below the waist, woman is the devil, the sulphurous pit, and stench. When Lear says to Gloucester, who has asked to kiss his hand, "Let me wipe it first; it smells of mortality," smell refers back to the diabolic female smell of procreation. My hand smells because it was born of woman.

Later in this scene, with "matter and impertinency mixed," Lear counsels patience to Gloucester. "We came crying hither"; we cried as soon as we first smelled the air of mortality and walked on the great stage of fools. To be born of woman is a calamity. Lear asks Gloucester to learn patience, but he hardly takes his own advice: "when I have stol'n upon these son-in-laws, / Then kill, kill, kill, kill, kill, kill."

At the end of IV.vii, the anger and violence are momentarily burned away. In "You do me wrong to take me out o' th' grave," Lear accepts his death as having already happened. He says to Cordelia, "If you have poison for me, I will drink it," consenting gently to suicide if that be her wish.

It is not easy to know what to make of "Ripeness is all." Edgar invites his father to move on after hearing of Cordelia's defeat. Gloucester pauses, with "a man may rot even here." And then, Edgar:

> What, in ill thoughts again? Men must endure
> Their going hence, even as their coming hither;
> Ripeness is all. Come on.
> (V.ii.9–11)

Don't feel so sorry for yourself, old man. Get used to dying, as we have to get used to being born. When fruit ripens, it falls or is picked from the tree. "Ripeness is all" may be the deepest word of all, or it may be a piece of off-hand therapy in the form of a Stoic commonplace. Edgar has a wiser (and clearer) perception of the relation of suffering and death: "O our lives' sweetness / That we the pain of death would hourly die / Rather than die at once!"(V.iii.185–187).

In the final scene of the play Lear and Cordelia are taken to prison, and Lear portrays the life he anticipates with his now beloved daughter. "Upon such sacrifices, my Cordelia, / The gods themselves throw incense." A decisive moment in Lear's understanding of love and death. Their new love is a sacrifice, a killing, a cleansing death: perhaps a final payment for his (and her?) earlier misuse of love. The love is now finally spoken by Cordelia: "No cause, no cause."

Dying Edmund, curiously delaying, finds that approaching death releases whatever fragments of decent love remain in him. He confesses his role in condemning Lear and Cordelia to death, and an officer is dispatched to rescue them. Albany, always pious, sighs: "The gods defend her!" And Lear enters with the dead Cordelia. So much for the power of the gods to defend. They exist, alas, and are both indifferent and cruel. Act V, scene iii, is the proof of that.

Act V, scene iii, from Lear's entrance to the end, takes only five minutes to read, a little longer to play. It has been called the most terrifying five minutes in literature. It is about but one thing, "the unconquerable fact of death," not only Cordelia's and Lear's, but ours.[7]

Lear is sane when he says "I know when one is dead and when one lives." Sane, but not purged of anger. "I might have saved her." That has been the case from the beginning, had he been able to receive love, and give it. Her death is on his hands. The guilt and the perception that she is gone forever shatter the fragile sanity recently restored. The return of madness brings the illusion that Cordelia lives. Sanity perceives her death, and the perception shatters the sanity.

Lear can find no hope in Cordelia's death except by denying it. Is there any meaning here at all, or is the only meaning the perfection of the negation of meaning? Cordelia does not die because she is flawed, but because she is innocent, confirming the principle both known and feared in the culture of the West that it is the fate of innocence to be destroyed and to cause the destruction of others. Perhaps all *King Lear* leaves us with is the ability to say "the worst is not / So long as we can say 'This is the worst.'" The horror of Cordelia's death is deepened—as Shakespeare, step by step, removes all possible escapes—by the horror of the perception that Lear's only relief from horror is a relief based on madness and illusion. Only if we are deceived and mad, like Lear at the end, can we discern the hands of the gods in the world.

> And it does look, after the death of kings and out of the ironies of revolutions and in the putrefactions of God, as if our trouble is that there used to be answers and now there are not.[8]

Once more, a moment before his own death, the joy and madness depart and Lear sees what is really there, a corpse.

> Why should a dog, a horse, a rat, have life,
> And thou no breath at all? Thou'lt come no more,
> Never, never, never, never, never.

There is no answer to this "Why?" There is only the final descent to madness. If Lear does die in joy, as some affirm, it is a terrible joy because it is deceived. Those "nevers" are the poundings of reality on Lear, and like the rest of us, he cannot bear very much of that.

Lear dies not because he is old, or exhausted, but because Cordelia has died; he has partly caused it, and she will never come again, either to this world or the next. To make a positive affirmation in the presence of death in this play, one must be mad. Whatever repose comes to us at the close of *King Lear* is the repose of nothingness and death. Whenever love is commanded, avoided, withdrawn, and quantified, there can be no peace. Kent prepares for a journey to death, perhaps by his own hand. At the end, in Edgar's "we that are young / Shall never see so much, nor live so long," even the death of the still living is affirmed.

III

Measure for Measure and *Hamlet* share an emphasis on another part of Shakespearean death: eschatology, the state of death, what is being dead like and what, if anything, lies beyond. In *Measure for Measure*, the Duke, disguised as a friar, offers a splendid, and most medieval, piece of theological counselling to the condemned Claudio.

> Be absolute for death: either death or life
> Shall thereby be the sweeter. Reason thus with life:
> If I do lose thee, I do lose a thing
> That none but fools would keep; a breath thou art,
> Servile to all the skyey influences
> That dost this habitation where thou keep'st
> Hourly afflict; merely, thou art death's fool,
> For him thou labor'st by thy flight to shun,
> And yet run'st toward him still. Thou art not noble,
> For all th' accommodations that thou bear'st
> Are nursed by baseness. Thou'rt by no means valiant,
> For thou dost fear the soft and tender fork
> Of a poor worm; the best of rest is sleep,
> And that thou oft provok'st, yet grossly fear'st
> Thy death, which is no more. Thou art not thyself,
> For thou exists on many a thousand grains
> That issue out of dust. Happy thou art not,
> For what thou hast not, still thou striv'st to get,
> And what thou hast, forget'st. Thou art not certain,
> For thy complexion shifts to strange effects,
> After the moon. If thou art rich, thou'rt poor,
> For, like an ass whose back with ingots bows,
> Thou bear'st thy heavy riches but a journey,
> And death unloads thee. Friend hast thou none,
> For thine own bowels, which do call thee sire,
> The mere effusion of thy proper loins,
> Do curse the gout, serpigo, and the rheum
> For ending thee no sooner. Thou hast not youth nor age,
> But as it were an after-dinner's sleep,
> Dreaming on both, for all thy blessed youth
> Becomes as agèd, and doth beg the alms
> Of palsied eld: and when thou art old and rich
> Thou hast neither heat, affection, limb, nor beauty,
> To make thy riches pleasant. What's yet in this
> That bears the name of life? Yet in this life
> Lie hid more thousand deaths; yet death we fear,
> That makes these odds all even.
>
> (III.i.5–41)

At first, Claudio seems content with this ducal counsel, but shortly his assurance collapses and terror takes over.

> Ay, but to die, and go we know not where,
> To lie in cold obstruction and to rot,
> This sensible warm motion to become
> A kneaded clod; and the delighted spirit
> To bathe in fiery floods, or to reside
> In thrilling region of thick-ribbèd ice,
> To be imprisoned in the viewless winds
> And blown with restless violence round about
> The pendent world; or to be worse than worst
> Of those that lawless and incertain thought
> Imagine howling, 'tis too horrible
> The weariest and most loathèd worldly life,
> That age, ache, penury, and imprisonment
> Can lay on nature is a paradise
> To what we fear of death.
>
> (III.i.118–132)

He is quite clear about what terrifies him: the decay of the body and the soul's final judgment. Claudio is not theologically untutored, he is afraid; his fear is not assuaged by his beliefs, it is caused by them. His fear does not turn him from the world, but passionately toward it, and just because of his love of life he is unwilling to die to maintain his sister's chastity. That faith creates fear of death is negatively confirmed by the drunken prisoner Barnardine. He has no faith and therefore no fear.

In this exchange between the disguised Duke and Claudio we see the breakdown of traditional Christian eschatology. With its otherworldly premise, it no longer comforts. Only drunken prisoners without the burden of faith are truly fearless before death. How does one overcome the fear of death in death-ridden Vienna? Not by listening to well-meaning nobles dressed up in monk's clothes. Recalling the procession of couples marching offstage at the play's end, should we conclude that only love can dampen the fear of mortality? If this is the word from *Measure for Measure*, we are back in the world of the sonnets, with their thoroughly secular injunction to marry, love, and breed.

Death, and above all, the state of death, lives at the center of *Hamlet*. We first see him discussing mortality with his mother, and in the first soliloquy he longs for death (I.ii.129–159). Later, Hamlet does some guiltless killing of his own, meditates on a skull, and a pervasive medieval *contemptus mundi* mood hovers over all. But *Hamlet* is not merely about killing and dying, it is about the hero's fear of death and what follows it. It is the ghost that embodies this problem of the state of death.

Who was the ghost, and what task did he give Hamlet? There is an ethical problem about the ghost's command, and a theological problem about the ghost's origin. If you decide that the ghost's command is an immoral one, you may conclude that the Protestant interpretation of ghosts is the correct one: they are real, but since there is no Purgatory they are not departed spirits, but the devil assuming a familiar form to do some mischief. The Catholic interpretation sees the ghost as a true spirit from Purgatory, returning to earth as part of its discipline, generally doing good deeds.

It is clear that Hamlet cannot decide between these two views. He asks whether it is "a spirit of health or goblin damned," Catholic or Protestant. The ghost himself refers both to tormenting flames (which suggests hell, from which escape is impossible) and to earthly crimes being purged (Purgatory). Hamlet declares to Horatio that it is an honest ghost, but at the close of "O what a rogue" he becomes uncertain again, with "the spirit that I have seen may be a devil." He is not sure, so the play within the play is designed to test the ghost, using Claudius' reaction as evidence.

The message of the ghost suggests the Protestant interpretation, for the ghost enjoins blood revenge, and if Shakespeare approves of revenge in this play it is the only one in which he does so. If the ghost is a devil, then Hamlet would be damned if he obeyed him. To be uncertain about ghosts is to be uncertain about the meaning of death, and that uncertainty is the theme of the great third act soliloquy.

> To be, or not to be—that is the question;
> Whether 'tis nobler in the mind to suffer
> The slings and arrows of outrageous fortune
> Or to take arms against a sea of troubles

> And by opposing end them. To die, to sleep—
> No more—and by a sleep to say we end
> The heartache, and the thousand natural shocks
> That flesh is heir to. 'Tis a consummation
> Devoutly to be wished. To die, to sleep—
> To sleep—perchance to dream; ay there's the rub,
> For in that sleep of death what dreams may come
> When we have shuffled off this mortal coil,
> Must give us pause. There's the respect
> That makes calamity of so long life.
> For who would bear the whips and scorns of time,
> Th' oppressor's wrong, the proud man's contumely
> The pangs of despised love, the law's delay,
> The insolence of office, and the spurns
> That patient merit of th' unworthy takes,
> When he himself might his quietus make
> With a bare bodkin? Who would fardels bear,
> To grunt and sweat under a weary life,
> But that the dread of something after death,
> The undiscovered country, from whose bourn
> No traveller returns, puzzles the will,
> And makes us rather bear those ills we have
> Than fly to others that we know not of?
> Thus conscience does make cowards of us all,
> And thus the native hue of resolution
> Is sicklied o'er with the pale cast of thought,
> And enterprises of great pitch and moment
> With this regard their currents turn awry
> And lose the name of action.
>
> (III.i.56–88)

When you describe death as a country from which no one returns, you are Protestant because you are denying Purgatory. But "To be or not to be" is not altogether Protestant. It is partly about suicide, but mostly it is about the state of death in the shadow of that uncertainty about the ghost. I think Hamlet is saying this: "If the ghost is a true one, if my Protestant professors at Wittenberg are wrong and there really is such a thing as a true Purgatorial spirit, then the death I may receive (from the courtiers or guards, for example) after killing Claudius may be like a sleep. But if the ghost is a devil out to tempt me, then after killing the king I will end up being eternally damned."

The problem of the ghost does not exhaust Hamlet's interest in the state of death. From the jokes about Polonius' guts on, Hamlet seems fascinated with corpses, skeletons, the vanity of life. The graveyard scene shows a clown–grave-digger and a cynical prince talking about a dead court jester, as if all were folly, even folly itself. Hamlet's views about death are close to those of traditional medieval theology (especially when we recall that he finally does go with the Catholic interpretation). The same views that make Claudio afraid make Hamlet bitter. He dies with "the rest is silence" on his lips, suggesting his earlier meditations on nothingness and sleep. This final "silence" has a deeply skeptical color: there is nothing beyond, no rest leading to something new. Hamlet's silence is Lear's "never" and Prospero's non-theological sleep of nothingness that rounds our little lives.

IV

This study has really had but two themes: how can love stand against death? and what happens when I die? The first called upon the sonnets; we found love hopelessly at death's mercy in *Romeo and Juliet* and *Othello*, and—in a different way—in *King Lear*. We tried to look at the blinding light of Cleopatra, in whom love and death collided, then merged, as sensual love turned into eternal *eros*. The second theme, more theological, contained some bitter and despondent answers to the question about what happens after death: Claudio's "'tis too horrible," Lear's "never", Hamlet's silence.

At the close of Shakespeare's literary life, we move into a different kind of air, a bit like the world of *Antony and Cleopatra* without its splendid vulgarity. Death in Shakespeare's last plays seems to own less power, to have lost its sting, but this final world of death seems even more secular than the Shakespearean world that came before. It may be that Shakespeare faced his own mortality with more serenity at the end of his life, with *Cymbeline* and *The Tempest*. This we do not know. But these last plays do give us something new, and *Cymbeline* offers an example. In the final act, Posthumus is in jail and he thinks he is guilty of his wife's death. He gently accepts his life's end.

> Most welcome, bondage! for thou art a way,
> I think to liberty. Yet am I better
> Than one that's sick o' th' gout, since he had rather
> Groan so in perpetuity than be cur'd
> By the sure physician death, who is the key
> To unbar these locks.
> My conscience, thou art fetter'd
> More than my shanks and wrists; you good gods, give me
> The penitent instrument to pick that bolt.
> Then free for ever! Is't enough I am sorry?
> So children temporal fathers do appease;
> Gods are more full of mercy. Must I repent,
> I cannot do it better than in gyves,
> Desir'd more than constrain'd. To satisfy,
> If of my freedom 'tis the main part, take
> No stricter render of me than my all.
> I know you are more clement than vile men,
> Who of their broken debtors take a third,
> A sixth, a tenth, letting them thrive again
> On their abatement; that's not my desire.
> For Imogen's dear life take mine; and though
> 'Tis not so dear, yet 'tis a life; you coin'd it.
> 'Tween man and man they weigh not every stamp.
> Though lift, take pieces for the figure's sake;
> You rather mine, being yours. And so, great pow'rs,
> If you will take this audit, take this life,
> And cancel these cold bonds. O Imogen!
> I'll speak to thee in silence.
>
> (V.iv.3–29)[9]

The climax to this essay on Shakespearean death comes, to no one's surprise, in *The Tempest*. This play is about mortality. Even if Prospero had not assured us that on his return to Milan "Every third thought shall be my grave," we would have assumed that he and his creator were getting ready for retirement and what comes after.[10] Prospero's "revels" speech (IV.i. 148–163) is about the mortality of all things, about how all that is earthly will dissolve, about how our life is ended with a sleep. Hamlet worried about the meaning of sleep, but nothing was settled. Prospero is not uncertain. When he declares that "our little life / is rounded with a sleep" (IV.i.157–158), he is at peace, and he makes us so. This is a secular peace.

When eschatology is Christian in Shakespeare, it causes fear and bitterness. Here, at Shakespeare's end, dreams and sleep lead on to—nothing: the nothing that so decimated Lear is now the basis for Prospero's serenity.

Prospero uses death language as he gives up his magic.

> I'll break my staff,
> Bury it certain fathoms in the earth,
> And deeper than did ever plummet sound
> I'll drown my book.
>
> (V.i.54–57)

"Fathoms" and "drown" finally bring us to Ariel's song. If Cleopatra's death was a visionary erotic eschatology that solved the problem of love and death, "Full fathom five" may be taken as Shakespeare's last answer to the other problem: "What happens to my body and soul after death, especially since Christian belief produces so much distress?"

A consoling spirit speaks to Ferdinand, who believes his father has drowned in the tempest.

> Full fathom five thy father lies;
>   Of his bones are coral made;
> Those are pearls that were his eyes;
>   Nothing of him that doth fade
> But doth suffer a sea-change
> Into something rich and strange.
> Sea nymphs hourly ring his knell:
> *Burden.*   Ding-dong.
> Hark! now I hear them—Ding-dong bell.
>
> (I.ii.397–405)

The terrifying vision from Clarence's dream in which skeletons and jewels mingle on the sea-floor in an underwater disaster is transfigured into a vision of order. Ten years before, the ideas of skeleton and corpse had exercised an almost prurient fascination for Hamlet, by the side of Ophelia's grave. Claudio could not face the reality of his own dead body, and Cordelia's corpse was cause of both the madness and death of Lear. Here, the corpse of the father, the death of all fathers, is transfigured as—in its decomposition—it is turned into treasured pieces of beauty. Neither death nor decomposition are denied; they are faced as brutal reality. It is imagination that makes immortal, not God.

IV

The Inquisitor's Argument

Theology today is lackluster, either pious or ideological. Literary criticism is bad French farce, closing in New Haven. We are drowning in interpretation. What do you do when this happens? You turn to a close reading of your primary sources. Close reading without interpretation? Who can tell? I propose such a reading, against interpretation, of a portion of "The Grand Inquisitor" chapter from *The Brothers Karamazov*. In this, Dostoevsky, the author, writes about what Ivan, an author, wrote about a sixteenth-century cardinal who talked to the returning Jesus. I am going to concentrate on what Dostoevsky said about what Ivan said the cardinal said.

In this text, there are four different centuries to juggle. First, there is the century of the reader, this dreadful end of the twentieth century. We are in an apocalyptic time; we have known political and religious tyrants; we are wary of all Big Brothers. Then there is the century of the writer, the nineteenth. Dostoevsky is, after all, writing about his world, not ours. He has a problem with Russian Orthodoxy; he has contempt for revolutionary politics; he is trying to extrude a personal faith from the crucible of doubt.

But the nineteenth-century writer who has written a sacred twentieth-century text has located his tale in the sixteenth century, during the Spanish counter-Reformation, and this means that the story is not only about fascism and communism and Orthodoxy, but about Catholicism. And finally, the tale is about the first century, for it is about the visit to the sixteenth century of the first-century man, Jesus. Dostoevsky presents us with what he claims to be the real New Testament Jesus, and one of the things the reader must do is test that claim: is Dostoevsky's silent yet eloquent figure in fact the real Jesus, if there is any such thing?

Introduction

The cardinal is initially uncertain about his prisoner's identity, and so are we. He solves his uncertainty not by collecting evidence but by ignoring his uncertainty and by proceeding as if it were Jesus. And this is what the reader does as well.

Cardinal: (in effect, to "Jesus") You have no right to add anything to your recorded words, for if you spoke anything new, today, you would violate the freedom of all those who followed you, sixteen centuries ago, and since.

Reader: This is the central fact about Dostoevsky's Jesus: he was an utterly non-coercive call to freedom, with no authority behind him, no promises or demands for the future. Just a call to follow. And this is in part what the New Testament says. Jesus *is* singularly evasive, obscure, or silent when it comes to defining himself in public.

Cardinal: I plan to treat you to a heretic's burning tomorrow, but let me first tell you something about myself. We have added something to that old freedom you offered. The men and women we take responsibility for think they are free, but they have in fact turned their freedom over to us.

Reader: That "us" is the problem. It is Hitler and Stalin and the last pages of *1984*. It is Orthodoxy and Catholicism and all religion. It is left and right; "all those smelly little orthodoxies contending for our souls," as Orwell elegantly says in another place.

Cardinal: We have done some simple surgery on the lives of our people. We have taken away their freedom and

The Inquisitor's Argument

replaced it with happiness. In fact, we have defined happiness as the giving up of freedom. You surely understand me; you once thought about doing the very thing we have done.

Reader: The cardinal, of course, refers to the temptation in the wilderness at the beginning of Jesus's ministry. The rest of his monologue is a free-wheeling exegesis of Matthew's record of that event.

Cardinal: Could any wise man, I ask you, "have invented anything equal in depth and force to the three questions which were actually put to you at the time by the wise and mighty spirit in the wilderness?" (p. 295, Penguin edition). Those three questions anticipate and summarize all of human history that has transpired since. Who has been proven correct, you or your Tempter?

First Temptation

"If you are the Son of God, command these stones to become loaves of bread." Matthew 4:3 (R.S.V.)

Cardinal: This is what I think the Tempter was saying to you back them. "You want to begin your earthly ministry with nothing but a promise of radical freedom, freely chosen without constraints. Don't you know anything about real men and women? They are simple people, terrified of the freedom you offer. Don't be so hard on them. If you really want their permanent and grateful obedience, turn these stones here into bread. Feed them, and they'll follow you, not for the miracle but for the food."

Then you replied to the Tempter that man needs more than bread. This is both obvious and true, but let me remind you that for the sake of bread, hungry man can and will rise up and destroy the beautiful world of spirit and freedom that seems to fascinate

154   *The Inquisitor's Argument*

Reader: you. People say, in effect, feed us, and then you may ask anything you like of us, even virtue.

Reader: We learn several things about Dostoevsky here. He has great contempt for the liberal world which sees no crime, only hunger. And he profoundly mistrusts the secular revolutionary movements of his own time. He expresses this mistrust in a complicated vision.

Cardinal: The new socialists (remember the anachronism here; the sixteenth-century cardinal is talking about the nineteenth century) are building a tower of their own, a new tower of Babel, and they will ultimately destroy your tower, your church based on freedom, not bread. Had you only begun by offering a combination of bread *and* freedom, you might have shortened man's suffering by a thousand years. They will finally come to us after living for some time in their tower, and we will give them the happiness they will fail to find in revolutionary politics.

Reader: The reference to shortening the suffering by a thousand years probably points to the unity of political and Christian Europe under Charlemagne, who was crowned in St. Peter's in 800 A.D.

Cardinal: We will pretend to help them finish their new tower in which there is no sin, only crime and hungry people. We call the new tower that we've helped them complete the Church. We will, of course, be lying, for we will assure them that our replacement of your message of lonely freedom with well-fed happiness is really done in your name. They will agree with us that they really couldn't handle freedom, and they will admit they are weak and worthless.

Reader: The cardinal has some interesting twentieth-century agreement for part of his argument. One thinks, of course, of Brecht's bitter remark from *The Three-*

penny Opera: "*erst kommt das Fressen dann kommt die Moral.*" And recall this apparently non-ironic comment from George Orwell, in "Looking Back on the Spanish War."

> The major problem of our time is the decay of the belief in personal immortality, and it cannot be dealt with while the average human being is either drudging like an ox or shivering in fear of the secret police. How right the working classes are in their "materialism"! How right they are to realize that the belly comes before the soul, not in the scale of values but in point of time!

The debate between the loquacious cardinal and the necessarily mute Jesus might have been helped by Orwell's distinction between the belly's priority in value (no) and priority in time (yes). Leaving behind his extended metaphor of the two towers, the cardinal continues.

Cardinal: You may, with your freedom and bread from heaven, capture a few thousands over the years, but we will win "scores of thousands of millions." Are you really only interested in those few strong ones that are capable of living with nothing but your offer of radical freedom? You are an élitist. We love all the weak ones that can't handle your freedom. They may be rebellious, but they'll give us their obedience in the end. We'll tell them we're doing all this in your name; we'll be lying. We know it but they don't. This is what that first question from the Tempter involved. This is the meaning of your rejection.

Reader: Now the cardinal makes a rather abrupt, even ungainly shift. Up to this point, to use the jargon of our century, the cardinal has been accusing Jesus of ignoring or misunderstanding the economic basis of human reality. He has been a Marxist accusing Jesus of bodiless idealism. Suddenly he takes another tack,

	and starts defending the religious *a priori* of the nineteenth century.
Cardinal:	Can't you understand? Man needs something absolutely incontestable and absolutely universal to worship. The only kind of god that really delivers happiness is a god everybody believes in. For such a god, man will kill. He will say, "Give up your gods and come and worship ours, or else death to you and to your gods!" (p. 298). Something incontestable and universal to worship—something to lay your freedom before—these are one and the same. Jesus: you are not that incontestable and universal reality. Bread is.
Reader:	There is a difficult passage on p. 298. The cardinal is speaking.

> With the bread you were given an incontestable banner: give him bread and man will worship you, for there is nothing more incontestable than bread; but if at the same time someone besides yourself should gain possession of his conscience—oh, then he will even throw away your bread and follow him who has ensnared his conscience. You were right about that. For the mystery of human life is not only in living, but in knowing why one lives. Without a clear idea of what to live for man will not consent to live and will rather destroy himself than remain on the earth, though he were surrounded by loaves of bread.

I believe the cardinal is saying something like this.

Cardinal: Jesus, you offered only freedom, and left man's conscience alone. I (and others like me) came along and captured his conscience by capturing his belly. We have had no trouble recruiting from those who initially thought your bread from heaven was sufficient. Incidentally, you were right when you observed that the way to destruction is easy and many follow, while the way to life is narrow and hard and few find it. You see, we don't give only bread. We give bread in your name, so we give meaning along with bread, and that is how we take possession of the conscience. You gave no security, no certainty at all; just that vague call to follow. You, who were supposed to have given your life for all men, proved that you really didn't love those weak men and woman at all. You were tragically mistaken when you thought that man can "decide for himself what is good and what is evil, having only your image before him for guidance" (p. 299). Part of your contempt for man is a contempt for ethics. Your image won't do the trick. Man wants the knowledge of good and evil.

Reader: This is what Dostoevsky means when he says that Jesus came offering only freedom, refusing to capture man's conscience, refusing to be worshipped, refusing to be incontestable, refusing to offer bread.

Cardinal: It is your miscalculation, Jesus, that explains the decline of your influence. You simply did not realize that there are only three forces that can capture the consciences of these weak rebels and give them happiness in exchange. Bread, of course, but more important: miracle, mystery, and authority.

Reader: This final part of the exposition of the first temptation is not entirely clear. Bread is an essential part of the cardinal's alternate gospel, but he admits that his weak rebels need meaning as well as bread. Indeed, the cardinal really does not deny Jesus's reply to Satan: "man does not live by bread alone." Authority has been already touched on in the discussion of freedom and the weak man's need to give it away. Miracle is the central theme in Dostoevsky's study of the second temptation; authority is the theme of the third.

Second Temptation

"If you are the Son of God, throw yourself down; for it is written, 'He will give his angels charge of you,' and 'On their hands they will bear you up, lest you strike your foot against a stone" (Matthew 4:6).

Cardinal: Of course, you rejected that one too; proudly, like a god. You seemed to know that in submitting you would have tempted God, lost your faith, and lost as well your life on the rocks below. Satan wouldn't have bothered to save you; he would have rejoiced in the pious suicide.

Reader: I think this is the meaning of that elusive sentence on p. 299: "Oh you understood perfectly then that in taking one step, in making a move to cast yourself down, you would at once have tempted God and have lost all your faith in him, and you would have been dashed to pieces against the earth which you came to save, and the wise spirit that tempted you would have rejoiced." According to this, Jesus does not so much reject the idea of a miracle as turn away from an act that would give Satan pleasure. We should recall that Dostoevsky made nothing of the rejection of miracle in the first temptation; all that interested him there was the rejection of bread. His interpretation of the second temptation has Jesus rejecting miracle.

Cardinal: Man simply cannot live on the basis of a "free decision of the heart," that uncoerced and uncertain invitation you have always offered. Man needs miracles—

Reader: It seems a bit odd that Dostoevsky now starts to have his cardinal attack Jesus for rejecting miracles, when his earthly career clearly included them and when his first act upon returning to Seville was the giving of sight to a blind man, and his second act was to bring a little girl back from the dead.

Cardinal: —and to ask him to reject them is to ask him to reject

God. Your refusal was virtually an invitation to godlessness. If man cannot get validating miracles from you, he'll go elsewhere. You refused to come down from the cross because to do so would enslave man. I agree. Freely given love is all you ever asked for, and I don't agree—

Reader: Exegesis was not the cardinal's best subject in seminary, apparently. There *was* an element of respect for freedom in Jesus's encounters with men and women. But the gospels also tell us that he asked for much more than this naked free choice. He asked those he called to discipleship to reject their pasts and to take up a wholly new life. He asked of those who would be healed something like faith.

Cardinal: —but man is weaker than you imagined. In seeming to respect man, you actually loved him very defectively. If you had truly loved, you would have asked less, taken him as he was, forgiven without condition.

Reader: At no point is our sentimental century more likely to fall in love with the cardinal than here. We, who wallow in all that dreadful language about acceptance and forgiveness and I'm OK and you're OK, are tempted to suspect that the cardinal here becomes the true Christ-figure, preferable to the silent one. But we are wrong in trying to love the cardinal. He doesn't know anything about love. He is really an editorial advisor for *Psychology Today*. What he has forgotten is that acceptance does not exhaust the meaning of love. Tillich's "You are Accepted" has become the ideology of the hot-tub. Love (and friendship) often has a harder office—to hold another to the highest, the noblest standards of conduct and action. To love yourself is to expect much of yourself. To love others is to expect much of them. Every lover and every parent knows that. The blindness of the cardinal is perhaps yet another argument against a celibate clergy. But let us allow the old man to go on.

Cardinal: People are really corrupt and childish rebels, you know. They try faintly, from time to time, to rebel against the sacred and to undertake violent revolutionary strategies, but they can't tolerate themselves for very long as rebels. They blame God for making them so corrupt, they become ashamed of their blasphemy, and they crawl back to us. In Revelation 7, the author has a vision of the redeemed as totalling 144,000. Was it just to these pathetic few that you intended to speak?

It is our love that has led us to correct your work, to base the new Christian message not on freedom but on miracle, mystery, and authority. Men rejoiced at this correction, for we took away that freedom that gave them so much uncertainty and suffering. How can you claim we were wrong? We lightened the burden of their lives; we allowed them to sin with our permission; we made it possible for them to accept themselves as weak, base, and rebellious. We are not on your side, of course. We are on the side of the Devil, the very one who tempted you so long ago, and we have been with him since the ninth century and the time of Charlemagne.

Reader: Here for the first time the Cardinal admits that his "correction" of Jesus is really a pact with the Devil. This identification has led some contemporary apocalypticists to treat "The Grand Inquisitor" itself as a piece of apocalyptic literature, to interpret the cardinal as either Satan or the man of lawlessness according to 2 Thessalonians 2, and to read the appearance of Jesus in sixteenth century Seville, as recorded at the end of the nineteenth century, as the beginning of the second coming, the start of the end time. Although this makes Dostoevsky dreadfully relevant to apocalyptic times like our own, this apocalyptic temptation, like all temptations, should certainly be resisted.

Third Temptation

"Again, the devil took him to a very high mountain, and showed him all the kingdoms of the world and the glory of them; and he said to him, 'All these I will give you, if you will fall down and worship me' " (Matthew 4:8–9).

Cardinal: Of course, you turned down the final gift of the Tempter. He offered you political power; you said no. We said yes, some six hundred years ago, and some day we will complete our goal of uniting you and Caesar in a perfect harmony. Man needs not only someone to worship, someone to give his conscience to. He needs to live in community. You forgot that, though the great pagan conquerors did not. With possession of their consciences, with giving them the bread that makes them content, we have established our political control. They may play their secular political games—

Reader: Here the cardinal hints that these longings for political freedom may have some connection to the gift of spiritual freedom that Jesus initially offered.

Cardinal: —but they will fail, and they will return to us and ask for mystery. In that mystery is their peace. We are very patient. Secularism and science will destroy some, but the rest will return and ask us to save them from freedom and the modern world. We will not turn stones into bread, but we will perform something far more welcome than a mere miracle: we will distribute back to them the bread they have made and given us.

You destroyed the natural human community when you called individuals away from family and work into freedom and discipleship. We are joining together what you have torn asunder, and the weak shall be happy again. They will forget that you taught them, for a brief moment, how to be proud. We will turn them into humble children again, as they were before you deceived them.

We will make them laugh, we will make them work, and we will cover every sin they manage to think up. This we do because we love these weak children you turned your back on. They will not have to make any tormenting decisions about their lives; we shall make them for them.

They will be happy, but there is a price. *We* shall be unhappy. We know we are liars when we console them with heaven, but perhaps their happiness justifies the lie and consoles the liar.

I was once with you, but I awoke and become one of your correctors. My happy constituents will gladly feed the flames which I will prepare for you tomorrow.

* * * * *

The cardinal finished his long monologue and paused, expecting some sort of answer, if only anger. But the prisoner made no reply. He looked at the cardinal with great gentleness and said nothing. Suddenly, he approached the old man and kissed him on the lips. This was his "answer" to the Grand Inquisitor. But what *was* that answer? Jesus is not, after all, burned at the stake. The cardinal sends him out of the prison into the streets of the city.

Before we let Karl Barth and his friends persuade us that Jesus' final kiss on the Grand Inquisitor's lips is a message of "radical forgiveness," and before we are beguiled by D. H. Lawrence into reading that same kiss as an admirable admission of Christological complicity in the old man's demonism, a brief look is surely required at the other kisses in the novel. Before we flee into culture and presupposition, let us attend to what the text may have to say.

The first kiss to be summoned as possible interpretation of that of Jesus is Alyosha's "double" or imitation kiss on Ivan's lips at the close of "The Grand Inquisitor" chapter. Ivan had just admitted to Alyosha that he had recently said, and believed, that "everything is "permitted" because of the death of God and immortality. Sadly and bitterly, Ivan supposes that "there's no place for me in your heart" (p. 309), since he can never repudiate "everything is permitted." Then Ivan, to Alyosha: "but you will repudiate me for it, won't you?" The kiss of Alyosha is a response to that question. It is, at the very least, a repudiation of a repudiation, a refusal of piety to reject Ivan's nihilism. Does this help us with the kiss of Jesus?

The novel's full theology of kissing, like the rest of its theology, is both unsettling and confusing. I find three kiss themes in *The Brothers Karamazov*.

First of all, the kiss is a sacrament of dishonest love or dishonest piety. Piety first. In the tavern scene, Ivan tells Alyosha the story of the murderer Richard who was converted to Christianity just before his execution. Before he died, Ivan tells us, Richard was covered with the kisses of his new Christian friends, as they kissed him off to his death. So much for Christian kisses. As for dishonest or disordered love, we must cite the powerful scene with Katerina, Grushenka and Alyosha in Katerina's house. Grushenka mysteriously enters the sitting room after Alyosha has arrived, and Katerina rapturously kisses her new friend on the lips and hand, as if she truly loved her. Grushenka first considers returning Katerina's kisses a hundredfold, then decides not to kiss her at all. "You see," she says, "I want you to remember always that you kissed my hand, but I didn't kiss yours" (p. 177). Grushenka doesn't know whom she loves in this scene; probably not yet Dmitri, certainly not Katerina.

Second, the kiss—even in this novel—can be a kiss of passionate human love, present or past. Dmitri, early in the novel, admires Grushenka's superb body, and confesses that he has kissed her toe—and only that. Later, at Mokroye, just before the arrest and after her Polish friend has been dismissed, there is a good deal of kissing between Dmitri and Grushenka. She says to him, "Kiss me! Beat me, torture me, do what you like with me . . . , Oh, I deserve to be tortured" (p. 516). But she adds (almost implying that kissing isn't really touching), don't touch me, I'm not yours yet. After the trial, in their farewell scene, Katerina kisses Dmitri's hand, confessing the integrity of her old and insane love for him (p. 901).

Kissing as deception; kissing as sensual love. But the third and most important kissing of the novel remains; the kissing of Zossima. As elder, he kissed only the earth, but in his story of the "mysterious visitor" (pp. 354ff.), there is a fascinating preparation for his religious teaching on the kiss. After he resigned from his regiment, the young Zossima made the acquaintance of a mysterious man with a Tolstoyan view of the indwelling Kingdom, and a Dostoevskian view of the responsibility of each for all. One night he confessed to Zossima that he had committed a murder in the past. After the confession, Zossima wept and kissed his friend. This is , I suspect, the only pure kiss of forgiveness in the novel, and it entails a first mixture of kissing and tears that Zossima will later become a specialist in and pass on to Alyosha.

Leaving Zossima's room one night, the friend suddenly returns. He later admitted to Zossima that he had intended to kill him as the only possessor of his secret, but what the confessed murderer actually did on his sudden return was to kiss Zossima. This exchange between the murderer and Zossima sounds very much like a dress rehearsal for the elder's mature teaching.

There is another anticipation of Zossima's teaching on the kiss: that almost-kiss early in the novel when the elder kneels and touches his forehead to the earth before Dmitri, bowing—he later said (p. 334)—before the great suffering in store for him; a suffering, as it turned out, of the innocent. As if to restrict the kissing of the earth to Zossima (and his disciple), Dmitri (p. 122) admits that he loves the earth, but does not kiss it.

The central passages on Dostoevsky's theology of kissing

come in the exposition of Zossima's *theoria* (pp. 378ff.) which is to become Alyosha's *praxis* in the world. Fall upon the earth, he advises again and again; kiss it, water the earth with your tears, and the earth will bring forth fruit. This kiss, like the kiss in foreplay, is fruitful, leading to something new. It is related to tears and to the watering of the earth; it has all the passion of the kisses between Dmitri and Grushenka, and something more. When we remember that Zossima's very last act before his death was to kiss the ground (p. 382), we are obliged to say that Zossima's mature kiss is a kiss of death and resurrection, a simple sacrament for the book's motto: "Verily, verily, I say unto you, except a corn of wheat fall into the ground and die, it abideth alone; but if it die, it bringeth forth much fruit" (John 12:24). To kiss your lover is to give yourself to the lover so that something new may come forth. The Zossima kiss is a kiss of utter self-giving to his lover, to the ground, the earth, the nation and all that live within it, that a resurrection may happen, a new birth, an Alyosha.

Alyosha was thrown into despair when the miracle of incorruption did not occur; he did not know that *he* was to be the miracle, the resurrection from the dead. So, when he fled from the monastery chapel in which the Johannine passage was being read, fully aware that "his elder was stinking the place up," he ran out into the night, threw himself on the earth, kissed it, and watered it with his tears, just as his beloved mentor had advised. And he rose, we are assured, "a resolute fighter" (p. 426).

Deceit; passion; death and resurrection? Are we any further along the way toward an understanding of Jesus' strange kiss of the cardinal of which Ivan darkly said: "The kiss glows in his heart, but the old man sticks to his idea"?

V

God as Monica's Breast?

Fernand Braudel has persuasively argued that the culture of the Mediterranean cannot be fully grasped until we see how deeply it was shaped by the production and distribution of food. Christian theology has often made its way in the world by co-opting fashionable ideologues (even French ones), and I see no reason to exempt M. Braudel from this process. If we consider every Christian's favorite Mediterranean playfellow, Augustine of Hippo, will we discern any hints of the products M. Braudel has taught us to look for? I propose a brief look at Augustine's *Confessions*, I–IX, to see what we can learn there about food, and especially drink.

I do not intend to make anything of the profound fact, currently exciting some structuralist critics, that the *Confessions* are built around a central core consisting of two fruit-trees: the pear-tree (II.4ff.) for man under law, and the fig-tree (VIII.12) for man under grace. Apart from these trees, Augustine in this work had an unusual food and drink obsession, I believe, not merely because he was a sensitive Algerian Berber, growing up and working most of his adult life in a tropical climate with agricultural problems. What were the implications of those Manicheean years in his third decade? What did the young aspirant actually do during the weekends and summer vacations picking and carrying all those zucchinis and eggplants to the elect, so they could belch and fart the light particles into freedom?

What is the function of food and drink in the autobiographical section of the *Confessions*? At the beginning, with the *inquietum est cor nostrum, donec requiescat in te*, do we not have a faint suggestion of a restless and hungry infant becoming stilled at last on his mother's breast? That God nourishes (*nutriens*), we first read in the great hymn of praise in I.4. Later, the idea of nourishment is developed as Augustine contrasts the empty and false food of the Manicheans that did not satisfy, with God, the food that never perishes (III.6, IV.1). He finds himself wondering what food Faustus would offer (V.3), and then declaring that his thirst was not slaked by the coming of the Manicheean leader.

> I had learned that wisdom and folly are like different kinds of food. Some are wholesome and others are not, but both can be served equally well in the finest china dish or the meanest earthenware.
> (V.6)

Close to God as nourishment is God whose sweetness (*dulcedo*) is to be tasted or savored (II.1, VIII.4 and 6). I do not think it is merely Augustinian biblicism that imports the link between God and nourishment into the *Confessions*. A psalm or two is reflected; Psalm 145:15, "thou givest them their food in due season" in VI.10 and 14. But the psalmist here is talking about real food given by God, and Augustinian language is entirely metaphorical.[1]

The Manicheeans give solid food, and it is false; God's nourishing food is almost always liquid. There are some exceptions. There is a beautiful passage just before the plotinian ecstasy (VIII.10): "I am the food of full-grown men. Grow and you shall feed on me."[2] And in a passage from VII.18, God, or more exactly the Eternal Son, second person of the Trinity, is both food and drink in the same sentence, mixing eating, nursing, and Incarnation in a striking way:

> He it was who united with our flesh that food which I was too weak to take; for the Word was made flesh so that your Wisdom, by which you created all things, might be milk to suckle us in infancy.

Nevertheless, perhaps because of that painful autobiographical connection between Manicheeism and vegetables, these nine books of the *Confessions* are most comfortable with liquid grace. God is, of course, water. Baptism guarantees that. God pours himself over us (I.3), fills all things (*ibid.*), fills the heart (I.5),

God as Monica's Breast? 169

and is the fountain of life and water of grace that washes clean (III.8).

Water-language and wine-language are mixed (just as, in the ancient world, water and wine were mixed) in a curious passage. Nebridius, now dead, is imagined to be drinking at God's heavenly fountain, drinking God himself!

> And I cannot believe that the draught intoxicates him so that he forgets me, for it is you, O Lord, whom he drinks in and you are mindful of your servants.
>
> (IX.3)[3]

Augustine is uneasy with the wine metaphor for God, perhaps because of his mother's wine problem, both as a child (IX.8) and on her arrival in Milan (IV.2). The beggar was happy because of wine, of course, but it is "the wine of error" that Augustine's early teachers forced on him when they insisted he learn about all those sex-crazed deities (I.16). This world is drunk with the invisible wine of its own egotism (II.3). But the Psalms again save him from excessive priggishness, and he can speak to God about "the richness of your corn, the joy of your oil, and the sober intoxication of your wine" (V.13, a reflection of Psalm 104:14–15).

But deeper than all language about fountains and washing, more central than metaphors of water or wine, is the language about milk. The true fountain is not what provides mere water, but the true God; and God's true food, like Monica's, is milk. The sweetness of God is the sweetness of breast milk. The bond between grace and lactation is established early in II.6, as the physiological process is compared to the unbidden and gratuitous character of grace. Later, mother's milk is identified with the very name of Jesus, as suckling becomes union with Christ, or faith. Augustine recalled "the time when my mother fed me at the breast [and] my infant heart had been suckled dutifully on his name" (III.4). God's milk appears again in IV.1.

It is in the Christian ecstasy with Monica (IX.10) that all this comes together, and the fountain, milk, and food are identified. Augustine and Monica become one flesh in this experience, it is said, noting the powerful orgasmic rhythm of their "straining" followed by sighing. But in this vision Monica also becomes God. "We laid the lips of our hearts to the heavenly stream that flows from your fountain." Then they passed beyond their separate individualities to that place of plenty where "you feed Israel forever with the food of truth." Monica, partly the subject of this ecstasy, along with her son, is—more significantly—the source of that sweet food that flows to Augustine. In Ostia, Augustine nursed at his mother's breast for the last time. For Augustine to experience the Christian God, Monica had to become Him. In Michelangelo's *Madonna Medici* (see Fig. 2), the infant Jesus appears to be nursing. But this infant is a young Hercules, too old for nursing. What he is in fact doing is embracing Mary, seeking union with her. She knows this, for she has crossed her legs.[4]

Monica has always been central to any serious reading of the *Confessions*. A formidable, perhaps even a good woman, she effectively kept her son from Christianity for a decade because he could not discover a form of it the choice of which could not be read as capitulation to her. He finally found what she did not will for him—celibacy. We are accustomed to say that Augustine always needed a strong woman, a Monica, a mother for Adeodatus, and finally, when one was dismissed and the other dead, a mother Church which ruled over the world. I do not think that the church takes over for Monica, at least in the *Confessions*. Nor do I think it is accurate to say that Augustine needed a strong woman. What he did need, like many highly-sexed men, was a woman he could submit to, be a child before, who would feed him when he cried, give him rest when he was restless. This is what Monica was for him, before she died, and after. Augustinian grace is Monica's milk.

If Christian feminist theology is looking for new places to stand, I would be inclined to observe: "Stay away from gnosticism. That stuff gets stuck on your hands and it is impossible to wash off. Next thing you know you'll be reading Jung, and then it's all over. To deserve the maternal darkness of the divine, which is certainly there in gnosticism, you will have to pay the price of hating your bodies, and neither good feminism nor good theology permits that. Try instead the mother–God of the Bishop of Hippo."

VI

To Cast Fire Upon The Earth

Let me say what I am not going to do. I am not going to flatter you (the hope for the future, the brightest and best), for that would cause severe moral deterioration, and I wish to postpone your moral deterioration for as long as possible. I am not going to give you advice. You wouldn't take it, even if I did try, and you are probably adviced-out as it is. Besides, you should never take advice from anyone who is not at least twenty years younger than you are, so you have a wait. I am not going to rattle nuclear weapons over your head in order to terrify you into piety or virtue. For all I know, you may well be pious and virtuous already, and fear rarely creates admirable behavior. Besides, the nuclear crisis is so palpably a part of our present consciousness that we do not need to be reminded of its presence, power, and danger.

Finally, and more seriously, I am not going to offer you the ultimate meaning of existence. Let me make a small aside to tell you why I am not going to do that. It is not that I have the answer and I don't think you are ready for it. It is not that there is an answer but I don't know it. It is because there is no answer to the question about human existence's meaning. There is nothing out there waiting for you to find it. Life is very close to nonsense; this is an imbecile universe and Shakespeare's *King Lear* is the key to it. Life itself is an accident; life after death is a lie, and there is no reason for being here except just being here.

Now this proposal that there is no "ultimate meaning" out there is not a cause for despair. It is really good news, for it means that you and I have to make our own meaning and sense. It will not be given to us, for there is nothing to give, and no one able to give it. This frees the mind considerably, for it means that much of what seems to matter doesn't. You cannot *find* meaning, but you can *make* it for yourself and for the people and things you love. So, if you don't have a god or gods, fine; don't patronize those who do. If you have a god or gods, fine; don't patronize those who don't. You are both right, or wrong, or both. (May I quote Nietzsche here? "He who no longer finds what is great in God, will find it nowhere; he must either deny it or create it.")

Despair is by no means a necessary conclusion from all this; the antidote, the preventive, is the capacity of your own consciences, skill and knowledge, to resist the massive social pressures out there, just down the road, to homogenize you and turn you into a consumer. Real ethical action *is* possible today, and it will always be in the form of rebellion against such pressures.

So much for why you will not receive the secret to the meaning of the universe this morning. I have finished with my aside, and with talking about what I will not be talking about.

But—if I do not have corrupting flattery, nuclear terror, advice, or the meaning of existence to offer, I am not exactly empty handed. Here comes my text, which all baccalaureate sermons are required to have. It is from Luke 12:49: "I came to cast fire upon the earth; and would that it were already kindled!" One of the strangest, yet most historically trustworthy sayings of Jesus. What does it mean? It is not about the fires of judgment, I am sure. Jesus was very little interested in such matters. It is a piece of self-description, it is about his own ministry, his way of being in the world. And it is for us.

What I have for you is not flattery or advice, but a *metaphor*, the one hidden in this dark saying. Now a metaphor is, among other things, a lie. If I say that the new moon is a fingernail clipping, I am lying, because that is not what the moon is made of. It is my brief function to persuade you that this metaphor says something priceless about what kind of men and women we should be in our particular world.

Yet, I already hear someone say: "What an appalling idea that the idea of fire has anything useful to offer us, here at the tag end of this awful century, the century of death." (It was Theodore Adorno who said, "Of the twentieth century, one cannot be too much afraid.") There are the fires of the crematoria, with all the good Germans listening to Mozart after doing their duty all day. There are the fires over London, and then "our" good fires in Dresden, and Hiroshima and Nagasaki. Then the napalm fires in Vietnam, unable to distinguish between men, women, and children, combatant and civilian. And there is that final nuclear fire that I am not going to mention. How dare I claim that to understand Jesus *and* to understand our proper function in the world, the metaphor of fire can help?

Let me briefly remind you of the amazing richness of this metaphor. Fire can be dangerous, as we acknowledge when we speak of "playing with fire"—often with sexual overtones. Fire warms us, it cooks—turning the inedible into the edible. It gives light; it is evil and it destroys. God himself is a destroyer, a "consuming fire" in Hebrew scriptures. William Blake, in what may be the greatest lyric poem in our language, builds his meditation on God's relation to absolute evil by identifying his "tyger" with fire:

> Tyger, Tyger, burning bright,
> In the forest of the night:
> What immortal hand or eye
> Could frame thy fearful symmetry?

And there is my beloved Captain Ahab (*Moby-Dick*) removing all temptation to goodness from himself by uttering a blasphemous word of worship—to fire: "Oh! thou clear spirit of clear fire."

Yet fire is immensely useful as well as evil, perhaps even useful because it is evil. It cauterizes, it refines, it destroys evil that good may persist. Think of these who fight our forest fires, making the backfire to slow down and control the advancing flames. We pay tribute to their courage when we speak of "fighting fire with fire." Fire is evil, fire is useful, and it is very beautiful, as anyone, at the end of day, looking into a campfire or a logfire in a fireplace, can remind us.

We are to *be* this fire, to bring warmth and comfort where needed, to bring light to someone's darkness, beauty to ugliness, justice and healing to injustice and suffering.

You see, I have an overt moral and political agenda after all. I am not playing Andy Rooney or Erma Bombeck, discoursing charmingly on the trivial. Our lives today are deeply determined, and will be for years to come, by the fact that Ronald Reagan has been our President. This has meant a brilliantly successful revolutionary transformation of our whole society, removing the federal government from every aspect of our lives, except that of serving and rescuing the manufacturing sector of American industry. Robbing the poor to help the rich. This brilliant, radical, effective and deeply insensitive revolution is rarely mentioned by those from whom we derive our daily information fix; it will affect our lives for years to come. It will take years to undo, should the citizens of our country ever decide to feel ashamed of what their nation has become. There *is* an enemy waiting for you, and it is formidable. It is called privatism: that despair about social change, that retreat into the private world of "relationships" and money and the consumption of shoddy products and culture, leaving the world to be run by the knaves and the fools. (This plausible evil may be related to those nuclear anxieties I have promised not to mention.)

What is the alternative to this debilitating and tempting retreat to the private? The strident and vulgar voices of much of Christianity today (apparently so irresistibly drawn to racism, sexism, and anti-semitism) make it difficult for all of us, believers or unbelievers, to discern the deep strength and power of the great religions of the West: Judaism, Islam, Christianity. How can I articulate that strength? These traditions each say, in their own way, that we are not our own, that we are not absolutely free to do with our bodies and souls and lives whatever we feel like. We belong in particular places in this world: alongside suffering and loneliness, fighting injustice, making humor and truth and beauty when we can, keeping our natural order intact.

If you make such a decision for your life, no gratitude can be counted on; your decency may never be acknowledged; you are not likely to make a lot of money, and you may not even have the satisfaction of a hostile audience. But you know this. You know that virtue is generally defeated; this is what tragedy means; this is what the New Testament is about. This need not distress you, for it means that your choices of decency, loyalty, honesty are based—not on expected result or reward—but on your own moral nature, on your character (as the old word has it). We must resist with every ounce of our strength what this sorry century calls success. Success on America's terms is failure.

This is what I think Jesus meant by his fire. This is what my metaphor does. My claim has really been quite modest. I have merely sought to explain: the meaning of Jesus, the meaning of the twentieth century, and what you and I ought to be doing. Let me close with two superb passages, saying well what I have been saying less well. The first is from George Bernard Shaw. (Ignore the male bias):

> The reasonable man adapts himself to the world; the unreasonable one persists in trying to adapt the world to himself. Therefore all progress depends on the unreasonable man.

The second is from the distinguished radical historian, the Englishman E. P. Thompson, one of the spiritual leaders of the contemporary European peace movement:

> If we are to control our future, we must understand and control ourselves. We must, as Shelley once wrote, "imagine that which we know" [i.e., really know and feel passionately the little that is given us to understand]. And if we are to imagine our place in the brief human record at a time of crisis so extreme that it threatens that record's continuance, then I suspect it may be poetry that we will need most of all.

Incredible. A great social scientist suggesting that poetry, that metaphor, may save us. "I came to cast fire upon the earth; and would that it were already kindled!"

VII

The Second Coming of the Death of God

Now that it has been agreed that the first American coming of the death of God in this century was either a media event or a mildly useful emetic, it is now time—in these apocalyptic days—to examine the second coming. There have always been two kinds of death of God experience: "the detective," where a body is found, and "the killer," where a death is required. Twenty years ago, we had one of the first kind; the death of God controversy then was part of a broader debate on the possibility of what used to be called "God-talk." "Reformulate" (or "secularize") advised the revisionists; "do without", said the radical theology. This old debate has now been securely folded into establishment theology, both Catholic and Protestant. It is now possible both to reformulate and do without (use *fides historica* or eschatology or earnest language about transcendence) without losing your credentials.

Today, the death of God experience in its second coming is less like Angela Lansbury finding an unexpected corpse on Sunday night in her kitchen and more like the murderer who put the corpse there in the first place. We have moved from the frightening silence of God, illustrated by Ingmar Bergman, to the more frightening danger of God—not silent or dead at all, but very much alive, murderous and needing to be killed. And "illustrated" by your own choice of imams, generals, politicians, TV shills. In its present form, the death of God experience suggests that the God of the great Western monotheistic faiths—at least in the First and Second Worlds—is too male, too dangerous, too violent to be allowed to live. Death of God today is not finding a body and figuring out who and why. It is the capture, understanding, and abolition of a dangerous twentieth century ideology. God, who used to be recommended as an antidote to idolatry, has become today, in our culture, pure idol without remainder. God, who only yesterday was defined as the power of the future summoning us forward, has disappeared as nuclear terror has obliterated that very future. God, who was but yesterday our excuse for not capitulating to corrupt political authority ("we must obey God rather than man") has become part of that reactionary authority it is our duty to disobey. The second coming of the death of God means that the killer must be killed, divested, locked up and abandoned in a cable TV studio.

I have no wish to pose as an expert in the danger of other Western gods beyond the largely Protestant–northern–American–European male I am concerned with. Jews, not Christians, should make recommendations about the God of Begin and Sharon's foreign policies. Muslims, not Christians, should speak to the evil killer-Allah of Iran, Syria, Libya today. We should become experts only in the danger of the god of our own tradition and place.

The danger of God is really an old idea: neither relevant nor particularly up to date. At the beginning of the century Shaw's John Tanner wrote: "Beware of the man whose god is in the skies." I wish merely to bring out an implication of that old maxim—beware also the god.

Of course it is not natural for an American to see that God is a danger. It was only yesterday (I think it may have been in 1975, with the confluence of Watergate and our deserved defeat in Vietnam) that we managed to relinquish the idea that we were the redeemer nation, chosen or almost chosen, on God's side and therefore both invulnerable (*pace* Vietnam) and virtuous (*pace* Watergate). Americans ordinarily believe that belief in God is either necessary or a harmless option for people who need that sort of thing.

The danger of God will take some getting used to. I am suggesting that it is an idea illuminating, as no other idea can, vast areas of our private and public lives today, from Guyana to Teheran to Beirut to Rome to Northern Ireland to Washington, D.C. What is there about the claim to the possession of God that makes some men (and women, I am obliged to say) so dangerous? The terrible cry of Nietzsche suggests the beginning of an answer: "If there were gods, how could I endure not to be a god?" To have a god, to believe, to have faith in one of the monotheistic gods, is more a moral than an intellectual defect. It entails a claim to possession, and thus a claim to uniqueness and special status, conferring superiority over the one who does not so possess. For example, Christianity, even when it wraps itself in the language of brotherhood, even when it says the correct things about liberation and Karl Marx, has real trouble in not giving the impression that it is a little richer, wiser, fuller than the world of Jewish faith. Here is how faith seems to be working today. Saying "yes" to God not only distinguishes you from those who say "no," but it involves saying "no" to the "no-sayers." Those whom I negate I am bound to deny, to deny their right to deny my affirmation, and finally, to deny their right to be. To possess God is to possess the most powerful possible instrument of self-approval our times have devised, and the mirror of self-approval turns quickly into a sword of judgment. The God I am speaking of—Christian, Western, bourgeois,—is transforming his advocates into self-righteous and dangerous sinners.

Are there not perhaps moderate or revisionist strategies that will enable us to avoid the "extreme" language of divestiture or death? The great religions of the West did not "intend" that this dangerous use be made of their God, that their God become a killer. Can we not make this God a little less masculine here, a little less bourgeois–Western there? Can we not rescue God by aligning him with some of the great moral and political movements of our time, with sanctuary, with the cause of the poor? This is, of course, happening, and in many ways it should happen. But it is not at all clear that this moral investment needs the killer God to inform it. Religion without God is a surprize only to those who have forgotten the great Buddhist tradition.

Work for decent causes does not require faith and does not prevent it from turning to self-righteous hatred of enemies, expanding and exploding all over America.

Only the radical strategy against the current danger of God will work. To protect ourselves, and to protect others from ourselves as believers, we must learn to do without God. This is the second death of God. Whatever God may have done for his people in the past: courage in the face of overwhelming odds at the time of our country's founding, or consolation in time of distress today, the past and present goods weigh too lightly in the balance. God makes men evil more often than not; we must divest ourselves of God and learn to be wary of those who do not. We may or may not become more desolate, more bereft. But we will also become more human, more tentative, more able to live easily with both adversaries and friends. In one of his prison letters, Bonhoeffer wrote: "*Vor Gott, ohne Gott*", which is officially translated "Before God, we are without God." It might also be construed in this way: "Before God we once were, and may be again; now, it is imperative that we are without."

VIII

Consenting to Die: A Meditation on Mortality

This is an essay on death, but not exactly. It is really about mortality, the fact that we die, and about what we do with that fact. "Thoughts about death are always more or less fruitless," André Malraux wrote in his last book, which contained a good many "thoughts about death."[1] Some writers on this subject build impressive historical schemes, telling us what we used to believe, what we believe today, and why we have changed. Others earnestly psychologize, advising us to shun rebellion and welcome acceptance. I want to begin on a more ordinary note: death has recently become a public event in our time; it is frequently spoken of, and the fact that it is so frequently spoken of needs speaking about.

I agree with the usual wisdom about accepting our mortality, though this is not as easy as it seems. But I do want to deny that acquiescence in death's presence is always the ultimate wisdom. Consenting to die, I am arguing, can include both the acceptance of mortality and rebellion against its necessity. "And life is the destiny you are bound to refuse until you have consented to die."[2]

Some deny death by denying that it is a problem. The idea of "my death," they claim, has no content. When it comes we will not be there, so "it" will not be. If that helps anyone, they are either lucky or fooling themselves. What we ought to conclude from the apparent fact that we will not fully experience our own deaths is that mortality is more like a mystery than a problem. We explore it and wonder about it because we can never get it entirely clear.

Love levels all ranks, and mortality abolishes our differences. Some think that gender and religion make a difference in the way we look at death (our gender, does seem to make a difference in the modes of suicide we choose), but finally, confronting the corpse, each of us says "I will be this." Corpse and tomb speak a common word, erasing our differences: *hodie mihi cras tibi, sum quod eris*: today me, tomorrow you; I am (now) what you will be.

We are all going to die; even children are catching on to this earlier than they used to. We all age and approach our deaths at the same rate, one day at a time. Are there right times or wrong times in the life-cycle to consider our mortality? Malraux observed that "the proximity of death does not encourage self-examination; it repels it."[3] What he may mean by this inversion of conventional wisdom is that if you have never been particularly introspective, and if you have never really faced your own mortality before, the time of your terminal illness will not be the best time to do so. There may be a "too late" for our mortality thoughts. After all, not all of us are guaranteed a decent reflective interval between diagnosis and death.

Can it ever be too early to reflect on mortality? Some argue, or used to, that children live in an illusion of deathlessness, convinced that an unending bloc of time stretches before them, and that really to face mortality you have to be forty-one and a half, or ill, or have lost both parents, or had too many contemporaries die. There is something to this illusion of immortality: "it's not going to get me." Husband to wife: "When one of us dies, I'm going to live in Venice." It isn't easy to consider our not being. How dare the world imagine that it can do without us? Freud has argued that the unconscious cannot conceive of death at all, the cessation of consciousness. But this remark may be neither as interesting nor as profound as first appears. What he may have meant is something quite simple. When we try to imagine our lives without our being there, we are still very much present in the act of observing our absence. If Freud meant that the imagination cannot construe a world without its own presence, I think he is wrong about the imagination. Some imaginations can; some cannot, some will not, look at their own deaths.

We deceive ourselves on this. We scan the obituary pages with anxiety, noting particularly the ages of those who have died. It is with a feeling of achievement, or relief, that we find we are not listed there. We slow down on the highway when we pass a serious accident not because we are drawn to blood, but as a kind of assurance that we are not in the wreck. Seeing someone else wrecked improves our chances of avoiding trouble. Do we deny our mortality because we fear death?

Something peculiar is happening to death in America. It is becoming fashionable. Television covers it, talk-show hosts have become very sincere about it, we diet and run to avert it. It was not always so. Until just the other day, everybody told us we were a death-denying people. Jessica Mitford wrote a book telling us so, and we got used to being lectured at by civilized overseas types, explaining how our uncultured barbarism could be inferred from the business habits of some people in the funeral business. But today, denial is out and Woody Allen is in. Who bothers attacking funeral homes when there is real corruption to be found in Beirut, or Detroit, or Washington.

As a matter of fact, Mitford's *The American Way of Death* suggests a way to date the transiton from repression to chic. It was published in 1963, assuring us that Americans avoided death, and at the close of that year President Kennedy was killed in Dallas. Something about that assassination seemed to shatter our denials of death, and it indeed turned out to be but the first episode in a veritable pageant of public deaths that (at that time) made us think that something had become seriously undone in our national life. Then the pageant unfolded. Malcolm X was killed in 1965; Martin Luther King and Bobby Kennedy in 1968; Jimi Hendrix and Janis Joplin had their semi-suicides within three weeks of each other in 1970. There was Jackson State and Kent State, and there was Vietnam.

By the end of the 1960s, death had found its way into our living rooms, and deeply into the lives of our children, who were supposed to be unaware of such things. It was as if death itself were exacting a price for our old habit of ignoring it.

In Vietnam, America became a killer nation in a new way. We lost that war because we should have lost it. That war, the last part of the pageant of public death that began in Dallas, guaranteed that death would never again be the sole possession of the aging and the aged. It became a presence for us all, as children, parents, grandparents, shared a common climate. Death came no longer just from illness or accident; it came from the center of our political lives. To experience this pageant of death was to be reminded once again of the very great fragility of our civilization, so vulnerable not only to the weapons we are collecting, but to famine, pollution, climatic shifts, secular and sacred terrorism, and our own locally grown economic egotism and greed. Death became public and has remained so. Repression, even reticence, is gone. Death is equidistant from everyone—the young and the old, the rich and the poor, the healthy and the sick.

We no longer deny it; we talk about it, even chatter about it. We do not repress it, we are open, and this openness is said to be good for us. Perhaps, but things said to be good for us usually turn out not to be. We have been through this supposedly beneficent revolution before, this move from repression to openness, on the subject of sex, and it is not at all clear that our moral health was much improved. We now have the problems of openness instead of the problems of repression. Sex, in the open, has become something worse than vulgar; it has become both boring and politically dangerous.[4] Death in the open is at least as fashionable and as exciting as sex in the open, and I am proud to be able to report that in some parts of the Western United States death is known as the "ultimate high."

Cosy familiarity may be no better than repression as a way of managing our consenting to die. Fashionable chatter about death may be just one more protection against the serious business of facing it. We have received conventional wisdom from muckraking journalists, and more recently we have been intellectually insulted by psychologists playing with the new openness about death, assuring us that there is one right way to face our mortality—to "accept." The seriously ill must be guided along a spectrum from bad anger and rebellion to healthy and productive acceptance. The grieving should make the same move; so should we all. When I talk about consenting to die, I am not thinking of those strategies of acceptance sponsored by thanatologists like Dr. Elizabeth Kübler-Ross. She clearly has some very real clinical skills, but as a dogmatic moralist, manipulating us from rebellion to acceptance, she does not persuade. She may even be inadvertently sponsoring bad medicine. A study of breast cancer patients at Johns Hopkins Hospital established that responses to the disease of anger, anxiety, guilt and depression led to a longer life expectancy that did a response of acceptance beloved by our popular psychologies.[5]

We ought to feel that there is something unfair and inexplicable in every death before which the only decent response is anger and rebellion. When we truly consent to die, acknowledging our mortality, we do not deny such anger, we affirm it. Dylan Thomas cried out to his dying father, suddenly serene and pious on his death-bed:

> Do not go gentle into that good night,
> Old age should burn and rave at close of day;
> Rage, rage against the dying of the light.[6]

Such anger before death should not be demoted to the lowest level on some psychologist's scale. It is a good anger, and we all need it as part of our consent. The poet is a wiser guide than the thanatologist defending acquiescence because secular demands for submission to inevitability are as dangerous and corruptible as any reactionary–religious other-worldliness.

There is no paradox in insisting that consenting to die must include a raging against the dying of the light—all light, old and young, enemy and friend. Consenting to die, recognizing that we are neither immortal nor gods, can effect something both wonderful and strange. Such a consent can become the precise opposite of morbid. When we really come to acknowledge our mortal limit, the present moment is returned to us with a greater intensity and freshness than ever before. When we come to see that we do not have all time, the little we do have becomes more precious. We can learn to be suspicious of many of our (Protestant?) strategies of postponement, putting this or that off until some better time that we may never have, consigning the present to an emptied mediocrity.

Only when we perceive the transiency of things can we really value and enjoy them. How anti-platonic, even anti-Augustinian this is. Time and things do not lose their value by virtue of their impermanence, they achieve it. Our hearts are restless until they consent to their mortality. The great lesson of the knowledge of our mortality is this radical this-worldliness. The value of our death is not in the room it creates for others. It lies simply in being there at the end of our series, compelling us to attend passionately and carefully to the rest of the life we have left. There is not time enough for everything, but only for a few things, and the present is at hand for present service and enjoyment. You may say if you wish that this life is good because created by God, or you may more simply confess that consenting to die gives you back an elusive present. Consenting to die requires a high valuation of this life, and requires as well a rage against whatever vitiates this life: poverty, injustice, death. The this-worldliness inherent in our consenting to die has an interesting biblical source.

I

"I tell you we must die," Brecht and Weill sing. Yet, consenting to die, we must rebel against our deaths and against all in life that is death-dealing: pain, disease, injustice, and pious justification for them. Let us turn to the two most decisive death stories in our cultural history to see how they illuminate these tensions. The deaths of Socrates and of Jesus.

Simply as ways of dying they are strikingly different. Socrates's is courageous and impressive, worthy of imitation. Jesus, according to Mark, dies alone, deserted by his followers, in something like despair at the end. It would not occur to anyone,

Consenting to Die: A Meditation on Mortality 187

even to a Christian, to claim that this is a death for imitation. Jesus instructs in something other than the art of dying.

The records of both these deaths were assembled by devoted followers; they are interpreted history, shaped by believers. Yet it is still instructive to reflect on their differences.

In 399 B.C. Socrates was condemned to death by the Athenian court because of the effect his teaching was having on the young. Impiety or atheism was the charge, and when political power charges atheism it usually means "not believing in my gods." In Plato's dialogue, *Phaedo*, Socrates' attitude to death is given extended attention. Fear of death is never proper for the good man, he declares, for the only thing the good man has a right to be anxious about is doing good itself. There is a deep sense in which death, far from being an object of fear, is really the chief good and greatest blessing for Socrates, and it is important to see just why. Through Socrates, by way of the Orphic mystery cults, a profound suspicion of the body and life in the body was inserted into Western thought. Christianity picked up this suspicion from the platonic tradition, and to our day there are still some who deem this hostility uniquely Christian. It is, in fact, uniquely Socratic. For Socrates, the center of all war, all evil, all passion, was the human body. The body is the tomb, *soma-sema*, as the Orphic tag put it. The human body is imperfectly wedded to the eternal and immortal soul, defined as man's unique capacity to grasp eternal ideas of the good, the true, and the beautiful. The aim of philosophy itself is to separate by thought the good soul from the ponderous body. Death does in fact what philosophical thought attempts in theory. Philosophy *is* mediation on death, for in death the desired separation, only imperfectly achieved in life by contemplation and rationality, becomes the welcomed reality. The strange legacy of platonism is nowhere more obvious than here, at the point of its candid celebration of death as the pinnacle of both goodness and wisdom.

Socrates in prison, preparing to die, rejected all the proposals by his friends for escaping his legal fate. Suicide was ruled out because prohibited by the gods. He would not promise to stop teaching. This refusal, incidentally, was not a moral refusal based on conscience or freedom of speech. It was a religious decision: he had no choice but to refuse, he argued, because he never obeyed himself, only the god or *daimon* in him, and the *daimon* said "don't stop." The court's sentence of death, Socrates claimed, was a good, not an evil, because death itself is a good. Look at the alternatives, he said. Either there is nothing after death, and a perpetual sleep would surely count as a blessed relief, or one really does proceed to the house of Hades and face the judges there. Socrates has no fear of this journey to the underworld because he has a clear conscience—he had always done what the god told him to do. Proposals to save his life by escape from prison and flight from Athens he rejected on the interesting basis that even unjust laws are to be obeyed. No hero of civil disobedience.

Socrates' approach to his own death is thus composed of two elements, both of which are difficult for us to understand today. He is convinced of his soul's immortality, and he is persuaded of his own virtue. "I believe, my dear Simmias and Cebes," he declares, "that I shall pass over first of all to other gods, both wise and good; secondly to dead men, better than those in this world; and if I did not think so, I should do wrong in not objecting to death."

There is something in man that doesn't die. This is what immortality means in the Greek philosophical tradition. (In Christianity, this inherent deathlessness is not the primary meaning; central rather is the affirmation that death is not the end.) Immortality of the soul is a complex belief for Socrates, validated in two ways: religiously, when he says that his god has assured him of his own immortality, and philosophically, as analyzed in the *Phaedo*. In that dialogue immortality is grounded on the basic Socratic principle that all knowledge is recollection, and knowledge as recollection is proof for the Socratic belief in the pre-existence and eternity of the soul. The knowledge of geometry that Socrates is able to elicit from the untutored slave-boy Meno is knowledge that Meno received through the same soul in an earlier bodily existence. This soul, eternal both forwards and backwards, is the organ in man that receives the knowledge of the realm of ideas. The soul is strengthened by the good done in this life so that when judged in the kingdom of the dead, it will be more likely to be judged favorably.

Thus death for the good man, and preeminently for Socrates himself, is no evil to be feared, but a positive good to be welcomed. In prison at the close of his life, he rejects suicide, escape, compromise, and silence, taking the hemlock not just with serenity and confidence, but with an almost playful humor, utterly certain of his virtue and destiny. How shall we bury you, a sorrowing disciple asks.

> "How you like," said he, "if you catch me and I don't escape you." At the same time, laughing gently and looking towards us, he said, "Criton doesn't believe me, my friends, that this is I, Socrates, now talking with you and laying down each of my injunctions, but he thinks me to be what he will see shortly, a corpse, and asks, if you please, how to bury me! I have been saying all this long time, that when I have drunk the potion, I shall not be here then with you; I shall have gone clear away to some bliss of the blest, as they call it. . . ."

This is not a denial of death, but it is a denial of its tragic character. Not an enemy, but a friend. Not something to be redeemed from, but something that redeems. Socrates dies confident and merry, almost a martyr, if you define a martyr's death as that death for righteous cause that we desire to emulate.

Turning from the fourth century B.C. in Greece to the first century of the Christian era in the world of the eastern Mediterranean, and looking at the New Testament records of the death of Jesus, we find ourselves in the presence of a very different way of dying. I want to look particularly at two passages from the gospel according to Mark. This is the earliest of the gospels, but even so it represents a mixture of history and interpretation that is not easy to break apart. To the question: Do we have Jesus himself here, or Mark's Jesus? the answer is both, and just how they are to be distinguished is virtually impossible to be certain about. In Mark 14:32–42 there is an account of a bitter inner struggle undergone by Jesus as he faces the inevitability of his own death. This is how Mark records that scene in the garden of Gethsemane, the night before the crucifixion.

> And they went to a place which was called Gethsemane; and he said to his disciples, "Sit here, while I pray." And he took with him Peter and James and John, and began to be greatly distressed and troubled. And he said to them, "My soul is very sorrowful, even to death; remain here, and watch." And going a little farther, he fell on the ground and prayed that, if it were possible, the hour might pass from him. And he said, "Abba, Father, all things are possible to thee; remove this cup from me; yet not what I will, but what thou wilt." And he came and found them sleeping, and he said to Peter, "Simon, are you asleep? Could you not watch one hour? Watch and pray that you may not enter into temptation; the spirit indeed is willing, but the flesh is weak." And again he went away, and prayed, saying the same words. And again he came and found them sleeping, for their eyes were very heavy; and they did not know what to answer him. And he came the third time, and said to them, "Are you still sleeping and taking your rest? It is enough; the hour has come; the Son of man is betrayed into the hands of sinners. Rise, let us be going; see, my betrayer is at hand."

How different this is from Socrates' words about his own approaching death in the *Apology*. "I will tell you," Socrates says in this dialogue, "really this that has happened to me is good, and it is impossible that any of us conceives it aright who thinks it is an evil thing to die." In Jesus' Gethsemane prayer we find no Socratic serenity about the next world, no confidence in his own virtue, none of that untroubled acquiescence deemed desirable by some contemporary analysts of dying. Jesus rebels against the idea that his death should be taken as God's will. He asks that the hour of death not come, that the cup of suffering and death be removed. His own will and God's are at odds, and he says so, and only finally does he add that God's will and not his own should prevail. The scene is one of bitter conflict and, unlike Socrates, Jesus is utterly alone.

Mark's account of the actual moment of death presents a Jesus, if anything, even more anguished.

> And when the sixth hour had come, there was darkness over the whole land until the ninth hour. And at the ninth hour Jesus cried with a loud

Consenting to Die: A Meditation on Mortality 191

voice, "Eloi, Eloi, lama sabachthani?" with means, "My God, my God, why hast thou forsaken me?" And some of the bystanders hearing it said, "Behold, he is calling Elijah." And one ran and, filling a sponge full of vinegar, put it on a reed and gave it to him to drink, saying, "Wait, let us see whether Elijah will come to take him down." And Jesus uttered a loud cry, and breathed his last. And the curtain of the temple was torn in two, from top to bottom. And when the centurion, who stood facing him, saw that he thus breathed his last, he said, "Truly this man was a son of God!"

(15:33–39)

The final words of Jesus as recorded by Mark combine in an astonishing way both prayer and separation from God. "My God," Jesus cries out, as if the father were truly present; "why hast thou forsaken me?" as if the father were truly absent. No final word of acceptance here, rounding it out, making the death more psychologically attractive. Matthew, writing a little later, keeps close to Mark's account and includes the same cry of dereliction. But Luke and John are not content with the unresolved tensions in Mark. They omit the cry and add other words from the cross that turn the actual death into something closer to a triumph.

Socrates confidently expects his own immortality and successful weathering of the judgment in Hades. Jesus, according to Mark, does not appear to expect his own resurrection, nor did his disciples, who fled in despair the night before at the time of the arrest. It is true that earlier in Mark's gospel Jesus is recorded as predicting his own resurrection three times in the disciples' presence. But the record of Jesus' desolation and the disciples' despondent flight makes it difficult to accept these predictions as historically trustworthy. The devout hand of the early church should probably be discerned in them.

There is, of course, a resurrection at the end of Mark, but it is quite a different thing from Socratic immortality. Resurrection, in Christian belief, is given by God's grace and has nothing to do with a deathless soul. In Christian resurrection, death is total; all of man dies, body, mind, soul, and he is raised a whole man, body, mind, soul. Socrates reminded his friends that his corpse was not Socrates. Jesus' friends felt differently about him.

Another difference underlies these two deaths. In the Hebrew and the Christian traditions, the human body is part of the good creation. It is not exempt from the fall, but it is not the cause of it. Life in the body is good, not maimed or incomplete. It would be impossible to imagine Socrates talking about the body as the temple of the spirit, or the word becoming flesh. Disobedience and pride play the same role in the Hebrew and Christian traditions as the body plays in the Socratic–Platonic world. In the *Phaedo*, Socrates insists that the body is the source of all evil and distress. In Jesus' teaching, his most decisive moral indictments are directed towards sins of the spirit—hypocrisy and self-righteousness—not sins of the flesh. Towards these he is remarkably open and non-judgmental. Let him who is without sin. . . .

A final point of difference, though I am not sure just what it means. Jesus' death has rarely been taken as a marytrdom by Christians. A martyr is one whose death, after a certain kind of life, has a special visible and instructive character that makes us wish to emulate it. In that sense Socrates died a martyr; we found his death an admirable one. But Jesus does not so die, and whatever else they may say about Jesus' death, believers have never turned to it as a way of dying to be imitated: it is part of a larger story that speaks not of a martyr, but a savior, a redeemer, a lord. This redemptive context tends to shift the focus away from the actual moment of dying, and re-directs it in two ways: to God as the one who wills the death of the Son, who in fact may be said to kill the Son; and to the life and work of the one dead. Socrates didn't save or redeem anyone (except, perhaps, a few middle-class Frenchmen in the eighteenth century); he simply died well. Jesus didn't die well, but his redemptive death doesn't call attention to itself, but to the God who willed it.

It is nonetheless a death, both at Gethsemane and on the cross, that contains both rebellion and acceptance, though an acceptance far more anguished than Socrates' playful welcome of death as good friend. I don't mind citing that mixture of rebellion and acceptance as justification for my own claim that both moods belong in our attitudes to our own deaths. Resignation before the fact of mortality, this is what I am calling consenting to die, acknowledging our human limits, our nondivinity—but rebellion against particular deaths, our own, our loved ones, the aged, the useless, the famous and forgotten. Consenting to die is consenting to mortality, but we still must find our own way to rage against the dying of the light.

The contrasting shadows cast by these two ancient deaths do not overcome our ambivalence about mortality, but they do illuminate it (if shadows can be allowed to illuminate in the world of metaphor). If we choose to think about mortality, we soon discover there is no orthodoxy or heresy, no consensus, no right and wrong, no consistency. It looks as if we are bound to be open and reticent, rebellious and consenting afraid and unafraid.

II

Our century has finally received its proper name. It took some time. At my first World's Fair in Chicago in 1933, it was the Century of Progress. A war later, a poet christened us with "anxiety." Better, but not good enough. We are the century of death. Once whispered guiltily about, it is now shouted in the streets. The very events that have blasted death into the front of our minds are the events that justify our century's name.

We have just recently found our right name, but it was predicted early in the century. Viscount Grey of Fallodon looked out of his office window on the evening before the British declaration of war against Germany in 1914, and stumbled upon a very ancient metaphor for death: "The lamps are going out all over Europe; we shall not see them lit again in our lifetime." At just about the same time, in a poem about the death of God, Wallace Stevens in "Sunday Morning" prophetically stated that "death is the mother of beauty." And, in a work that has led Leonard Bernstein to refer to him as *the* musical prophet of our century of death, Gustav Mahler's massive Ninth Symphony (1910) was singing of many deaths: Mahler's own, along with the deaths of tonality, of culture, and of God.[7]

It is not only that we have killed more in this century than in all the others combined. It is not only the genocide. Death has taken over our language as well as our history; or better, has taken over our language because it has dominated our history. I am speaking of the persistence of the metaphor of death, of the omnipresence of the proclamations of the death-of-something. We speak about our times as we would speak about an end. We experience things in their absence. We actually kill and we actually die, and we make death into a favorite metaphor. The death of nearly everything has been announced. It matters little if the reports are validated or not. In our part of the century death is on our lips as well as in our organs and bloodstream. From the death of God and the death of the city, to the death of language and the death of psychoanalysis, the twentieth century has become the century of the death-metaphor.

In a way, "death" is only a metaphor expressing a certain kind of absence or loss. When we talk about, say, the death of God, we are not saying something utterly unlike what the mystics have said when they spoke of God's absence or silence or disappearance or eclipse. Perhaps the difference in metaphorical flavor is slight. These non-death words speak of absence, but of an absence that is expected to go away, an absence that will turn into presence if the seeker will but patiently wait. Out of the silence will emerge the word, the eclipse passes quickly, and the disappearance of God disappears. So to speak of the death of something is to speak about an absence a little more intensely. The loss or not-having lasts a little longer. It may last a part of a lifetime, a full lifetime, a generation, an epoch. If things like gods can die metaphorically, they can experience resurrections, metaphorically, as well.

We would not, of course, be dominated by this death-metaphor had we not experienced the peculiar and terrible historical reality of total death. The pervasive metaphor has come from the pervasive killing. Our contemporary history of death, that history that finally gave us our right name—what Robert Jay Lifton calls technological and absurd death—begins, I believe, with the reaction of the British air force to the German Luft-

Consenting to Die: A Meditation on Mortality   195

waffe's low-level bombing of unoccupied European towns and villages in 1940. This shattered the moral resistance of the British to bombing strategies with highly probable civilian involvement. Up to 1940 the Allies had believed that the air war could and should respect the distinction between civilian and combatant. But when the enemy showed such contempt for that distinction, respect for the distinction proved to be a military limitation, and strategic bombing began. It continued as a fundamental bombing strategy in Europe until the end of the war in 1945, and the American Air Force quickly went along with British practice. Loosening of moral constraints often takes place invisibly and necessarily. The enemy's initial practice functioned as sufficient mandate for the Allied side. The European air war from 1940–1945, and the dropping of the atomic bombs over Japan, constituted the Allied portion of the pattern of twentieth-century total death. To place these military strategies on a list that includes the death camps is not to suggest a similarity of culpability, but just to show the pattern of killing, ranging from the justifiable and necessary to the unbelievably criminal.

The death camps themselves remain the most unassimilated event of modern history. The struggle to answer the question "Why?" continues, long after the barbarian hypothesis has been abandoned. Indeed, as Richard Rubenstein and others have been persuasively reminding us, the death camps proceeded from the best things in our Western civilization, from our religion, from our organizational, technological, and scientific genius, from the very economic system that has so splendidly enriched a few in our time.

In addition to our continuing engagement with the historical questions, Christians and Jews have been drawn together in a new and serious attempt to determine whether any kind of meaning can be extruded from our new studies of the victims and the executioners. Given the death camps, what happens to theodicies, and gods, and indeed to any system claiming to offer historical meaning? How do Christians and Jews face each other in this dark shadow? How can those who were there speak to those who were not? How can those who essay explanation face those who are offended by explanation? The death camps are not all there is to the century of death, but they are the climax.

The bombs on Hiroshima and Nagasaki are a little alike, and utterly unlike the deaths of the Holocaust. I am not referring to difference in numbers. I am calling attention to the decision to drop the bomb; to that persistent belief in 1945, based on the best intelligence material we had, that the Japanese were not close to surrender, that religious–military fanaticism was not at all amenable to diplomatic rationality, and that without the atomic bombing of population centers, the Japanese empire could not be brought to surrender without a massive Allied invasion of the mainland at Tokyo Bay. General MacArthur and others were predicting that such an invasion could cost a million Allied lives.

I am a very untrustworthy witness on the subject of the morality of the dropping the bombs that ended World War II. I was in training for that Japanese invasion in the summer of 1945, brushing up on aircraft identification and gunnery so I could serve on the bridge of an aircraft carrier to make more rapid identification of kamikaze fighters than we had been able to do up to that point. And then the atomic bombs were dropped and the war was over and the invasion did not need to take place and I went home. When observers, younger than I, write about Hiroshima and Nagasaki, noting accurately the destruction it brought to life, property, genetic health, and ask from all Americans an unambiguous *mea culpa*, my inclination to join the criticism is tempered by the not at all irrational conviction that those atomic bombs may have saved this life, while they took the lives of so many others. This doesn't make me proud, but it does make me alive.

The bombs may not have been needed, revisionist historians assure us today. Fine; that is what historians are for, to remind us on how frail a basis so many of our most fateful political and military decisions are made. Let the bombs on Japan be part of the genocidal story, part of the century of death, but only amnesia or self-hatred will identify the ovens of Auschwitz with the mushroom clouds over Japan.

Consenting to Die: A Meditation on Mortality 197

If I have attempted a kind of exculpation of my own country for Dresden, even for Hiroshima, I cannot make any such attempt for the final item on our list describing the century of death, the war in Vietnam. This is still an undigested part of our recent past. Political discourse today is virtually silent about that war. No one remembers it, no one was to blame, and no one even apparently defended it at the time. Vietnam is still unatoned for; the nation's wounds inflicted on soldier and civilian both, though in greatly unequal amounts, have not been "bound up." Will it take us as long to begin to confront the effects of our Vietnamese adventure on our national life as it took us to face the consequences of that other unassuaged event in our past, the Civil War? Will it be a hundred years, once again, before we even look? The Watergate scandals followed hard upon the end of the war in Vietnam, and Watergate gave us just what we needed, a large, public event that was very easy to judge morally. It took no discrimination or courage to find Watergate and its participants contemptible. In our orgy of domestic self-criticism we forgot, perhaps with some relief, that war we lost and should have lost. And that war still festers in the land. None of the national leaders responsible for this episode have had to confront publically their criminal culpability. Some are dead; some are running foundations, teaching our young, writing books, living just off Fifth Avenue. When things are tight economically, only crime pays.

The participants in that war are beginning to write and their witness is proving utterly essential to the task of understanding and learning. Some films are beginning to appear. For the most part we still must depend on the journalism of the time. Here is a piece from *The New Yorker* that says most of what needs to be said about Vietnam's contribution to our understanding of death and to our citizenship in death's century.

> Our current bombing campaign in Indo-China is something new in the history of warfare. . . . our air force over Indo-China is the most powerful ever assembled in a single theatre of war, and the Indo-China theatre is a small one. Moreover, this latest form of intervention in the Indo-China war represents a culmination of our century's tendency

toward mechanized killing. In this campaign, the growing American official indifference to human life has come close to perfection. . . . Our new strategy has done away with one of the most fundamental restraints on warmaking. It used to be that those who would kill also had to be ready to die. Even large armies facing small armies knew this and felt it, and, by extension, the societies they belonged to knew it and felt it. There was a feeling of equality in the face of death in wartime which touched both sides and formed the basis for whatever codes of honor have appeared in war. The nearness and sureness of death gave war its solemnity, its feeling of great weight for an army or a people. It could not be undertaken casually—not for very long, anyway. But the present policy aims precisely at making the waging of war casual and acceptable. It confronts the innocent and the supposed foe alike with an army of machines, and rests on the assumption that although we don't like to die we don't mind killing. The war that this country's government is waging now is war trivialized. Never has a nation unleashed so much violence with so little risk to itself. It is the government's way of waging war without the support of its own people, and involves us all in the dishonor of killing in a cause we are no longer willing to die for.[8]

And so, the century of death, and particularly that definitive fragment of it we are recording here—from Dresden to Vietnam, 1940–1975—has significantly changed our lives by changing our consciousness of death. Those deaths are no longer private events, having to do with illness and aging, taking place in nursing home or hospital. Our deaths have become public and political. Strategies for postponing death now must go beyond diet, exercise, giving up smoking. Postponement of death has become the primary task of politics. If we decide to join the current bandwagon that deems politics impossible, institutions and nations unworkable, turning to domestic and private delights, then we will have capitulated to death without even a whimper. For in the century of death, it is not weapons that keep apocalypse at bay, it is rational discourse in the public arena. Whatever your favorite apocalyptic metaphor may be: nuclear annihilation, slow environmental poison, melting icecaps engulfing us, terrorism secular or sacred, death is no longer a matter just for the middle-aged and aging. It is equidistant from all of us, and from all continents. It could easily be total, and it could easily be tomorrow. We are just beginning to see that something utterly new has entered our lives, and we are just beginning to see our techniques of forgetfulness failing. Small wonder we no longer are able to be silent about death, why we chatter about it, and watch movies and plays and television that swallow it up. Thanatology is becoming our secular theology.

Thanatology as our theology leads to a final point. The public deaths of our century that have forced death out of the shadows into the full light of consciousness have removed something from that consciousness as well. They have removed God; almost, it would seem, they have caused the displacement of the experience of God by the experience of death. The century of death has seen the decisive triumph of the death of God or, more exactly, twentieth-century death has killed God by defining him as a killer.

How has this come about? The answer is simple, and terrible, and it gets us directly to the heart of that central spiritual event of our day, the death of God. Let us begin with the death camps as a definitive piece of our history—the deaths, at the hands of totalitarian power, of something like ten million Jews and non-Jews. Next let us turn to the Christian doctrine of God. What does God mean in the Christian tradition? Two elements must always be present when that question receives a responsible answer. The idea of God, if it is to remain recognizably Christian, must include both the idea of goodness or love and the idea of Providence, power, sovereignty, lordship. The Christian God both cares and effectively rules. You can, when you are dealing with the problem of suffering, shave a little from one of these two fixed points to protect the integrity of the other, but you cannot proceed very far along the road of compromise without leaving Christian territory. You might be tempted, for example, to insist on God's love as your single non-negotiable absolute, and ascribe all human and natural evil, say, to a Devil. God's love is saved, but his power is lost, and your consequent dualism might be fully consistent, but it would not be Christian, if God is only love without power. Or you might take the opposite tack: stay with Providence and power, ascribe everything (even the worst) that happens to him, and you have lost the goodness and love. The Calvinist tradition comes very near to this; so does Islam. Isaiah 45:7 permits it: "I form the light, and create darkness: I make peace, and create evil: I the Lord do all these things."

The death camps have happened in our history. We have argued that far from being eccentric and inexplicable they proceed from the very heart of Western values and in some ways they illuminate those values. The Christian idea of God, we have observed, contains the idea of Providence at its center. What exactly does Providence mean? It means that no event happens to man on the horizontal line of his earthly life that does not come directly from the hand, the will, the purpose of God. All events, of course, have their full complement of worldly causes—historical, psychological, all the rest. Providence does not deny these, it simply adds another interpretive story on top of the horizontal one. You can never be out of God's hands. In prosperity, in adversity, in the best and worst of times, he is not only present, he had directly sent you whatever it is that has defined your prosperity and adversity. To confess Providence is to confess an absolute security—there is no escape from the direct causal presence of God.

He has, therefore, caused, sent, and willed the mass murders of the mid-twentieth century. The doctrine of Providence, and therefore a true Christian doctrine of God, must not shrink from this. Evasions can be found, of course, but they all cut too deeply into the power or the love of God. Some say that God permits but does not will, or that he does not will everything but wills something in everything, or that he wills all our adversity for our own good, for discipline and the perfection of our characters. Dietrich Bonhoeffer has uttered perhaps the most radical rejection of Providence and thus of the Christian doctrine of God of any of the great modern theologians: "only the suffering God can help."

Applied to the event of the death camps, the Christian doctrine of Providence makes a choice. It chooses to remain with its central message of the sovereignty of God, and in so doing it transforms the character of that sovereign into that of a brutal and capricious killer. The intersection of the century of death and Christian Providence has made God into a monster. A monster in control, but monster nonetheless.

This is what it means to identify the century of death with the death of God. Our century has been able to hold on to the Christian God only by insisting that he wills, wants, causes the mass death. It has defined him, if he is indeed in control of his world, as evil, as himself deserving of death. What has "died" in the death of God is the possibility of a dialectic between power and love in the face of the horror of our times that can remain recognizably Christian. Death of God means that God, if alive, is evil, and that human compassion and liberation require his removal. The death of God in the twentieth century, clarified by the century of death, has made the identity of God and death inevitable. Thanatology has become theology because God has become death.

III

The mystery of mortality is not exhausted by reflection on how we ought to receive our own deaths. Death is not only something that happens; for which we wait, in courage or fear, rebelling or accepting, making metaphors to hold it at arm's length. Death is also something we inflict on others, something we do. Consenting to kill is part of our consenting to die.

These are the death-inflicting activities I have in mind: killing in self-defense, euthanasia, killing in a just war, abortion, capital punishment, tyrannicide, martyrdom, and suicide. Suicide I want to look at in the next section of this essay; the others I will deal with here. Each entails a killing, or something like a killing, that is both legally and socially mandated. But the odd fact is that few of us are consistent in our responses to these activities, and it may be there is no reason we ought to be. Supporters of capital punishment are often opposed to abortion, and vice versa. Unless we are willing to claim that life must never be taken in any circumstances, this world of mandated killing is a morally messy one.

Our legal system allows killing in self-defense. It is important that our law enforcement officers have, and are known to have, the right to use force in their own defense. Of course, some ethical systems (the Sermon on the Mount comes to mind) prohibit retaliation in one-to-one relationships, and thus would not allow killing in defense of self or loved one. But my point here is not the obvious one that absolute norms are frequently irrelevant to public policy. It is this: when our codes and customs justify self-defensive actions that include inflicting violence and the taking of life, our attitudes to our own deaths become subtly changed. We have become killers; there are times when we may kill, even when we ought to kill. This is what I mean by death as something we not only suffer but do.

Euthanasia for the terminally ill is a topic in the forefront of contemporary discussion and by now most of us know how to distinguish the passive from the active, deciding not to take a particular heroic life-maintenance strategy as against actually terminating some system of life-support. Both kinds of activity are said to be common in hospitals, with or without the consultation of family, patient, and medical, legal, and religious interests. Written statements, living wills, are coming to be used to validate such decisions. Decisions for euthanasia are decisions to let die, and there is not a vast moral difference between letting die and killing. Such decisions, even if we grant their validity under some conditions, need some deep patterns of deterrence to keep them from becoming casual or corrupt. Respect for life is one such deterrent, and fear of malpractice suits is perhaps even a better one. If we know that there can be such a thing as arbitrary, exhausted, depressed, greedy, and corrupt kinds of medical and family interventions into a patient's life, and if we are sensitive to all the moral and human controls and limits, then we may well decide that love itself may lead to some forms of euthanasia. If we say this, we must also say the next thing, that in euthanasia love can lead to the willingness to kill.

Killing in a just war is a moral problem, of course, only for the non-pacifist. The absolute pacifist, who can be secular or religious, speaks his "no" against any kind of participation in any war, whether it be a relatively decent one like World War II was believed to be, or a corrupt and corrupting one like our invasions in Vietnam and southeast Asia. Incidentally, one of the most acute tensions between the generations today is precisely at the point of this idea of a just or moral war. Many young men and women today, whose idea of war has been shaped by Vietnam, cannot understand why their parents and teachers will not join them in opposition to all war. The parents have a different model, one in which resistence to obvious tyranny was not only permitted but required. We may not in fact have been saving Western civilization when we fought, but we did not laugh when we were told we were, and it is barely possible that we were. It may be that war will not become inconceivable until the last veteran of that war is dead, or Hitler is forgotten, whichever comes last.

Moral discourse justifying war, one form of which is the just war theory, goes back a little before Pearl Harbor. It goes back at least to Augustine, and it is developed with great care throughout the medieval period. We should recall some of the traditional marks of the just war, even if only to suggest that no conceivable war in our time, with our weapons, could meet those tests of justice. If the absolutists are indeed right and if there can indeed be no justifiable wars any more, then we are in some trouble. Moral discourse will have lost a very valuable piece of middle ground, where each war as it emerges into possibility can be studied both with moral sensitivity and realism. If moralists can only say "no" to the wars of today and tomorrow, then there is no possible discourse between morality and the realities of power—such as just war theories provided—and morality becomes what corrupt power and corrupt defenders of realism have always claimed, an irrelevant, civilian luxury, worthy of being ignored or devoured by our defenders of self-interest and self-aggrandizement.

A just war, traditionally, was one in which the distinction between civilian and combatant could be made and respected in the waging. Killing, other tests for justice permitting, could only be done to combatants, defined as those on the other side out to kill you. This test practically merges with the traditional justifications for killing in self-defense. Civilians no, combatants yes, and until yesterday such a distinction was possible. Today it surely is not. When we went to strategic bombing in the European theater in 1940 we moved to obliterate the distinction. In Vietnam, our infantrymen found it quite impossible to distinguish between civilian and combatant, because in fact there often was no distinction. The guerrilla fighters of the north were fighters during the day, civilians at night. Some civilian criticism of our soldiers' action in southeast Asia forgets how devastating it was to be unable to discern the difference between enemy fighter and enemy non-fighter.

Another test for a just war is that it must be one that resists aggression. Governments often feel the force of this tradition, even when they have no intention of respecting it. When we couldn't discover solid enough an aggression to justify our deepening involvement in Vietnam in 1964, we invented one and called it the Tonkin Gulf incident. If resistance to aggression is required for a war to be just, and if there was a just war anywhere in southeast Asia in the 1960's and 1970's, it can be argued that North Vietnam's response to our aggression was just.

A just war, the tradition states, must enforce justice and must be in obedience to lawful authority. This latter category was designed by the moralists to exclude local and regional feuds from the sanctioned category. It is interesting to look at this category of lawful authority in relation to the Vietnamese war. Some of the strongest anti-war voices of the 1960's rejected the war by rejecting the legitimacy of the authority that had "declared" it. It was illegal, undeclared, unconstitutional, because no constitutional body formally declared it, and illegitimate authority ought not to be obeyed. Both Wayne Morse and Noam Chomsky, so different in their attacks on that war—Morse so much the law-school dean, Chomsky the academic moralist—based their rejection on this moral-legal point.

It is our weapons that make the phrase "just war" such an

Consenting to Die: A Meditation on Mortality 205

incredible one today. We work to avoid conflict not because our moral categories can't find a war to fit them, but because we are afraid of being destroyed. This legitimate self-interested fear of incineration, not moral scruple, has kept us recently from global military adventure. As a nation, indeed, America actually may be becoming less aggressive, less inclined to impose its will by force (though Latin America may be an exception to that hope). It is with great relief that we watch the end of America in its original sense, the eschatological nation, the city on a hill, the beginning of the last days, that mystical union that shall not perish from the earth. This theological nation, armored in Christian self-righteousness, itself part of the great drama of salvation, not needing but bearing salvation—it was this nation that went to war in southeast Asia. The defeated nation that came home from that wreck, secularized, weaker, less expansionist, is a safer nation—safer to the rest of the world, less destructive. At last we may be willing to confess that we are not part of God's redemptive plan, but just a nation, like any other. More secular, we are less sure of bearing God; weaker, we are less likely to kill for God and for our ideas of what other peoples' freedom should be.

The just war tradition may have lost some of its power of discerning the distinctions between permitted and forbidden wars, and many may feel, given our instruments of genocide, that no war at all can conceivably be "moral" in our time. But that tradition was, and still is, a great one because it tried to think unsentimentally about matters of great concern. I do not believe our weapons can prevent us from the moral task. I would not support a war to rescue the oil states of the Persian Gulf from external aggression, but I would certainly support a military response to a non-nuclear attack on my own nation. So long as such distinctions still can be made, war is still a possibility and should be. If some conceivable wars are politically possible, then some can be deemed more moral or less immoral than others. Our moral defenses of war in the days to come, even when less self-righteous and more tentative than before, will be defenses of killing, and of killing that cannot always be limited.

To consent to the possibility of war, is to consent to kill, and to a killing that could lead to genocide.

In placing abortion on a list of activities implying a consent to kill, I wish to stop short of any rhetorical identification of abortion with murder. I support full freedom of choice on the abortion question, partly because of a deep distrust of many forms of opposition to that freedom: celibate males with no economic anxiety, so certain of abortion's immorality, seem to me perfect contemporary models of Christian immorality. But I am convinced, as some defenders of abortion appear not to be, that a decision for abortion is a morally serious one. The choice for it must be as uncoerced as possible, free from pressures from guilty potential father or shame-ridden parent. It is serious because, unlike the decision for birth control, it has to do with both life and death. This is the truth hidden in the error of the most strident anti-abortion pickets, for all their anger, intolerance, and middle-class complacency.

If the discussion about abortion is vitiated by an identification of abortion and murder, it is possible to imagine a definition of it that might be assented to by both parties in the bitter debate. Would not both sides agree that conception is the start of a process that can end in birth? From conception forward there is at least the potential for life, whether or not we go on to say that there is life itself present. Decision for abortion is decision to arrest a potential process. It is therefore about life and death, even if we stop short of naming it a killing. This minimal definition permits us to avoid the vexing question about the viability of the fetus, the question about the origin of the soul, and we have not even needed to call upon "the sanctity of human life," that splendid phrase of such marvellous generality that no one can ever be found to deny it.

I think there is a flaw in the positions of both pro- and anti-abortionists today. The anti-abortionists fail the test of tolerance whenever they seek more than their own rights to believe and to practice. This willingness to take away the freedom of those they disagree with is so serious that it virtually destroys their claims to moral leadership. Ideologues can always be found who glibly assure us that tolerance is the virtue of people who don't believe in anything. But in our increasingly nasty, polarized, and vicious ideological nation, that soft voice enjoining tolerance must continue to be spoken. It need hardly be observed that conservatives are not the only ones who systematically fail this test.

The flaw of the pro-abortionists (one of the sure signs of the death of language is the way we have allowed this issue to be described as "pro-life" against "pro-choice"; who could possibly be against either?) is less dangerous and more interesting. (The flaw may be an inevitable one in a particular stage in the women's movement.) The defender of abortion tends, I think, to misunderstand the human body, to tumble—perhaps inadvertently—into an unacceptable psychological dualism. A split, an alienation, of the body from the self. Notice how the language goes. I insist on having control over my own body. I am free to do with it, or to it, what I wish. The claim of freedom in such language is not false, but the latent dualism surely is. I mean the implication of such language that "I" is pure mind or will, and that this "I" carries around a body, a kind of thing or machine or "it" that the "I" is free to use as the "I" chooses. Not "I am a body" but "I have a body." The body is not me, or part of me; it is something outside me. Lurking in the shadows of this language in defense of abortion lies the Cartesian ghost in the machine or worse, Socrates' Orphic religiosity preferring spirit to evil flesh. Such language has trouble taking the body seriously because it does not see the body as part of the self. Perhaps feminism's deep-rooted rejection of what it calls Freud's anatomical bias is behind this dualistic–spiritual rejection of the body.

The decision for abortion, having to do with life and death, is a decision that has to do with that consenting to kill that I am examining.

Capital punishment is another issue at the center of journalistic, moral, and political discussions today that is related to the problem of permitted killing. It is interesting to note that language against capital punishment is rarely moral. It is more often secular, social, political, and it is often about matters of fact. The fact of deterrence, for example. Does capital punishment deter capital crime? Much of the debate reduces itself to that question. The answer appears to be "no," but we cannot be sure. Murder is frequently committed in the grip of irrational passion, or under alcohol's influence. In such cases, rational calculation about deterrence is not likely to be present. Some even argue that capital punishment might even encourage capital crime under certain conditions. When a witnessed murder is committed, then reflected on, the murderer may feel that his escape from the consequences of his crime will be more likely if the witnesses are also killed. A recent study of executions in New York State between 1907 and 1965 showed that in the month following each execution there was an average of two more murders than normal.

Beyond the inconclusive argument about deterrence lie other arguments. Does society belong in the vengeance business? Our legal systems are not so flawless that mistaken verdicts are inconceivable; innocent men have been executed. Imprisonment, at least, is revocable. There is finally an interesting political argument against capital punishment that has been especially active since World War II, and that seems to surface whenever our own rulers seem to go beyond ordinary ineptness to something more dangerous. In the past fifty years, this argument runs, state crimes have been more heinous than individual ones. Therefore, we certainly do not want to place capital punishment in the hands of a nation that might not be averse to using such a legal means of disposing of dissent. We should not only be reflecting on the fascist and communist totalitarianisms of past history, but of those more recent visions of America, held by Mr. Nixon and Mr. Reagan and some of their friends, that showed no anxiety about compassing the violation of both moral and legal norms.

If one is to oppose capital punishment, it is well not to oppose it just because it entails killing, unless one is willing to reject all other activities implying consent to kill.

We may seem to many to be too soft on killing. Only with

capital punishment do I come even close to wanting something like absolute prohibition. There is even a kind of murder, and one not mitigated by accident or self-defense, that belongs on my permitted list. I am thinking of tyrannicide, of the extent of our right to kill unjust or wicked rulers. I am thinking of our own rulers, I should add, and not of some C.I.A. incursion into someone else's politics. There is a strong tradition of Christian political theology, stemming largely from Paul's infamous thirteenth chapter of the epistle to the Romans, that suggests that even unjust rulers should be obeyed. The Lutheran tradition tilts toward uncritical obedience slightly more than the Calvinist, as any student of anti-Naziism can bear witness. During the resistance movement in World War II, it was not a matter of simple obedience, or flight, it was often a question about the legitimacy of murder, murder of the tyrant and of his surrogates. Many Christian, and others, wrestled grimly with this issue: if disobedience to unjust rulers is rarely allowed, what does this mean about murder? Is the killing of a tyrant justified only when it is during a war, borrowing the justifications of killing that war grants? It was understandable and right that the Christians and non-Christians in the plot against Hitler's life had to overcome a deep resistance to murder. But they did overcome it; the act was seen not as a tragically necessary evil, but as a liberating good. It failed, and hundreds of the finest men of Europe died as a result. To read the story of the resistance is to hope one would have had the courage to be with them.

No student of the *Oresteia* will make facile statements about justifiable homicide, ever. Orestes chose to kill his mother, urged on by a bloodthirsty Apollo, and yet in that act of violence he broke the chain of violence binding the house of Atreus. His violence destroyed violence because he hesitated before he killed. In that hesitation, the killing became a crime of reflection, not of passion; a rational act in which the results were foreseen. Today our magistrates are neither Clytemnestra nor Hitler. They are benign, and we can deal with them with strategies far milder than tyrannicide: ignoring, laughing, voting them into oblivion. But we have no guarantees that Clytemnestras and Hitlers may not visit us again. When they do, there should be some who care so little for themselves and so much for others that they will dare to run the risks of tyrannicide, that form of consenting to kill of which our moral approval should be far more than grudging.

Finally, a word about that special form of suicide, martyrdom, in which I choose my death and choose something that transcends my death at one and the same time. Is there anything worth dying for in a world with nothing, save a few loved ones, worth living for? Among the most alluring of the dissenting opinions of Justice Holmes was his frequently-uttered remark that the finest thing a man could do was to die for a cause he didn't believe in. Clever as an attack on patriotic moralism, charming in its skepticism, but insensitive and vulgar when read in the light of the veteran of the war in Vietnam.

In our wars, even in the recent nasty ones, we reserve our highest honors, our Congressional Medals, for those who throw themselves on a grenade, dying to save the lives of a few. Are such deaths martyrs' deaths? What do we learn from them? How do they instruct? Perhaps two kinds of martyrdom should be distinguished: those that take a death they cannot avoid and turn it into a death that instructs. Dietrich Bonhoeffer's death at the hands of the Nazis in 1945 was of this kind. Or, one may choose a death that could have been avoided, and the refusal to escape becomes part of the instruction the martyrdom offers. Socrates' death was like this. Jesus' death was not exactly a suicide, and martyr is not a term usually applied to him, at least by Christians. But part of any full understanding of his atoning death, as it is called, must include the fact that he died in part because he chose to, because he chose to go to the city where he knew the hostility was intense. Partly suicide, partly martyrdom, after all.

It has been argued that the deepest moral obliquity of the German death camps was not simply that lives in such incredible numbers were taken. Something almost more precious than life was taken—the possibility of dying visibly in the presence of a human community that might learn from the dying. The Nazis not only took lives, they took the possibility of martyrdom away. Both the actual deaths and their anonymity and invisibility define the unique evil of the Holocaust. When we think of ways in which we consent to kill, we must think of gods, and saviors, and martyrs. I wonder if we want to live in a world where martyrdom is impossible, or unintelligible. Perhaps we already do. A world with room for martyrdom is a world in which consenting to kill ourselves for something beyond ourselves may be part of our full consenting to die.

IV

Suicide, like the world it would escape, is too much with us. Teen-age suicides ebb and flow like fashions in dress. The elderly, faced by the shadow of irreversible illnesses like Alzheimer's disease, seek suicide as a plausible release from a life of loneliness and dependency. Even pre-pubescent children, once thought to be immune, are now attempting suicide, and sometimes succeeding.

Religious, moral, and social constraints have weakened, present just faintly enough to create guilt in the survivors. None of us can be as clear as the suicidal Hamlet that the Almighty has fixed his canon 'gainst self-slaughter. So we are rediscovering the rational suicides of the Greek and Roman worlds, and contemporary suicide is taking on, apparently like death itself, an almost smiling face. Not a crime or a sin, but an eloquent problem-solver. After all, the very medical skills that prolong our lives are also prolonging our terminal illnesses. When medicine does finally discontinue its last attack on our last illness, we turn to palliatives. Why, we ask, should a drugged, nauseated, semi-comatose "life" be our only option? The Hemlock Society, whose membership list has grown past 10,000, answers: "Good life, good death through control and choice."

Even our good friend "the media" have taken to selling suicide as a courageous choice. In the fall of 1979 a play by Brian Clark called "Whose Life Is It Anyway?" opened on Broadway (and later, as a movie). A decent enough play, made better than it deserved by a bravura performance by Tom Conti as Ken, the young sculptor who ruptured his spinal column in a motorcycle accident and who, as the play opens, is alive but paralyzed from the neck down.

Ken decides he does not want to live, and he requests discharge from the hospital. The chief surgeon refuses on the grounds that Ken would be dead in a week without his support systems. Exactly, Ken replies; that is what I intend. The play is a study of the impact on others of Ken's desire to carry out his project of active euthanasia. That desire is consistently portrayed as courage, while those who oppose Ken are uniformly bewildered, foolish, or evil.

Ken tells us that he does not want to live because what is left to him is not life. He can no longer do what he wants to do, sculpture and orgasm, primarily. Nor does anyone in the play give Ken an intelligent reason to stay alive, as if any argument against suicide were hopelessly out-of-date and unworthy of respect. The anti-suicide forces are arrogant or inept. The surgeon fights the discharge request because he is by oath committed to the preservation of life, and this Hippocratic loyalty is made to appear insensitive. The doctor further argues that Ken is not medically competent to make the decision to terminate treatment, and besides, anyone wanting to commit suicide is probably clinically depressed and so should be enjoined from doing so. Ken reports on the incredible contribution of the (invisible) hospital chaplain to the debate: Ken should be happy to stay alive, the chaplain is reported to have advised, so he can serve as a vessel into which people could pour their pity. Thus the anti-suicide forces are represented by the arrogant doctor who saved his life and doesn't want his surgical handiwork wiped out and a theological argument from what must surely be the most incompetent hospital chaplain in twentieth-century literature.

A legal procedure is finally assembled in Ken's room, and a kindly judge finds that the law does in fact give Ken the right to request discharge and thus to will his own death. The moment the judge finds for Ken, the audience (the night I was there) broke into applause, identifying with the courageous hero choosing suicide against arrogant medicine and inept religion.

Consenting to Die: A Meditation on Mortality 213

With the subject of death becoming chic, suicide was bound to follow suit. I must confess to a touch of uneasiness with this movement towards acceptable suicide, suicide with a friendlier face. Since Émile Durkheim at the end of the last century, the subject of suicide has been in firm control of the specialists; the sociologists first (suicide virtually invented sociology); and, shortly after, the psychoanalysts. Both professions have of course done able and humanitarian work in both classification and treatment. Durkheim's three-fold distinction is still useful: suicide as egoistic, when one is lonely and isolated, insufficiently integrated into society, in need of attention or help (explaining, therefore, why Protestant countries have more suicide than Catholic); as altruistic, when one is too fully absorbed in a group (the Buddhist monks in Vietnam twenty years ago); as anomic, when there has been a great change or loss in life. The contribution of psychoanalysis dates from a symposium on the subject in Vienna in 1910. It was there that Wilhelm Stekel uttered what is still an abiding presupposition of the psychoanalytic approach: "No one kills himself who does not wish to kill another." Suicide, thus, is saying to someone, "You'll be sorry." Incidentally, this is not a debate between a social science that insists that suicide springs only from a sick society and a medical science claiming a more psychological source. Suicide can be anomic for the sociologist, and Stekel at least discerned the dyadic nature of many suicides.

It appears, finally, that we often kill ourselves to show that we do in fact have some residual control over our own lives, to show that we are free and not bound. In the midst of the pointlessness of modern life we take up weapons against ourselves as if to say, "You see, I can do something right." The last way of bringing order to a life of disorder; we order by ending.

In the midst of this new openness, and all of these plausible explanations and defenses, I still think it may be worth looking for a language with which to speak a modest dissuasive word to suicide, though I am not at all sure that such a word exists apart from the traditional religious one. I cannot wholly applaud the disappearance of the taboos, the loosening of the constraints. In that Broadway theater, I found myself uneasy with the audience's instinctive reaction to the play's climax, in which the charming egoist, deprived of orgasm, should be accounted a hero because he wanted to die. I am no sociologist or psychoanalyst; moralist or theologian, if anything, and I am not at all sure that dissuasives are possible. But neither am I sure that the more suicide is tolerated the more civilized the society. I do not believe that all words spoken against suicide can automatically be labelled superstition. I am not even sure that "rational suicide" is a particularly useful phrase, since we have learned so much in our time about how deeply irrational our rationality can be.

Is there a way of speaking against suicide that does not depend on religious prohibition? I am not looking for a paragraph that can be printed on a card and handed to anyone who happens to be standing on a building ledge. Insofar as many suicides are prepared at a deeply non-rational level, rational discourse—what I am calling a dissuasive—can be singularly ineffectual. In his fine book on suicide, Alvarez argues that all suicides are impervious to solace.[9] Very well. Then I must offer my post-Christian (and post-existentialist) dissuasive not to an impervious individual, but to the idea of acceptable suicide as it is taking shape in our own strange time. Suicide is not only a problem to be sociologically understood and psychoanalytically cured, it is a power each of us possesses, a unique mark of our humanity, and therefore a proper subject for us all.

If the disappearance of God lies behind the loosening of the constraints against suicide, then we may no longer put all of our trust in religious argument. If God is silent or dead, the warning not to play God is gratuitous. That argument went like this: the length of our days is not in our control; to take our own life is to deny God's purpose, and in effect to blaspheme. I suspect many of the traditionally religious have become aware of the insufficiency of this argument. It really can work only if you grant that the beginning of life is wholly in God's hands as well. Birth control has introduced an element of choice at the beginning of life. Why should not the same choice be permitted at life's

Consenting to Die: A Meditation on Mortality 215

closing? Is there any other language to be uttered against suicide, or are we doomed to accept the new tolerance?

The language of the new tolerance merits brief notice. It often goes something like this: "We must be willing to take full responsibility for the whole spectrum of our lives, their beginnings, their durations, their endings." Now ignoring the slight flavor of a *Psychology Today* editorial or a guest specialist on *The Phil Donahue Show*, this is generally unobjectionable democratic–secular language of responsibility and freedom from moral tyrannies. Yet two things should be noted. First, this is not inadequate because it disenfranchises the gods and surrogate gods seeking to impose their moral wills upon us: presidents, parents, priests, and so forth. Our lives are our own to make or mar, and I shall not argue otherwise. Second, this tolerant language about suicide has a darker, more "California" or Yuppie side. It not only abolishes the gods in favor of a proper autonomy, it also abolishes the brother, the neighbor in need. This language defending civilized suicide is a language incapable of ethics, a language suitable for no community larger than can be inserted into a hot tub. Any new dissuasive language must find a way of saying that life is not something the individual is utterly free to reject, even though he has come of age and the gods have fled. The individual's right to take his own life should be no different and no greater than his right to take the life of another. Both are lives; the distinction between mine and thine does not change the fact that suicide is killing, a form of murder. This is the truth behind the medieval Christian conviction that suicide is a sin because it violates the Commandment "Thou shalt not kill." Affirming that we are responsible for ourselves does not mean that we live outside any moral or social context. If the defender of rational suicide insisting on human responsibility really means "I am responsible only for myself, and no one is responsible for me," what can we say to him? Is the privatist in the hot tub indeed the moral wave of the future?

The beginning of an answer might go like this. To be sure, we can no longer say with John Calvin, "*nostri non sumus . . . sed Dei,*" there is yet a post-Christian sense in which our lives do not wholly belong to ourselves. Human survival, if not the gods, permits us to say that we belong not just anywhere we fancy where we don't happen to be hurting anyone too greatly, but at some point or place in the worlds of work and love where we can be of use, at the service of somebody's need, making something beautiful or useful, telling an honest truth, relieving suffering and pain, laughing in spite of everything. The death of God does not abolish the neighbor, it brings him to the fore.

Some brief historical remarks may be in order. Plato, and later the Stoics and Epicureans, argued that when life becomes intolerable, either because of disease or constraint, suicide is not only a permitted but a rational act.

The New Testament does not appear to oppose suicide; that of Judas can be construed as an act of repentance. But by the beginning of the fifth century, largely because of Augustine's brilliant syncretistic assembling of practical–political, classical, as well as biblical arguments, an ethic against suicide began to take shape in Christian Europe. It had four main parts.

Political—No private citizen is allowed to take the life of a guilty person on his or her own initiative. This is the business of the courts, civil or ecclesiastical. The suicide is by definition guilty, and thus this law applies to him. This is a strained interpretation of a principle designed to control anarchy, and of course it is profoundly conservative, defending the legitimacy of established legal institutions.

Biblical–legal—"Thou shalt not kill" refers to any life, your own or another's, and suicide is thus a form of murder, prohibited by the commandment. This is, incidentally, the only biblical component in the emerging ethic.

Stoic—The noble and devout soul must learn to bear his own suffering; to try to escape it is weakness, the opposite of courage, that classical virtue also cherished by Christians. There was a Christian form to this argument: sufferings are deserved because of our sin, and they can be fruitful as discipline for character.

Eschatological—Suicide, defined as sin by the commandment

Consenting to Die: A Meditation on Mortality 217

against killing, is in fact a far more serious sin than any conceivable sin you might escape by killing yourself. It is more serious because it is a sin that cannot be repented of, for repentance must follow sin, and nothing earthly can follow suicide. Without repentance, every successful suicide condemns himself to eternal damnation.

Institutional Christianity officially comes out against suicide in the sixth century, and in spite of the Greek elements in the emerging ethic, it really was something new in European thought—that life is good because it is a gift created by God, living man being made in the divine image. To kill the self is to kill the divine image, the gift, and in some way to kill the giver, God himself, This is why it is seen as the deepest blasphemy, worthy of damnation. It is not so much that suicide plays God, but that he kills him. Suicide, I suspect, even today can never shake its religious character.

Exceptions to this ethic of prohibition soon emerge, mostly from the world of monasticism. How can martyrdom be accorded the highest honor if the prohibition against taking your own life is too strenuously enforced? How can we prohibit suicide and still honor that life lost because of excessively enthusiastic monastic privations? How can we honor the maiden who takes her life to protect her virginity? The Middle Ages, even while working toward a profound ethic of the sanctity of life, still could not shake loose from that strange Christian fascination for death as something truly marvellous because it is a portal to a real life lying beyond. Nor could the medieval mind, devising exceptions, resist that growing hostility to the body and to sexuality emerging concurrently from Augustinian thought and monastic practice.

With the Renaissance, a return to Greek and Roman tolerance was to be expected. For Montaigne, suicide is a subject to be discussed, not a sin or a crime. John Donne reflects his own pre-conversion melancholy in his defence of suicide in *Biathanatos*. Shakespeare does not seem to condemn his suicides at all:

not the love deaths of Romeo and Juliet; not the suicides of Brutus and Othello, marks of their nobility and honor.

The Christian argument against suicide, even though qualified by the death-laden and anti-sexual bad conscience of parts of medieval Christianity, has a profound truth embedded in its now inaccessible and eschatological language: that life has been given to us, and that our freedom to end it has profound ethical limitations. We are not our own. On that point, the post-Christian wishing to speak against suicide and the Christian can agree.

Today we live in both worlds: the world of Renaissance tolerance and the world of Christian prohibition. Pieces of both worlds show themselves when we find ourselves adopting the protective fallacy (like the doctor in the play) that insists that all suicides are in fact insane at the moment the act is committed. This is a form of rejection, and therefore Christian. But behind this fallacy is the even deeper illusion, more Renaissance–liberal than Christian, that the natural state of man is sane rationality.

In Albert Camus' *The Myth of Sisyphus*, the existentialist tradition uttered its distinctive word against suicide. Camus' essay is a mixture of medieval prohibition and Renaissance tolerance, of theological earnestness and rebellion against the gods. As argument, it is not particularly rigorous; as essay, it is suggestive. Camus starts with three presuppositions, stated rather than defended, and from them his rejection of suicide follows: we must reject all the gods, we must hate death, and we must invest whatever passion we have in life itself. Camus' anguished persistence in holding on to life itself, for all its meaninglessness, is as far from our contemporary civilized friendship with suicide as is the medieval Christian ethic of prohibition. Suicide is a temptation, Camus suggests, when life becomes too much, when both God and meaning have withdrawn. What he contributes to the current discussion is to sever the logical nexus between the perception that life has no meaning and that life is not worth continuing. His argument is not that life is not absurd. It is, but absurdity need not lead to suicide.

Nadezhda Mandelstam has movingly written about the relationship of suicide to modern totalitarianism, the context from which Camus' perception of the absurdity of existence emerges.

> The thought of this last resort had consoled and soothed me all my life, and often, at times when things were quite unbearable, I had proposed to M. [her husband, the poet Osip Mandelstam] that we commit suicide together.[10]

She is insisting on her right, like the Greek, Roman, and Renaissance traditions before her, to control her own life. Her husband always rigorously rejected her proposal, with the words: "Life is a gift that nobody should renounce," and, most interestingly, "Why do you think you ought to be happy?" Nadezhda becomes persuaded by her husband's refusals that there may be something persistently true, beyond the incredible theological form, in the Christian prohibition. Mandelstam's query "Why do you think you ought to be happy?" is equivalent to Camus' argument that there is no necessary link between absurdity and suicide. Meaninglessness has always been the nature of lived life, and indeed it is better thus, for life "will be lived all the better if it has no meaning.[11] Better, presumably, because living contentedly with meaninglessness keeps one from the temptation of escape into some other-worldly system of explanation.

Perhaps the talk about civilized suicide is oozing back into our lives because we have come to believe the false promise that we can be happy. So, when we are not, we become tempted to reject the world that has disappointed us so bitterly. America today is some distance in time and space from the political oppression that Camus and the Mandelstams knew, and some ideological distance as well from the Christian idea of the fallen world. We still somehow believe we have a right to be happy, and so we are furious or self-pitying or despondent when we are not. Christians have never expected the fallen world to provide their beatitude, so they didn't break apart when it failed to do so. Today, without the Christian God to warn against the expectation of happiness or to console when unhappiness comes, we seem to have only happiness itself remaining as god, after both God and ethics have been swallowed up in the comforting language about being responsible for ourselves. When earthly happiness is taken away, and it will be, neither divine prohibition nor an ethic of responsibility to others stands between our misery and suicide. Pain and suffering sometimes turn out to be less redemptive and purifying for our characters than piety had promised, and happiness itself turns out to be as unstable a god as God was.

Camus' persistent claim that life is meaningless and absurd means less than first appears. When he rejects meaning, it is only ideological or religious meaning that he wants to reject: Communism and Catholicism, to be exact. He readily acknowledges a sweetness to life that the imagination knows, even though ideologies fail to convince. He can speak of "the poetry of forms and colors" of "the soft lines of these hills and the hand of evening on this troubled heart."[12] Life itself, the actual living and feeling it—not the scientific or theological attempts to master or explain—that is what we have, that is all we have, and it is enough to live by and for. The Christian world justifies its exceptions to the prohibition against suicide by its assurance that something more important than mere life lies beyond it. Political ideologues as well can readily take life, others' and their own, to serve an expected future beyond the present. The broken eggs for which the omlet is the justification. But if they are wrong, if it is wrong to define life's meaning by something transcendent or something future, and if life is and ought to be its own justification, then endurance in that life becomes something very close to an absolute, and even the exceptional and sacrificial justifications for suicide lose their power to persuade.

> The luxury of sacrifice—by which I mean the strategic choice of death to resolve irreconcilable moral conflicts—is meaningless in a world where any person's death only contributes to the success of evil.[13]

Edgar, in *King Lear*, concealed his identity from his father, Gloucester, in order to bring the old man out of his suicidal pessimism. He was a great prophet of endurance as the only thing we really have—"ripeness is all." His therapeutic task led him to two remarkable affirmations of life as its own justification, requiring neither God nor an eschatology for its value. Even at the moment he first saw his blinded father, Edgar could confess that life in any form is better than death.

> The worst is not
> So long as we can say 'This is the worst.'
> (IV.i.27–28)

Later, speaking to Albany,

> O our lives' sweetness
> That we the pain of death would hourly die
> Rather than die at once!
> (V.iii.185–187)

Camus, though more haunted by theology than any of the non-theological existentialists, rejects suicide for the same reason he rejects faith in God. Both suicide and faith are forms of escape from life; both are species of acceptance or acquiescence; both imply rejection of rebellion, that persistent absolute in Camus' ethic, that one action ever asked of us in the time of the deaths of the Christian and political gods. Even though medieval Christianity found a language with which to make a condemnation of suicide, Camus' argument helps us grasp an even deeper truth about Christianity by perceiving the affinity of suicide and faith. Both Christianity and suicide are in ultimate service to death, and therefore to be resisted. "It is essential," Camus writes, "to die unreconciled and not of one's own free will."[14]

Lurking behind this affinity between Christianity and death is the anguished presence of the writer who has taught the twentieth century more about both God and death than anyone else— Fyodor Dostoevsky. I am thinking primarily of Kirillov in *The Possessed*, both his tormented discussions of suicide and his actual suicide. An examination of Kirillov will enable us to press through and beyond the new–old tolerance and the Christian and existentialist prohibitions.

He first appears in the novel as a man whose only interest is in exploring why people don't kill themselves. There were two things, he suspects, that used to dissuade: pain (that pain entailed, presumably, in the act of taking one's life—surely avoidable, with the proper precautions) and fear of what might lurk in the world to come. Kirillov knows that neither of these deterrents are any longer effective. Putting God aside, believing only in his own free will, he argues that motiveless suicide (the old deterrent being too fragile to prevent) is the purest possible expression of that freedom which is all that remains after the departure of God.

But we soon discover that suicide is but his secondary passion. His primary passion is how man can live without God. Suicide matters only as it illuminates that. Since man in fact invented God in order to avoid killing himself, and since for Kirillov that God is dead, he sees himself as the first modern man consciously to live without God. Why not turn to suicide at once?

> I cannot understand how an atheist could know that there is no god and not kill himself at once! To realize that there is no god and not to realize at the same instant that you have become god yourself—is an absurdity, for else you would certainly kill yourself. If you do realize it, you are a king and you will never kill yourself, but will live in the greatest glory. But he who is the first to realize it is bound to kill himself, for otherwise who will begin and prove it?[15]

Kirillov is struggling to say and to believe that the truly free man should not care whether he lives or dies. He certainly will not refuse suicide because he loves life. Such an argument infuriates Kirillov, because since life is fear and pain, to love life is to be in love with fear and pain.

This perfectly free man after the death of God, subject to none, able to live or die with equal ease, is what Kirillov defines as the "new man" in the making. Kirillov's theology of death is really an eschatology, and he sees himself (as did Jesus, and as does the Reverend Moon today) as the earnest of the new age. The new man will have conquered fear and pain (that which used to deter suicide and that which defines life), and through this victory he will become god. The other God will disappear as the new age and the new man–god appears, though wherever men are in fear or pain, the old God lingers. In *The Possessed*, the new man–god is free to kill himself or not (he finally does so), and this constitutes the freedom he has wrested from the old God. (Ivan Karamazov looked for the new man–god, and that led him not to suicide but to madness.)

For Kirillov the new age is neither wholly present nor wholly future. Like the kingdom in the New Testament, it is both. When it fully comes (and Kirillov, like Schweitzer's Jesus, seems to hint that he may have to force its coming by his own suicide), it will bring a new history, a new heaven and a new earth. World history is split in two, an old covenant and a new: from the gorilla to the death of God (accomplished by the overcoming of pain and fear, by the overcoming of history itself) is the old aeon; from the death of God to the "physical transformation of man and the earth" is the new. Kirillov stands on the edge. Surely modern Marxist language about the new man and the new history owes something to Kirillov's suicide and Ivan's madness.

What is Kirillov's perception of suicide's relation to this new man standing on the edge of the new age? Kirillov is not wholly clear about this, and Dostoevsky may not be either. On the one hand, Kirillov steadfastly insists that it doesn't make any difference whether he kills himself or not. On the other hand, the new man does not automatically kill himself when the old God dies and he becomes the new man–god, even though he certainly has the freedom to do so. He has no reason not to do so, because he does not have the God who was the only good reason not to. Kirillov defines his new freedom after the death of God as the freedom to take his own life. But is it not the case that the new man can truly become god or God only if he does in fact kill himself? Both the dead old God and the new–god seem to equal death, and thus to equal each other.

At the novel's harrowing close, Kirillov summarizes his eschatological theology of suicide. Two things are forever true, he says. God is indispensible (for the prevention of suicide, *e.g.*) and therefore must exist; and "I know there is no God and there can't be." The new man is the one tormented by the knowledge that both of these affirmations are true and who, at the same time, refuses to endure the torment of that contradiction. Suicide, not dialectic, is the only escape.

In reality, the atheist presupposition dominates, for Kirillov argues that since he is now the only god he must exercise his new freedom on the most important point, his own life. The act of suicide is both a consequence of the human freedom stolen from the dead God and a means of establishing that freedom. Kirillov very nearly ends up as the central actor in a new doctrine of atonement. As Jesus died for human sin, once and for all, making it unnecessary for men and women ever again to die for each others' sins, so Kirillov commits suicide at the threshold of the new age so the rest of us will not have to do the same after the death of God.

We are not astonished, therefore, to find that Kirillov's valedictory is not finally based on becoming God or the flight from life as pain and fear. It is based on Jesus. "That Man was the best on earth," he declares, and without him, the planet has become insane. He died for a lie; there was no resurrection, and so the planet since his death has been a lie.

Since there is no God, Kirillov has become god, and as such is free to take (or not to take) his life. Yet since he has become god he is sovereign and has no need to take his life. But he does so. His last action therefore proves that suicide must take place before there can be any new man–god. Therefore, one must not try to argue against the necessity of his suicide, for if you were successful, the new age would exist only in hope, in imagination. In order to become the first new man, to bring the new age after the death of God into reality; in order to enable others to live in (and not die for) the new age; in order to wipe out all subsequent justification for suicide, Kirillov shoots himself in the right temple.

I believe that Kirillov on suicide embodies some of the purest and truest Christian theology of the nineteenth century. He says he is killing himself to prove he is god, but he is also killing himself because he is not. In taking his own life, he takes over

Consenting to Die: A Meditation on Mortality 225

God's function of setting the time of his own death. He plays God, he kills the god within him, and he kills the god he has become in the absence of the Christian God. Kirillov kills himself in order to transcend mortality. He kills himself for precisely the same reason that other men and women have faith in God.

The important contribution the existentialists have made to the discussion of suicide is not in their particular arguments, which are often ineffectual, but in their identification of Kirillov as their model. It is his suicide that must be rejected if suicide in general is to be resisted. The secret to a dissuasive lies in Kirillov.

Camus is too good natured, too tolerant of Christians, to admit and confess the dark implications of Kirillov's death. As our dissuasive had to go beyond the Christian prohibition, it must also go beyond that of the existentialists. Kirillov's death teaches us the shattering theological lesson that thralldom to death lies at the heart of historic Christianity. As God's redemption can only come through the death of the redeemer, human redemption can only come through human death. Our contemporary tolerance for suicide, our civilized relief at being beyond superstition and taboo, our new willingness to take suicide seriously—this is really part of the dreadful religious revival of our time, a new form of that very old religious conviction (common to Plato and the New Testament) that death reigns because it is the portal to the realm of reality beyond. Suicide, like faith in God, gives death the victory. Christianity, far from effectually banning suicide, retreats from its prohibition, makes its exceptions, and finally offers its encouragement. "For me to live is Christ, and to die is gain. . . . My desire is to depart and be with Christ, for that is far better." (Phillippians 1:21,23) If God as redeemer is a filicidal killer, faith in him is suicide. God is in thrall to death, one with it. Death of God should mean the death of defenses of suicide, the death of our own love of death. To defend suicide is to defend death.

Man may or may not be determined by a death instinct, that instinct Freud found himself inventing in part because of the fact of suicide. It appears that a possible theological interpretation of the death instinct is to note its identity with the Christian God. The immortal combat between love and death is another name for the combat between man and God. Along these lines, a post-Christian, post-existentialist word against suicide might proceed.

V

I wish to bring this essay to a close by moving into a fictional mode.[16]

*   *   *   *

Patient

It all started a little more than two years ago when I turned forty. Submitting to my wife's urging, I agreed to get a full physical. The doctor's office called back several days later and said that everything looked fine but would I come so they could take some more blood and finish the lab work. I did, and after that the doctor called and asked me to drop by the office at my convenience. I don't recall if I was aware at that time of anything ominous on my horizon. There were those bruises on my left arm that I was not sure I knew how I got. But the doctor's "at my convenience" reassured me. I didn't know then that medical schools give full semester courses on how to say "drop by at your convenience" without upsetting the patient.

My internist began by saying something about my white cells, and it was clear that it had not yet been determined how much of the truth I was capable of receiving. We veered into a bizarre discussion about truth-telling in general. The doctor remarked that telling the truth was not a necessary moral absolute for a physician; that it sometimes confuses a patient who does not really want the truth even when he says he does; and finally that diagnostic truth can actually harm the patient by removing the will to fight.

I asked if it was really the case that doctors believed themselves in possession of a divine (or at least, a Hippocratic) mandate to lie, as long as they are persuaded that it helps. (Like the teen-age boy's lying "Of course I love you" in the back seat?) The doctor admitted that the situation often looked that way, but it was explained to me that the medical ethic is based on not doing harm, not on truth-telling. Medical ethics has become quite fashionable, I was assured; even medical schools have discovered it. Truth-telling is secondary? I asked. Yes, but this is not as paternalistic as it seems. Predictions about serious illness are not the same as "truth." Such predictions are tricky to make, often both hypothetical and inaccurate. The patient wants to know "How long do I have", and we never have that kind of truth. So we lie, or at least mystify, as a way of dealing with this most intellectually messy part of our science.

I then remarked that I had been taught by both books and experience to mistrust all human claims to semi-divine status, so that when someone claimed to know just what the right truth for me was, I tended to reach protectively for my wallet. Then we were finally ready to talk about cancer. That first discussion continued something like this.

Doctor

Leukemia is a cancer of the bone marrow, the blood-forming tissue inside the bones, and what it does is to cause an excessive production of immature white cells, crowding out the production of normal red cells. Your form is what we call chronic myelogenous leukemia.

Patient

I hadn't thought of leukemia as the cancer that would finally choose me. I'd anticipated tumors and surgery.

Doctor

There is a marrow transplant procedure that is sometimes indicated, but I'm not inclined to recommend that at present. I want you to be very clear about what I am saying. To say that you have this form of cancer is to say a little more than "You have a serious illness," but it is to say less than "You are doomed to an imminent death." You have a disease that may or may not be fatal.

Patient

Does your profession talk about "terminal illness" any more?

Doctor

One of our most unsatisfactory phrases. What is it supposed to mean? An illness from which one will die, or may die, or may die with better than even odds? To most patients "terminal" implies that we can predict the time of death. We can't, and we never should claim to. Why is it that laymen always seem to confuse science with prediction? I think that "terminal" is beginning to pass from medical usage, from muddying the waters of the doctor–patient relation, out into the wider literary world. The novelists are taking it over. According to *The World According to Garp*, we are all terminal cases. Banal enough for you?

Patient

I suppose some patients actually become more likely to die if they receive such a verbal death sentence.

Doctor

Of course. Even if "terminal illness" were a scientifically useful phrase, it is also a self-fulfilling prophecy. People die from terminal illnesses, and they also die from being told that they have terminal illnesses.

Patient

Should I ask about my odds?

Doctor

That is at least the right question. Most patients want an answer to another question: Is it cancer? If it is, they assume it is all over.

Patient

Why is cancer identified with imminent death, and cardiovascular disease is not? Cancer has almost become a demonic myth.

Doctor

We make myths when we do not understand.

Patient

I've always assumed that the myth-making function is something admirable in us, something uniquely human.

Doctor

Maybe it is, but it is also a deceptive lie when applied to cancer. It tends to grant to cancer more omnipotence than it actually deserves.

Patient

Some immortality myths are ways to relieve our fears. The effect of the cancer myth is to seal our doom.

Doctor

Freud liked to say that the unconscious believes itself to be immortal. It appears the cancer patient is the exception.

Patient

We are the ones, deceived by language into considering cancer an irresistible presence, who too quickly assume our inevitable mortality.

Doctor

Yes. Since we do not have a single cause yet, cancer is thought of as incurable, which it is not; therefore it is inevitable as death and equivalent to it. I suspect that both doctors and patients share the blame for this linguistic mistake.

Patient

What is it that mythologizing cancer makes us patients acquiescent? Can't we fight myths? Was Camus right, after all, in claiming that we must choose between understanding evil and fighting it? Maybe mythologizing is too much like divinizing, and we haven't been allowed to fight our gods in the good old Christian West. Your mythologized cancer is like demon possession, a foe striking irrationality, omnipotent. Must we believe in omnipotence?

Doctor

You're out of my field now. The real damage the cancer myth does may not lie in the fact that it leads to passive acquiescence (in some ways, I guess, I prefer acquiescent patients, truly patient ones), but the reverse—that it leads to an aggressive, totalitarian style of thought. The Jews were a "cancer" to the Nazis; Stalin a cancer to Trotsky.

Patient

Even little John Dean contributed to the myth when he testified that he told Nixon that "there was a cancer growing on the Presidency."

Doctor

Dean's language was very interesting. It seemed to take the perceived evil seriously, but it also blamed no one, not even the President. In Dean's phrase, Nixon almost seems to be the victim, the patient, the one who can't help it. And when you call something a cancer you approve the use of violence against it. This is why the disease has attracted military metaphors. We have governmental wars against it, cancer cells invade or colonize, the body throws up defenses. But the cancer myth also suggests that the disease is a demon, and alien intruder, an irrational guest, and as such not quite the sort of thing you fight—you exorcize it. Why do so many of our patients turn to non-medical forms of healing in their distress? When we doctors don't produce rapid enough effects, the patient bewitched by the mythological language turns to the exorcists or the apricot pits.

Patient

I don't want to give up some parts of the myth: the idea of the disease as enemy, for example.

Doctor

We can do our fighting without the myths or metaphors, just as we ought to fight our necessary wars without turning them into crusades. All I am claiming is that cancer is a disease, not a metaphor or a myth, not some Dread Presence out of Ingmar Bergman.

Patient

A good cigar is sometimes just a good cigar, as Freud is reported to have admitted.

Doctor

Myth-making inserts the idea of inevitable death into the discussion of cancer. That is both false and dangerous, psychologically and medically.

Patient

Can cancer be an evil to be fought without becoming a symbol of evil?

Doctor

I can hardly object to the idea of fighting evil; I am, after all, a physician with some knowledge of cancer. I distrust the American habit of escalating our wars into crusades, so I beg leave to dissent from the parallel move from disease to metaphor or myth. And I think I know how to resist that move. As an internist board-certified in hematology and who, a few years ago, somehow became an oncologist, I find I cannot look upon cancer as merely an irrational intruder. It seems more like a natural consequence of aging, a more or less normal way to die for those saved from earlier deaths by medical and public health advances. John Fowles, one of my favorite novelists, has put my scientific hunch in a more lyrical mode:

> Death contains me as my skin contains me. Without it, I am not what I am. Death is not a sinister door I walk towards; it is my walking towards.

Patient

Let me try to understand what you mean by cancer as a natural event. You are saying that my body has been producing cancer cells for some time now, and that this time my immunological system didn't happen to catch them in time.

Doctor

Yes. This permits me to demythologize cancer, to make it something natural, explicable, without for a moment denying that it is a foe we fight and over whom—I should say, which—real victories can be won.

Patient

I guess I am a little uneasy with your talk about illness and death as natural events. There seems such a little step between "natural" and "welcome," and I get the feeling that I am supposed to applaud death and disease as really wise things done by evolution.

Consenting to Die: A Meditation on Mortality 233

Doctor

This is the danger in my view. In trying to console by demythologizing I may become cruel in a different way. Maybe we shouldn't make up our minds about myth and metaphor too readily. I don't really want to abolish the poets from my academy, but I think I do want them out of my examining room. In any case, you will not find that my anti-mythic skepticism will tempt me to capitulate to your disease. A lot of progress has been made, just in the last few years, in the treatment of leukemia. In some forms of children's leukemia, acute lymphocytic leukemia, for example, if treatment continues for at least two and a half years, we can claim a survival rate after five years of 50%. Half of all the children's leukemia we see we can either cure or control.

Patient

I assume that the outlook for adults is less sanguine. Have you told me what you mean by "cure"?

Doctor

I did use the word, didn't I. It can be very deceptive. Surgeons especially like to use it about their results. It makes them feel successful in a specialty that has lots of failure in it. It may be true that the very idea of "cure" sometimes tempts surgeons into radical procedures that are avoidable. I usually use it, if at all, to describe non-recurrence within a four-year period. I would rather talk about extending life, or survival time. "Cure" connotes to the patient an exemption from the kingdom of disease, which none of us has and none can offer. Our decisions over the next weeks and months will have to do with the kind of life you are now living and the kind of life you can be expected to live in the immediate future. I can certainly offer you hope, without being able to promise a cure. The American cancer establishment, when out for grant money, is professionally optimistic. The clinical specialist is not.

Patient

You said that if we cannot cure we can sometimes control. What do you mean by that? I take it that the odds for control are a little better than the odds for cure.

Doctor

Yes. To control a tumor is to keep it from growing, or to reduce its growth rate. To control your leukemia would mean to keep the manufacture of defective white cells from increasing. Our primary mode of treatment in this first stage is chemotherapy.

Patient

Nausea, fatigue, hair falling out, treatment worse than disease?

Doctor

Five years ago, that might have been half true. Not so today. Now we can control nearly all of the side effects of the standard drugs. We start by putting together a combination of drugs, watching the results, adjusting the mix, observing, adjusting, until we are satisfied. You will be an out-patient, coming here probably every two weeks. I see no reason why your life should not continue, now at least, pretty much as it has been.

Patient

With a rather decisively altered consciousness.

Doctor

Of course. You have leukemia. But we have by no means ruled out the real possibility that the right combination of drugs will effect a cure, as I've defined it.

Patient

What if this right combination controls rather than cures. What does that mean?

Doctor

It means that we will have succeeded in turning your leukemia into a chronic condition, getting no worse and no better, with chemotherapy, and perhaps radiotherapy. Such control would entail a more or less normal life.

Patient

Is it possible this combination of drugs controlling my problem will have such unpleasant side-effects that I will decide it is not worth it?

Doctor

This is not likely during the first stage of treatment. The drugs we'll be working with are thoroughly studied, and the possibility of the uncontrollable side-effect is quite low. The problem you mention may come up later on.

Patient

What is later on? What comes after what you've called the first stage? What if nothing works?

Doctor

One of our options in that case would be to proceed to the use of somewhat more experimental drugs, not so thoroughly tested as those of the first stage. Then we might run into the side-effect problem. We can face that when and if we have to. I have tried to be as honest as I can with you, and I've already told you that we don't have to deny hope in order to be honest. We may get a result that can be called a cure; we may get something we can call control. We will be trying for a cure, but don't sell the idea of palliative treatment short, if that is what we have to settle for. Holding a disease in check without eliminating it is a common medical situation. Think of diabetes or kidney failure. Both can be serious illnesses, but we don't call them mortal or terminal, and both can be controlled in such a way that a virtually normal life is assured. What we achieve may not be full health, but it is not a sentence of doom. We will try to turn your leukemia into a chronic illness if we cannot eliminate it. If we have this modest success, then your life expectancy would still be about what it would be without the disease.

Patient

We may have effectively slaughtered the metaphorical cancer, transforming it from a myth to a mere disease, but my cancer suggests another problem, besides the medical one.

Doctor

I suppose you mean "Why me, and why at 42 instead of 62 or 72."

Patient

Of course, I'm not quite as blameless as Job, but I still have some right to a complaint. Have I done something to deserve this? What have I done, or allowed to be done to me (too many X-rays years ago?), that brings me my cancer ahead of schedule? I quit smoking six years ago. My consumption of alcohol has moved from "problematic" to "moderate." I'm a faithful husband, and my children seem to like me most of the time. I've never voted for a Republican presidential candidate and I don't read *Playboy*, even on airplanes. I was correct on Vietnam yesterday, and I am correct on abortion, the Middle East, and nuclear proliferation today. The world needs more like me, not fewer.

Doctor

Since no one in the history of the world has even satisfactorily answered that, I assume you don't expect me to. I will not play Job's comforter and insist that sin is the source of your suffering. One part of your question, though, I do know a little about. There is a strange connection between cancer and guilt that I sometimes see in my tumor patients. Healthy people treat cancer patients as unclean, as if their disease were communicable. This may be part of our myth.

Patient

Maybe my outburst was more influenced than I imagine by the popular psychology that tells me there are such things as heart-attack-prone and cancer-prone personality types.

Doctor

I hear a good deal about the cancer-prone personality in my line of work and I think it is a despicable idea.

Patient

Where does it come from?

Doctor

I haven't really tracked it down, but I have a suspicion that it comes from the early years of psychoanalysis and ultimately from Wilhelm Reich's obsessive, violent, and quite psychotic hatred of his mentor Freud. Reich thought Freud himself was the typical cancer-prone type, and he claimed that Freud's own cancer could be explained by his constricted emotional life. Reich so hated Freud's contention that civilization is based on necessary repression that the idea of the cancer-prone personality was his revenge.

Patient

I've always assumed that Freud's cigars might have had something to do with his cancer of the throat.

Doctor

Of course. The idea of a cancer-prone personality is the product of a scientific culture that naturally wants to know what the cause of cancer is. They are too sophisticated to blame God and unwilling to admit that they do not yet know the answer to the problem of cause. So they blame their patients and a personality type of which they do not approve.

Patient

I assume this theory relies on some kind of evidence.

Doctor

There are studies that show that a large proportion of cancer patients have reported feelings of depression at the time of the appearance of their first symptoms. But I suspect that we can always find "feelings of depression" at the onset of anything we do. The name for that fact is the human condition.

Patient

Any psychological determinism ignores the obvious fact that people get cancer in part because of certain things they, or others, have done: smoking, industrial sloppiness, lousy diet. I don't like to see bad psychology let American industry off the carcinogenic hook.

Doctor

It's the phony guilt generated by this myth that really bothers me. It is simply not true that either you or your personality bear responsibility for the fact that you have chronic leukemia. We are still some distance from a cancer cure, even some way from a solution to the problem of cause. There never may turn out to be a single cause. Right now, we are working with spectrum of causes: substances in the environment can cause cancers; we can be genetically tilted toward it; our immunological defenses against it can be weakened by illness, and maybe even stress. I recently came across a lovely experiment that will please you, though I'm not sure I know just what it means. At least it helps to bury the cancer-prone personality. It seems there is a certain strain of experimental rat with a high susceptibility to one form of leukemia. When we put two males of this species together in the same cage, the frequency of leukemia drops decisively.

Patient

What happens in the cage?

Doctor

Nothing X-rated, apparently. They fight, nip at each other, and seem constantly wary and on the alert.

Patient

Does this mean that intellectual alertness is protection against cancer?

Doctor

Stupider conclusions from animal evidence have been drawn.

Patient

Well, I will take note of my possible guilt and genuine anger. They haven't been cured, but they may have been controlled by our discussion.

Doctor

In spite of what some of my more holistic medical colleagues may say, we are not in the business of preventing death. Just of postponing it a bit. This I think we can do for you. The medical profession should not be over-rated; the death-rate in this country has remained virtually unchanged over the last twenty-five years.

* * * *

Patient

I will not rehearse all of my psychological responses to the announcement of my cancer then or since. I mentioned my rebellion, and I still have that. I have not followed the advices of the death-gurus in our culture by travelling obediently from anger to acquiescence, as if that journey were inevitably one from darkness to light. As I look back, one of my first, most infantile, and (I am told) most typical reactions to the knowledge of my disease was to blame my wife. It was her idea that I get the check-up initially, and I clearly must have felt, at some deep level, that if I hadn't known about the disease I wouldn't have contracted it. That irrational feeling must not be confused with the often quite sensible idea that to maintain our health we should stay as far as possible from all medical professionals.

I have been undergoing treatment for about two years. Chemotherapy all the time, radiotherapy occasionally. The drugs had some initial side-effects, but I tolerated them pretty well. At first, it appeared we had achieved a kind of stabilization of the disease, but this is not the case now. The doctors have told me that first stage of treatment is having no effect and that I have a new set of choices to face, I am not in pain, but I am generally quite tired, and—given the failure of the treatment at present—more than a little depressed. And, I suppose, afraid of what's coming up. Recently my internist and I talked over the situation.

Doctor

None of the drugs we have been working with up to now, singly or in combination, with or without radiotherapy, are having significant effect on your bone marrow. We have determined that continuing present treatment would be about as effective as no treatment at all. I recommend that we bring this first stage to a close. It was a failure in that it didn't give us a cure or long-term control, but it did give us nearly two years.

Patient

I thought oncologists never gave up hope, at least when talking to patients.

Doctor

I have no intention of giving up. I am simply recommending that we stop phase one.

Patient

What is phase two? Where do we go from here?

Doctor

The odds for either cure or control have worsened, but they haven't collapsed. At this time, I am inclined to put the matter into your hands. I can lay out several options but I can't make the choice for you, even if you would let me. We can move into experimental chemotherapy. There are dozens of new drugs, in various stages of testing and use, and we can take our chances with some of these. This would mean giving up your out-patient status, and being admitted to the hospital. With the new drugs, the side-effect problem is trickier simply because we know less about them.

Patient

How long can this experimental phase go on?

Doctor

Until we regain control of the cancer or, because of failure, we decide to stop treatment. The number of experimental substances is not infinite, but we can combine and experiment until such a time as it seems to both of us that your quality of life would be too unbearable if we continued.

Patient

Phase two, first option, experimental drugs. High risk, or at least high discomfort, and no promises. What else is there?

Doctor

We could decide simply to treat symptoms: relief of pain and relief of depression. When a patient moves from chemotherapy to relief of symptoms, a new kind of depression sets in, even when the patient himself has consented to the choice.

Patient

Respice finem.

Doctor

Partly, but also taking full notice of the interval between now and the end, which is called life. Up to now, your fatigue and depression have been moderate, and for two years you've had something close to normal life.

Patient

Whatever I choose, that normal life is clearly behind me.

Doctor

Yes. You will be connected to death in quite a new way. It will seem a lot closer, more inevitable.

Patient

Can I have any sort of life under such a sentence of death? Would I be taking the experimental drug direction just to postpone facing my sentence? You're never allowed to know the differences between false and legitimate hope beforehand. I really don't feel, after these two years, that there is any drug that can cure me. . . .

Doctor

I can understand how you might feel that way at this point, but you can see that there is no way I can either agree of disagree with you. Don't forget the ways in which you and I are alike, since you are likely now to be especially sensitive to our differences-you with cancer, me without. Both of us are going to die. You do not know your death date; neither do I know mine. Yours probably will come before mine, but that is not certain.

Patient

I'm not sure whether I want those months of bed-ridden semi-life, with daily shots and I-V feeding. I may have three months of your new drugs, or six, and twelve, or one. You can't tell me.

Doctor

No, and we are just as uncertain about how much time you have left if we discontinue the treatment altogether. Your life will probably be shorter if we do that, but we are not even sure of that.

Patient

Either way I will be very much the patient, having things done to me. Is it worth it?

Doctor

Is extension of life always a good?

Patient

Possibly not always, but surely most of the time it is. If I decide against the experimental drugs, I move into a surveillance and minimal care system. Pain relief and tranquillizers. Where would this take place?

Doctor

At home, until it has to happen at the hospital. Or, if you prefer, the hospice is fully qualified to administer the anti-pain and anti-depression medication we might decide on. The setting is quite unlike that of the hospital; to choose to go there would be to choose to die in a very straightforward sense.

Patient

That would be true of the minimal care program wherever we did it. I suppose I do have another option, though it is quite proper that you did not have it on your list. I am free at some time in my truncated future to take my own life if I come to the decision with a clear head, without self-dramatization or self-pity, and after full consultation with those I love. In my present feeling of powerlessness before a disease we have not been able to stop, I must admit that the sense of control that taking my own life implies has a slight appeal. I wish to thank you for the time you have given me, in every sense, and for your refusal to make my choice for me at this final point.

Notes

I

[1] Leon Howard, Introduction to Modern Library edition of *Moby-Dick* (New York: Random House, 1950), p. xiii. F.O. Matthiessen, *American Renaissance*, is excellent on Melville and transcendentalist theories of language (pp. 30–44, 119–132, 242–291, 421–466, 653–656).

[2] Loren Baritz, *City on a Hill* (New York: John Wiley, 1964), pp. 330–331.

[3] "Dead to the World: The Passions of Herman Melville," in *Essays in Self-Destruction* (New York: Science House, 1967), p. 27. Earlier in this essay, Murray remarked that "Herman Melville enjoyed and suffered from the most patent and protracted (overt as well as covert) Oedipus complex I have ever encountered in print or practice."

[4] Melville must have been brooding about the problem of speaking painful truth to a recalcitrant audience during the work on Moby-*Dick*. In "Hawthorne and His Mosses", referring to his beloved Shakespeare, he writes: "Tormented into desperation, Lear the frantic King tears off the mask, and speaks the sane madness of vital truth." In the April 16, 1851 letter to Hawthorne he identifies this "truth" with that perception of darkness and tragedy in Hawthorne (and Ahab) that he so admires:

> There is a certain tragic phase of humanity which, in our opinion, was never more powerfully embodied than by Hawthorne: we mean the tragicalness of human thought in its own unbiassed, native, and profounder workings. We think that into no recorded mind has the intense feeling of the visible truth ever entered more deeply than into this man's. By visible truth, we mean the apprehension of the absolute condition of present things as they strike the eye of the man who fears them not, though they do their worst to him. . . .

[5] In *Mariners, Renegades and Castaways*, the West Indian radical writer C. L. R. James interprets *Moby-Dick* as an attack on the nascent economic totalitarianism of America, and Ahab as a totalitarian fanatic. (New York: Schocken, 1984; originally published in 1953.)

[6] There is a fascinating parallel to Ahab's epistemology in a recent study of Tolstoy's theory of knowledge.

Knowledge through affective awareness is a way of knowing the reality in which one exists. It does not oppose a knowing subject and a known object out there. The subject exists in the reality and the reality exists in the subject's consciousness. Such knowledge is knowledge by participation: the subject goes forth into reality, takes part in it and takes that part of it back into itself. To be conscious of my finger, I must go forth from my center of awareness, where I reside, into my finger, become aware of the finger and then return that awareness to my center of consciousness, where now we both reside together. The process is a reversal and a return. Empiricist knowledge opposes the subject and the object. The knowing subject does not participate in the reality it knows; the objects out there impress themselves on the subject, but the subject does not take part in their reality nor actively take their reality into itself.

Richard F. Gustafson, *Leo Tolstoy, Resident and Stranger* (Princeton, N.J.: Princeton University Press, 1986), p. 240.

[7] Letter of November 17(?), 1851.

[8] *The Gay Science*, no. 125.

II

[1] *Michelangelo*, Volume I: *The Youth of Michelangelo* (Princeton, N.J.: Princeton University Press, 1969; second printing), introduction.

[2] "Michelangelo Pittore," *Apollo* 80 (1964), p. 445.

[3] Robert S. Liebert, *Michelangelo, A Psychoanalytic Study of His Life and Images* (New Haven and London: Yale University Press, 1983), p. 22.

[4] A priest friend wrote to Michelangelo in 1516 and in this rather effusive letter we can discern both the writer's interpretation of Michelangelo's piety and also a fascinating example of the Christian–platonic amalgam of the day. Deeply platonic, and deeply Christian, at the same time.

> ... I understand by your letter that you have reached salvation ... it seems to me that a perpetual brotherhood has been confirmed between us, since I realize that in visiting my father you recognize him as your own. ... You know love is not limited by time or place, especially that of God; and more than such love transforms the one into the other, that is, the lover into the thing loved, and makes a mutual penetration of souls: thus I ascend to you through the love I bear for you, I penetrate and understand you, if you think, if you speak, if you write: and this is enough for you. Let us love each other, then, in the Lord, as we have done until now, and we will understand and know the whole and the truth, and we will see it face to face if we live well and as Christians, as you sculpt with your mallet in good and virtuous works the imprint of Christ Crucified for us; this one does in faith and by faith informed of holy charity; in which may God keep you forever. *Vale et ama.* ...

[5] This conflict can be studied in another early pair of works: the Bacchus of 1496–1498 in which the pagan god has lost both beauty and divinity, and the famous Rome Pietà (1497–1500). Something about this Pietà (which, Howard

Hibbard has written, "became one of the images closest to Michelangelo's own spiritual aspirations," *Michelangelo*, [New York: Harper and Row, 1974], p. 46) disturbed the sixteenth-century Italian hierarchy, perhaps because at one level it is a statue of a beautiful young woman holding an exhausted young man on her lap. When a copy of this Pietà was placed in a chapel in Florence in 1549 it was called by one ecclesiastic a *"capriccio Luterano."* Why? Because the mother, like the Bacchus, was too little divinized?

Another early pair of works brings out the mixed inheritance of the young artist, Christian and neo-platonic: the serene Bruges Madonna (1503–1505) and the massive David (1501–1504). The David has always been taken as the supreme example of Michelangelo's High Renaissance style, celebrating man and his body without ambiguity. But there may be a dark undercurrent to this celebration. It is not always safe to celebrate the power of the body. Mary McCarthy tells a wonderful story illustrating the demonic side of the Florentine Renaissance.

> The Florentines, in fact, invented the Renaissance, which is the same as saying that they invented the modern world—not, of course, an unmixed good. Florence was a turning-point, and this is what often troubles the reflective sort of visitor today—the feeling that a terrible mistake was committed here, at some point between Giotto and Michelangelo, a mistake that had to do with power and megalomania or gigantism of the human ego. You can see, if you wish, the handwriting on the walls of Palazzo Pitti or Palazzo Strozzi, those formidable creations in bristling prepotent stone, or in the cold, vain stare of Michelangelo's "David," in love with his own strength and beauty. This feeling that Florence was the scene of the original crime or error was hard to avoid just after the last World War, when power and technology had reduced so much to rubble. *"You* were responsible for this," chided a Florentine sadly, looking around the Michelangelo room of the Bargello after it was finally reopened. In contrast, Giotto's bell tower appeared an innocent party. (*The Stones of Florence* [New York: Harcourt, Brace, Jovanovich, 1963], pp. 121–122.)

[6] Gilbert #18. The poetry will hereafter be cited in this form in the text. The translations are by Creighton Gilbert from the volume edited by Robert Linscott, *The Complete Poems and Selected Letters of Michelangelo* (Princeton, N.J.: Princeton University Press, 1980).

[7] *The Life of Michelangelo* (New York: Capricorn Books, 1962), p. 75.

[8] *Michelangelo*, Volume II: *The Sistine Ceiling* (1969, second printing), p. 117.

[9] *Op. cit.*, p. 154.

[10] de Tolnay, *Michelangelo*, Volume II: *The Sistine Ceiling*, p. 37.

[11] *Ibid.*, p. 40.

[12] Charles de Tolnay, *Michelangelo, Sculptor, Painter, Architect* (Princeton, N.J.: Princeton University Press, 1975), p. 35:

The Sistine Ceiling is the work of an artist at the height of his powers: it is the titanic flight towards the heavens of a man in his prime. By glorifying the boundless creative force of God, Michelangelo has at the same time made an image of his own supreme aspirations during this period of his activity.

[13] He had done so earlier in that glorious, insouciant Eve of the Temptation on the Sistine ceiling. (Fig. 3) There is perhaps one theological point of interest concerning this Eve, but it is highly speculative. Leo Steinberg has said about all there is to say about her famous right hand ("Eve's Idle Hand," *Art Journal*, vol. 35, no. 2, Winter 1975/6), but I am interested in the head. Rotate it 120 degrees clockwise and it becomes difficult to avoid the impression that she has just completed, or was interrupted during, an episode of oral sex with Adam. We know a little about the gnostic sects who, from the beginning of the Christian era, believed that oral sex was the form of sex practiced in Eden (since there was immortality, reproduction was not necessary) and that when the first couple fell they fell into genital sex. The gnostic enlightened ones believed that some of the conditions of paradise could be re-enacted even in the fallen world as an anticipation, one might almost say, foretaste. The activities of these groups, sometimes known as Patarenes or Adamites, are recorded in northern Italy into the late Middle Ages. There is no evidence at all that Michelangelo ever went to a gnostic party-meeting. We can say that, given his conflicted views on the human body, he would have been a push-over for a slick gnostic evangelist.

[14] Kenneth Clark has written, without his customary lucidity, that "every line of the Dawn's body is like a lamentation at the sovereignty of the senses. . . ." *The Nude* (New York: Pantheon Books, 1956), p. 253.

[15] The peculiar character of Florentine neo-Platonism appears in nothing more than in its insistence on man's power to seize reality by its own efforts; in its endeavours, one might almost say, to take the kingdom of heaven by force.

(Nesca Robb, *Neo-Platonism of the Italian Renaissance* [London: Allen and Unwin, 1935], p. 69.)

[16] Dr. Liebert has argued that both Michelangelo's character and his Christian faith probably kept him from overt homosexual expression (*op. cit.*, p. 294):

For Michelangelo it would have caused great emotional upheaval to witness in himself the failure of the Neoplatonic ideology through which he could filter out the need for actual sexual consummation.

[17] Tommaso married several years after he and Michelangelo met, and that may have been one of the reasons the artist came to see the futility of his homosexual impulses. Here is Liebert on this matter (*op. cit.*, p. 326):

Unable to consummate his desires, partly because of the guilt that he internalized from the social code of the day and from Christian teachings, he may have resolved to purge himself of this increasingly disturbing area of thought and interest. He was, after all, dwelling day in and day out on issues of judgment and eternal afterlife in connection with his work on the *Last Judgment*. So, as the harmony between Christian and classical thought shifted to antagonism, the obvious solution was to surrender to one or the other. With body failing and death approaching, and the image of a harsh "Christ the Judge," so central in the *Last Judgment*, already uppermost in his mind, Michelangelo surrendered to belief in the teachings and sufferings of Christ rather than to love for another mortal male. Even as early as the Doni tondo of 1503–1504 we can see evidence of Michelangelo's guilt and moral condemnation of homosexuality, albeit expressed quite ambivalently. As we recall, he represented the group of background nudes as homosexuals presenting themselves at the baptismal font to be cleansed of their sin. In the wake of Michelangelo's renunciation of homosexuality, it is understandable that he would turn to the relative safety of a female guide, although he perceived her as an unwomanly woman. In this respect, Vittoria could serve better than any male theologian, shepherding him toward what was to absorb him throughout the last seventeen years of his life—the Passion of Christ. . . . It can be inferred from his late works, and particularly from his unrelenting labors over those years on the Florence and Rondanini *Pietàs*, that the ultimate goal of Michelangelo's identification with the crucified Christ was the union between Jesus and the Virgin so poignantly expressed in those Pietàs. Perhaps Vittoria Colonna may be regarded as the transitional figure in this increasingly intense artistic quest for the loving union between son and mother.

When Michelangelo met Vittoria, five years or so after first meeting Tommaso, he made his choice. Homosexual temptation was abolished along with its imperfect justification and sublimation system; Vittoria and the crucified Christ and the union of mother and son become the dominant, and at the end, the only artistic and spiritual agenda.

[18] In Gilbert #59 and #85 love is again a renewing fire.

[19] Anthony Blunt, *Artistic Theory in Italy, 1450–1600* (New York: Oxford University Press, 1956), p. 65.

[20] Liebert, *op. cit.*, p. 345.

[21] "Michelangelo's 'Last Judgment' as Merciful Heresy," *Art in America*, 63 (Nov.–Dec. 1975), pp. 48–63; "A Corner of the 'Last Judgment,' " *Daedalus*, 109 (1980), pp. 207–273; "The Line of Fate in Michelangelo's Painting," *Critical Inquiry*, vol. 6, no. 3 (Spring 1980), p. 411–454.

[22] Leo Steinberg, *Michelangelo's Last Paintings* (New York: Oxford University Press, 1975), p. 40.

[23] Liebert, *op. cit.*, pp. 222–223. We should recall two poems already cited: Gilbert #44 where the poet suggests a theological interpretation of the unfinished statues, and #240 in which the resisting stone and rejecting mother are identified.

[24] Frederick Hartt, *Michelangelo's Drawings* (New York: Harry N. Abrams, Inc., 1971 [?]), p. 293.

[25] *Michelangelo*, Volume V: *The Final Period* (1971), p. 92.

III

[1] Phillip Ariès, *Western Attitudes Toward Death* (Baltimore: Johns Hopkins University Press, 1974), pp. 45–46. The Huizinga reference is to *The Waning of the Middle Ages* (London: Edward Arnold, 1924), p. 27.

[2] References to the plays will be in this form and in the text. I am using *The Complete Pelican Shakespeare*, ed. Alfred Harbage (Baltimore: Penguin, 1969).

[3] *Henry IV, Part I*, V.i.126. Feeble repeats this truism in *Part 2*, III.ii.222: "We owe God a death." Freud, who knew his Shakespeare, quoted this several times, and misquoted it as "we owe nature a death." As he taught us, little slips are significant.

[4] Eric Partridge, *Shakespeare's Bawdy*, p. 101, reminds us that "die" often bears a sexual sense in Elizabethan English, referring to the moment of exhaustion after orgasm.

[5] Stanley Cavell, *Must We Mean What We Say?* (Cambridge: Cambridge University Press, 1975), p. 341.

[6] "The Theme of the Three Caskets," *Collected Papers*, vol. 4 (New York: Basic Books, Inc., 1959), p. 255.

[7] The phrase is Granville-Barker's.

[8] Cavell, *op. cit.*, p. 52.

[9] Professor H. V. D. Dyson concludes his excellent B.B.C. talks on Shakespeare and death with a reference to this speech of Posthumus, which he calls "the profoundest interpretation of death as an element in man's experience." "This Mortal Coil: Shakespeare and Death," *The Listener* (April 9 and 16, 1964).

[10] Theodor Reik said this of the contrast between the mood of *The Tempest* and that of *Hamlet*, ten years before.

> *Hamlet* was written after the death of Shakespeare's father (1601). All the emotions of childhood were revived by this death, all the fears of childhood reawakened. The Dane meditates on the dissolution of the great men of this earth, and this reflects the poet's dual feelings of unconscious triumph at the death of the father and longing for him. Some ten years later *The Tempest* was written; the poet is weary of his revolt; the fame he has won has become meaningless. He has returned home to Stratford, and there is something about him now that suggests he is preparing for that other homecoming. Now that youth is over, now that he is slowly and heavily turning his steps toward the final peace, the prospect of death and his attitude toward it change. His phantasies sound wearier and more poignant now, and mellower, like a noble old violin. It is less of a victory over life than a laying down of arms before it. Death is now welcomed; it no longer means the terrible tyranny of fate, the dreaded end of all things. Children have been born to him; his daughter is of marriageable age; he has put his house in order. He himself, gathered closer to both his father and his forefathers, scarcely feels defiance any longer toward the authorities who represented the father. Now that he himself is an aging father he sees the position of the father differently, for now

he comprehends it. All the conflicts have slowly faded away, and the end is not triumph but resignation. (As Hans Sachs has put it in his beautiful study of *The Tempest*, "The puppets are now hanging on slack wires, for the puppeteer will soon go to his rest.") These, I believe are the wellsprings of the feelings which inspire Ariel's beautiful song.

"The Way of All Flesh," from *Thirty Years With Freud* (New York: Farrar and Rinehart, 1940), pp. 208–209.

V

[1] It is interesting to note that for all its interest in food the *Confessions* (I–IX) has nothing to say about the fruit-tree of Eden. There may be a faint hint of Genesis in Augustine's phrase "fruit of death" as the proper reward for his undefined sexual escapade in church (III.iii). Perhaps just because Genesis 2–3 identifies solid food with sin, the *Confessions* insists that God's food can only be liquid.

[2] An echo of the solid food–milk distinction from 1 Corinthians 3. Notice the unusual, almost Pelagian, implications of the final sentence of this passage. We might have expected, even from the early Augustine, something like "feed on me and you shall grow."

[3] There is that nasty, and fortunately infrequent, strain of cosmic egotism in our saint—hoping that the heavenly Nebridius won't get so drunk that he forgets his priceless friend still on earth.

[4] Cf. Leo Steinberg, "Michelangelo's Florentine Pietà," *Art Bulletin* (December, 1968), *ad. fin.*

> The Christ Child is an infant Hercules, sitting forward, straddling his Mother's thigh. His upper body swerves through an astonishing 180 degrees, and he appears to be nursing. But his left hand, grasping the Virgin's shoulder, leaves infancy as far behind as does the precocious athleticism of his physique.
>
> Why the crossed legs of the Virgin? Perhaps Michelangelo was alluding to an old Medicean image. In the cortile of the Medici Palace, the frieze decoration consists of relief tondi in which ancient gems from the Medici collection are monumentalized. One of these shows a nude child turning toward a seated woman, draped, her legs crossed; it represents the wedding procession of Eros and Psyche: divine love and the human soul about to be married in heaven. . . . What the crossing of the Madonna's legs accomplishes is to lift the Child far above her breast level; evidently the literal contact here was dispensable since the mere direction of the Child's turn would suffice to suggest sucking. But with the Madonna's legs crossed, the Child rides the high crest of her thigh. Now all his body, his straddling seat and his grip on her shoulder, reveal in the Child the divine love electing his spouse.
>
> Anatomy, said Freud, is destiny. In Michelangelo's hands it became theology.

VIII

[1] *Lazarus* (New York: Holt, Rinehart and Winston, 1977), p. 106.

[2] W. H. Auden, *Collected Poems*, edited by Edward Mendelson (New York: Random House, 1976), p. 274: from "For the Time Being, A Christmas Oratorio," Advent IV.

[3] *op. cit.*, p. 68. John Fowles has argued the opposite, making a good case for the conventional wisdom: "Death's rather like a certain kind of lecturer. You don't really hear what is being said until you're in the front row." (*Daniel Martin* [Boston: Little, Brown, and Co., 1977], p. 177.) Fowles's reflections on death in his little book of aphorisms are superb: *The Aristos* (New York: New American Library, 1975).

[4] All this garrulous attention which has us in a stew over sexuality, is it not motivated by one basic concern: to ensure population, to reproduce labor capacity . . . in short, to contribute a sexuality that is economically useful and politically conservative?

Michel Foucault, *The History of Sexuality*, Volume I: *An Introduction* (New York: Pantheon Books, 1978), pp. 36–37.

[5] "Psychological Coping Mechanisms and Survival Time in Metastatic Breast Cancer," by L. Derogatis, M. Abeloff, and N. Melisaratos, in the *Journal of the American Medical Association*, vol. 242, no. 14 (Oct. 5, 1979), pp. 1504ff.

[6] "Do Not Go Gentle into That Good Night," in *The Poems of Dylan Thomas*, edited by Daniel Jones (New York: New Directions, 1971).

[7] Bernstein's analysis of this work in the chapter entitled "The Twentieth-Century Crisis" in his 1973 Norton lectures is the high point of the book. *The Unanswered Question* (Cambridge, Mass: Harvard University Press, 1974).

[8] April 22, 1972, p. 33.

[9] A. Alvarez, *The Savage God* (New York: Bantam Books, Inc., 1972), p. 105.

[10] *Hope Against Hope* (New York: Atheneum Press, 1970), p. 105.

[11] Albert Camus, *The Myth of Sisyphus* (New York: Vintage Books, Random House, 1955), p. 40.

[12] *Ibid.*, pp. 39, 15.

[13] Terence Des Pres, *The Survivor* (New York: Oxford University Press, 1976), p. 100.

[14] *Op. cit.*, p. 141.

[15] *The Devils* (*The Possessed*) (Melbourne, London, and Baltimore: Penguin Books, 1953), p. 614.

[16] In working out this dialogue I have been helped by two books: *Concerning Cancer* by Lucien Israel and *Illness as Metaphor* by Susan Sontag.

Newman, Benjamin
SEARCHING FOR THE FIGURE IN THE CARPET IN THE TALES OF HENRY JAMES
Reflections of an Ordinary Reader

New York, Berne, Frankfurt/M., 1987.
American University Studies: Series IV (English Language and Literature).
Vol. 49
ISBN 0-8204-0442-X   200 pp.   hardback US $ 39.00/sFr. 59.00

Recommended prices – alterations reserved

Undertaken as if by an ordinary reader concentrating upon fundamentals of feeling and thought in the tales of Henry James, this study by Professor Newman is a probing, questioning, analytical search for the Jamesian figure, for the ultimate messages communicated by James, about his life and the world. Joining this distinctive perspective, a personalized style, and solid scholarly exploration, the book probes for meaning behind visions and metaphors over an expanse from *Daisy Miller* to *The Jolly Corner*, from the early years to the closing stage, the final years of recollection. As the odyssey progresses, its findings confirm for the author his conviction that there is indeed a «figure in the carpet», a consistent, coherent, and unified vision of James's life and of man's that runs through the tales, but modified in certain ways as the years passed. It is a complex design which, once uncovered and grasped, enables the reader to penetrate James's symbolic system, to resolve the so-called ambiguities and obscurities so often ascribed to him, and to interpret with confidence what James is saying to us as he writes about life and society, about art and personal passion and death.

PETER LANG PUBLISHING, INC.
62 West 45th Street
USA – New York, NY 10036

Paula M. Uruburu

THE GRUESOME DOORWAY
An Analysis of the American Grotesque

American University Studies: Series IV (English Language and Literature).
Vol. 45
ISBN 0-8204-0402-0 161 pages hardback US $ 29.00*

*Recommended price – alterations reserved

Moving from America's Puritan roots through the 19th and 20th centuries, *The Gruesome Doorway* examines the significance of the American Grotesque through an analysis of the works of Hawthorne, Poe, Crane, Norris, Anderson, West, and O'Connor. Dr. Uruburu explores the backgrounds and sources of the genre known as the Grotesque and reappraises the particular application of its «unconventional conventions» in American literature. The study reveals that this genre is peculiarly suited to a nation consistently torn between «high ideals» and «catch-penny realities,» whose inhabitants are pulled through the gruesome doorway into the landscape of the Grotesque.

Contents: Backgrounds and sources of the Grotesque – The American Grotesque – Puritan's analysis – chapter by chapter analysis of representative writers in the tradition – N. Hawthorne, E.A. Poe, S. Crane, F. Norris, S. Anderson, N. West, and F. O'Connor.

PETER LANG PUBLISHING, INC.
62 West 45th Street
USA – New York, NY 10036